Praise for *No One Left Behind*

"Ms. Yarsinske makes the case for the prosecution. She paints a picture of military ineptitude and deliberate cover-up that challenges conservative assertions that the Army is the only government agency that works. [*No One Left Behind*] is a challenge to those who cite the Gulf War as exorcising the demons of Vietnam. Until the mystery of Speicher is resolved, at least one demon still hovers."

—*Richmond Times-Dispatch*

"[Amy Waters Yarsinske], an expert in contemporary and historical naval aviation, drew her conclusions from interviews with government and military officials, diplomats, pilots, and Iraqi defectors and informers." —*The Orlando Sentinel*

"Thoroughly researched . . . *No One Left Behind* does demonstrate the continued viability of one of the hallmarks of our system: the overall civilian control over the military."

—*The Tampa Tribune*

"Drawing upon more than 500 interviews, government documents, intelligence case files, correspondence and other materials, Yarsinske describes an investigation allegedly plagued by mistakes and purposeful neglect."

—*The Kansas City Star*

continued . . .

Commentary about the
Lt. Comdr. Michael Scott Speicher case

"There is enough evidence to bring this whole situation into question. [The United States should] 'pursue every avenue' we can to find out what happened. . . . That's an American tradition."

   —Sen. John McCain (R-Ariz.), author of *Faith of My Fathers*

"The fact is, there continue to be reports from what would have some degree of credibility that he's still alive."

                    —Sen. Bob Graham (D-Fla.)

"My question is in reference to an overriding principle, it seems to me, of what we stand for within our military that is synonymous with our American values. . . . And I think it underscores the issue that we leave no one behind. I think unfortunately yet, due to past mistakes now viewed in eleven years of 20/20 hindsight . . . that that is what we did with reference to a young man by the name of Michael Scott Speicher, who was the first pilot shot down in the Gulf War, back in 1991."

                    —Sen. Pat Roberts (R-Kans.),
before the Senate Armed Services Committee

ALSO BY AMY WATERS YARSINSKE

Forward for Freedom

Mud Flats to Master Jet Base

The Jamestown Exposition

Wings of Valor, Wings of Gold

No One Left Behind

The Lieutenant Commander Michael Scott Speicher Story

AMY WATERS YARSINSKE

NEW AMERICAN LIBRARY

New American Library
Published by New American Library, a division of
Penguin Group (USA) Inc., 375 Hudson Street,
New York, New York 10014, U.S.A.
Penguin Books Ltd, 80 Strand,
London WC2R 0RL, England
Penguin Books Australia Ltd, 250 Camberwell Road,
Camberwell, Victoria 3124, Australia
Penguin Books Canada Ltd, 10 Alcorn Avenue,
Toronto, Ontario, Canada M4V 3B2
Penguin Books (N.Z.) Ltd, Cnr Rosedale and Airborne Roads,
Albany, Auckland 1310, New Zealand

Penguin Books Ltd, Registered Offices:
80 Strand, London WC2R 0RL, England

Published by New American Library, a division of Penguin Group (USA) Inc.
Previously published in a Dutton edition.

First New American Library Printing, May 2003
10 9 8 7 6 5 4 3 2

Library of Congress Cataloging-in-Publication data is available for this title upon
request.

Set in Janson Text
Designed by Eve L. Kirch

Printed in the United States of America

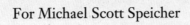

For Michael Scott Speicher

Contents

Prologue

President Theodore Roosevelt was giving a speech before a crowd in Springfield, Illinois, on July 4, 1903, in which he said: "A man who is good enough to shed his blood for his country is good enough to be given a square deal afterward. More than that no man is entitled to, and less than that no man shall have." It might have sounded like a pretty patriotic political speech delivered on a sweltering Fourth of July day, but it wasn't to the man who said it. To Teddy Roosevelt, a man and his country had a promise they made to one another when the man donned a uniform and the country asked him to go defend it.

Now, nearly one hundred years later, the sanctity of the warrior's code—the one that says we will leave no one behind—is being tested by the case of a naval aviator named Michael Scott Speicher, shot down on January 17, 1991, during the opening hours of the Persian Gulf War. While the war is considered an aberration to some who fought it, to Scott Speicher it is the interminable war, the one that won't go away because he continues to fight for his life every day in a country that took him captive because his own abandoned him. The U.S. government failed to rescue Scott, failed to even look for him when it knew he was in trouble, breaching the very premise of not leaving a fallen comrade on the field of battle.

Scott Speicher went into battle, but he never returned. He and his jet vanished that night and left behind a series of puzzling clues, jumbled further by government misstatements and mistakes. Lieutenant Commander Michael Scott Speicher would later gain a grim distinction: he is the only American from any war that the government changed from killed-in-action, body not recovered (KIA/BNR) to missing in action (MIA). What happened to Scott Speicher that January night tormented his family, battle-toughened pilots and intelligence agents for over a decade. His eleven-year journey back from the dead would eventually splash headlines and raise questions among civilian and military leadership as to how one of America's best and brightest pilots ended up behind enemy lines—and remained there unclaimed and seemingly unwanted through three presidential administrations and innumerable opportunities to bring him home.

CHAPTER 1

Iron Hand

On that afternoon of January 16, 1991, pilots stood around uneasily waiting for the mass briefing aboard the *Saratoga*. Everyone among the carrier's aircrew was on edge. This was no routine mission. As they waited pensively to hear from their battle group commander, some of them prayed to themselves. Others thought of their families and friends back home. All of them knew their mission down to the last detail. Iraq had let a January 15 deadline to withdraw from Kuwait expire. America was going to war. No one knew what to expect that night. The few combat-seasoned aviators aboard the carrier felt the same roiling emotions as the greenhorn pilots on their first cruise. In eight hours or less, they'd all be flying into combat. As Rear Admiral George "Nick" Gee started speaking, they listened somberly.

"Gentlemen," Gee said, "George Bush has called on us to do our duty, to liberate Kuwait, and that liberation is going to start tonight. There are several types of people back in the United States right now who will be watching as your bombs start dropping over Baghdad. It's going to be just about time for the evening news back home. There's going to be a guy sitting in a bar with long hair and a beard, an old hippie type, who is drinking beer and watching TV, and he's going to go, 'Fucking A, those are my boys, god damned U.S.' There are going to be moms out there that are crying and saying, 'That's my boy.' They are going to be watching you. You need to do this well. This will be with you for the rest of your lives. You will remember this night forever, so you want to do the best job you possibly can because if you don't, you will regret it until you die."

As he listened, VFA-81 *Sunliner* squadron pilot Lieutenant Barry W. "Skull" Hull felt his mouth go bone dry. He wasn't alone. "The very first thing we did was get a time hack so we'd all be on exact time," Hull remembered later. "We're synchronized. In thirty seconds it's going to be twenty-four after the hour, then ten, nine, eight and then he called 'Hack!'"

The atmosphere in the room remained somber until the mass briefing ended. Then the squadrons went to their own ready rooms for their individual mission briefs.

Hull, Scott "Spike" Speicher, Tony "Bano" Albano, Michael T. "Spock" Anderson, Philip "Chauncey" Gardner, plus scores of other Navy pilots, would soon climb into their F/A-18 Hornets and roar off the carrier *Saratoga* in the Red Sea, across Saudi Arabia toward Baghdad, initiating Operation Desert Storm. In the planning room, they reviewed the timing of the attack, their flight paths, and targets.

Originally, Speicher wasn't supposed to go. His commander had tapped him as the airborne spare. He was to fly in and take over if any of the other jets malfunctioned. As such, the spare had to know everybody's mission. But he had gone to his commanding officer, "Spock" Anderson, the day before and pleaded his case. He didn't want to be the spare, to be the one to have to turn around and come back to the ship without firing a shot. Anderson relented and let him join the mission.

Instead Spock assigned the spare position to Hull, but Hull balked, too. "I go, 'Wait a minute, I don't want to be the spare either.' It's not like I was some sort of big hero and the truth is, it's not like Spike was being a hero," said Hull. "I wanted to be in there with my buddies." To fix his predicament with the skipper, Hull went looking for Spike. "The skipper didn't like me very much," Hull confessed, so he figured Spike could help smooth things over. "I said, 'Look what you did for yourself. You gotta do it for me, too.' Spike goes, 'Yeah, sure.'" To assure Spike's success with Anderson, Hull told him that he'd get Conrad "Banker" Caldwell "and I guarantee you Banker will know every single mission." And he did. Hull was back on the mission. Later, he thanked Spike.

The mood of the Navy pilots is shown in a letter Barry Hull wrote home to his family a few days before. Saddam, he wrote, didn't appear to have his bags packed for a trip back to Iraq. "I suppose it could be arranged to send him back, maybe inside his own personal bag." There were no doubts about their readiness to go into combat. Hull was confident that the big picture was well in place and that they'd be able to concentrate on the details he and his squadronmates would soon face. "Occasionally we have the luxury to sit back and think, 'The plans are ready, now what else do I need to do?'" He ran the list of items all the *Sunliners* had to do before the deadline for Saddam's withdrawal drew closer. "We've sanitized our flight suits. That means all nametags and patches are removed. We wear our dog tags. Personal weapons are carried. My survival gear is so full of water that, you guessed it, my Oreos got smushed and I had to eat them and restock. Oh well. Wallets contain only military ID, family pictures, cash and credit cards. The SAR (search and rescue) guys tell us if we go down, we might be able to rent a car and drive out. Weird, huh?" Hull also carried sunscreen, Chapstick and, of course, his Vuarnets. "Would you rather be seen in the desert in Ray-Bans or Vuarnets?" he asked his sister. "One of our maintenance troops gave me a raghead hat, the turban thing, in case I need to go incognito."

Captain Dean M. "Milo" Hendrickson, Speicher's carrier air wing commander, was one of only a few pilots aboard the *Saratoga* who'd actually seen sustained combat. He warned the pilots of the first strike: "You're going to come back. Then you're going to look around . . . and one of you won't be here."

The *Sunliner* squadron's ready room was six decks down in the gigantic ship, and an escalator was used to carry the pilots and their sixty pounds of flight gear up to the flight deck. In the same letter, Hull describes the feeling of seeing the hatch leading outside. "A few deep breaths are taken at this point," Hull wrote home, "because I'm about to enter another world. It's dark and dangerous, and if you're not careful it will kill you." The hatch to the flight deck was always pitch dark and seemed to suck the light out of Hull's flashlight. The hatch led to a catwalk, a small flight of steps below the flight deck. The pilots stepped among fueling hoses and extra catapult wires and chocks and chains and yellow gear. The sodium vapor lights cast an eerie glow on the men and aircraft. Looking into the lights, only the outline of men could be seen. Looking away from the lights, there were only the reflections off goggles and more darkness.

On that flight run a couple of days shy of combat, there were several hundred men topside. Hull had to find a man with a *Sunliner* patch so he could tell him where to find his jet. "He knows what I want," continued Hull in his letter, "and just points without my asking." The twenty- to thirty-knot wind bent the men and the pilots over as they worked to get planes on and off the deck. "Your flashlight gives you a small tunnel vision to see clearly," Hull wrote, "and all the rest is noise and shadows. No faces, just helmets and goggles." Hull had once gone through an entire night launch and not known who his plane captain was—it was too dark to see and too loud to talk.

Before Hull could reach his jet, a Hornet slammed into the deck fifty feet to his left and startled him. Maybe the Hornet's pilot had boltered, for he gave everyone a light show as his hook dragged down the landing area at 150 knots spewing sparks and lighting up the night. All over the deck ordnance men were loading and unloading and pushing carts stacked with bombs and smart missiles. The steam from the catapults blew by, sometimes completely enveloping the men standing in it. As the steam cleared, Hull shone his light onto the Hornet he was looking for and there stood his plane captain, who would oversee the preparations for taking to the skies.

A half-hour before launch, the air boss came up on the loud-speaker: "Gentlemen, it's time to get into the proper flight deck uniform, sleeves rolled down, helmets on and buckled, goggles pulled down, life vests on and securely fastened. Let's check around the go birds for FOD [foreign object debris]. Whenever you're ready, gentlemen, let's crank 'em up, crank the go birds."

No matter how many times a Navy pilot hears those words, they still give him goose bumps. Mounting his Hornet and settling in, Hull looked back on the ladder to see his plane captain close behind. He helped him strap in. With a word or two, Hull's plane captain wished him a safe flight and scampered down to do one last preflight check of the Hornet. From his perch in the cockpit, all Hull could see was the outline of the nineteen-year-old plane captain and the glow of his blue wands. As the Hornet's engines fired up, the canopy came down with a thud, then slid smoothly forward and locked into place.

Fifteen minutes passed before Hull was ready to give a thumb's-up. The chocks and chains were removed from his Hornet, nose wheel steering was engaged, and he armed his ejection seat. Taxi directors in yellow shirts came out to guide his Hornet to the catapult, as he tried to do the takeoff checks and roger the weight board. This refers to calculating the gross weight of the plane, including ordnance, fuel, gear, the pilot's weight, etc. so that the correct thrust can be applied to the catapult that launches the plane off of the carrier. Hull spread the wings of the Hornet and made sure they locked. One last big turn and the jet was in place on the catapult. There is a rhythm and cadence to the men on the deck. Ten men scurried underneath the airplane to do final checks and hook up the launch bar. The taxi signals became precise—small and accurate movements. The ordnance men armed the Hornet's weapons and then passed the plane back. All stations checked "go."

Hull's heart was pounding. The yellow shirt checked with the catapult officer, and Hull got the sign to go for it and run up the engines. As he released the brakes—the hold-back keeping him stationary on the catapult—Hull added full power. His head tilted back and the lights came on—the nighttime salute. The catapult officer touched the deck, signaling launch, and five seconds later the Hornet lurched forward. Within two seconds Hull was doing over 180 miles per hour, pinned to the seat. Hurtled into the air, Hull said, "You better believe most of us tap afterburner." A few nights later, he and his squadronmates would roar off the *Saratoga* for the first air strike of the Persian Gulf War.

In the planning room, Speicher and Albano learned that they'd take off well after midnight and return around dawn. Hearing that news, they decided they'd better get some sleep and walked back to the stateroom they shared. Speicher crawled into the top bunk, Albano into the bottom. They lay still for forty-five minutes, hearts pounding, minds racing.

"I can't sleep," Albano finally said softly.

"I can't, either."

Around 1 A.M. local time, they put on their flight suits, boots and gear, and walked through the mess deck and up to the flight deck. Speicher, Albano and others from the *Sunliners* squadron slapped hands. "See you back on deck in a couple of hours," Albano told his buddy.

Scott Speicher had come to the *Sunliners* as a very junior department head. He didn't become a lieutenant commander until the squadron was under way on the Operation Desert Shield deployment. Scott Speicher had entered Aviation Officers' Candidate School (AOCS) in Pensacola, Florida, in July 1980. After completing training at the top of his class, he was commissioned as an ensign in the U.S. Navy on October 24 of that year. After he finished his flight training, he reported to the *Hellrazors* of VA-174 for his initial A-7E Corsair II replacement pilot training, then was assigned to the *Gunslingers* of VA-105, where he made deployments aboard the USS *Carl Vinson*, USS *Forrestal* and from a base in Iwakuni, Japan. For the next three years, Scott transitioned from the A-7E to the F/A-18 Hornet and qualified as a flight instructor in Strike Fighter Squadron 106 (VFA-106). His years as a flight instructor were followed by a rotation back to a fleet squadron. Scott was a patient and thorough flight instructor. No one who recalled him as a teacher would say otherwise.

Speicher and Albano had met long before. "We developed a close working and then a close personal friendship," Albano would say later. "We had similar personalities." They were also in a tightly knit squadron environment where pilots end up living together for six to nine months out of the year, in close quarters.

"We work together and rely on each other to save one another's life and provide both mutual support on liberty as well as in the air and in combat." There were times, recalled Albano, "that you tell your squadronmates things you never tell your wife." Albano had just rolled off the Carrier Air Wing 17 staff, where he'd been senior landing signal officer, to join the squadron. By chance he ended up filling a slot with the *Sunliners* that had been occupied by Scott's roommate, who'd left for his next assignment. "We became roommates and fellow department heads."

Bano had also just spent some time with Scott and some of the other *Sunliners* out at Fallon, Nevada, where the squadron had gone on workups—training exercises—before their scheduled six-month deployment. "Everyone goes to Lake Tahoe," he said, recalling a funny incident. "It's nice in the wintertime because you can go skiing. Everyone goes and gets a chalet. I remember Scott being passed out. I don't know if he was passed out or just got tired of being in the bar we had gone to, but he went out to the van and it was freezing out there." Scott had bundled up and climbed under all the coats piled in the backseat. "He's out there," continued Bano, "and everyone's getting in the car." Speicher was under all the coats, but no one knew it yet. "Where the hell is Spike?" they thought. Then someone jumped in the backseat, on top of the coats, and Spike started rising up like a hamster out of a pile of sawdust. "He just laid in the back of the van and went to sleep," recalls Bano. "I said, 'Spike, I gotta get you back. You're going to freeze out here. I'm going back to the bar, but I'm going to put you to bed, buddy.'" Spike murmured, "Thanks, Dad."

Later, during the Christmas holiday, the *Saratoga* pulled into Haifa harbor and put off liberty boats for the crew and air wing personnel to go into Israel to see the sights. One day, the pilots were relaxing at a hotel in Haifa where they'd set up a squadron admin, which means the pilots get hotel rooms and hang out and have a good time. They were several floors up on a balcony, having a cookout, and Spike looked across the street at some construction. "Twenty bucks I can hit that bulldozer with this kielbasa," Spike said, smiling broadly. "You're on," the other pilots told him. So Spike grabbed a whole kielbasa, ducked into the room to line up his shot, then quick-stepped to the railing and tossed it. It hurtled up, out across the street and then smacked right on top of the bulldozer. The operator looked over and started yelling, and the pilots cackled. "Direct hit! Direct hit!"

On Christmas Eve, Scott went ashore with his executive officer, Bill "Maggot" McKee, Albano, and Craig "Bert" Bertolett. "We toured around Jerusalem," Albano remembered warmly, "and then we went around Bethlehem that night." Several days later, they toured the area around the Sea of Galilee and tried to find the locations where the Sermon on the Mount and other sacred events in the Bible occurred.

Scott read the Bible regularly, both because of his faith and to gain some historical perspective. "He read the Bible a lot prior to us going to Israel," said Albano. "That's the kind of guy he was—very studious when he wanted to be, very passionate about learning things that he didn't have a clear understanding of . . . he wanted to learn more about a place we were going to go to."

But liberty did not last long. Around lunchtime on January 16, the *Sunliners* got sudden word they'd be going into combat. Adrenaline started flowing as the pilots went up to the strike planning rooms to look over the mission. Before they knew it, they'd be up on the flight deck, manning their Hornets. The hours flew past.

They were all anxious. Barry Hull knew he must be more uptight than he thought because his mouth was so dry. "I need a drink of water," he kept thinking as he stood in the paraloft—a room used to fix and store parachute gear—suiting up in his flight gear before heading up to the flight deck on the escalator. "I must be more nervous than I think I am." Then he remembered the Diet Coke and apple he'd packed in his pockets for the flight. "These missions are so long."

Though he high-fived his best friend, Tony Albano, Scott was quiet. No one was doing a lot of talking. It was time to focus—they had a mission to fly. It was a pitch-black night with just a sliver of moon. But at least it was clear. Once on the flight deck, the pilots could sense the seriousness of what they were about to do. "None of us had ever been in combat before," said Hull.

"We had aircraft turned up and launch safe," recalled Chief Terry Chandler, a *Sunliner* flight deck coordinator. "That night was an emotional period of time for everyone on the roof [the flight deck]. Everybody was ready." Despite the whine and roar of engines, the crew could hear the snapping and popping of the battle flags going up as they prepared their squadron aircraft for departure.

The *Sunliners* were lined up on the aft port side of the deck. Squadron leader Spock Anderson was up first in AA401—the jet he preferred—then AA406, 402, 404 and 403, Scott Speicher's Hornet. Banker Caldwell, the spare, sat in AA410. Gardner, Albano and Hull sat in between, completing final checks and focusing in their minds on the mission ahead. "We ran the lineups, and I shook each pilot's hand and told them we'd be there when they got back," recalled Chandler. "But by the time I got to Speicher, he'd already climbed into his Hornet and the engines were turned up. I told his plane captain to shut down his port engine. Mr. Speicher looked at me, but he trusted my judgment and knew there wasn't anything wrong. I let the boarding ladder down, climbed up and shook his hand like I'd done the others. I wanted him to know that we'd be waiting for him when he got back aboard."

They all took off without any problems. "He was in one of our best jets that night," said Chandler. "AA403 was ready to go."

The *Saratoga*'s crew launched forty-six aircraft off the cata-pults in twenty-five minutes. That means roughly every thirty seconds an aircraft was shot off the deck into the darkness. The pilots headed for their rendezvous point, a fuel tanker plane fly-ing over Saudi Arabia. The tankers flew a big circle in the sky to fill up inbound Coalition aircraft, including *Saratoga*'s Hornets. But the tankers were on a tight schedule. Up on Vulture's Row (an observation deck above the ship's bridge), Lieutenant Com-mander Mark "MRT" Fox watched Scott Speicher take off. Spike tapped the blowers as he lifted off the deck into the dark-ness, bound for his tanking point.

The first night's mission was going to be about five hours long. Most of the action was at least a fourteen-hundred-mile round trip from where the *Saratoga* floated in the Red Sea, so success at the tanker was essential. Though nervous that night, her pilots would eventually get used to tanking off the KC-135s, taking nearly ten tons of gas per jet, per mission. But the KC-135 could be very unforgiving to Navy pilots, especially at night in bad weather—the "goo" as the pilots call it. Designed for Air Force use, the KC-135 Stratotanker had to be adapted to the Navy's drogue method of refueling. There was a learning curve on both sides. For this method, a fueling basket was fitted to the end of a six-foot, barely flexible hose stuck on the end of the tanker's boom. Tanking at night was no cakewalk. Not getting enough fuel the first go-around wasn't good either.

When Barry Hull wrote his folks back home in South Car-olina that previous October during the battle group's simulated air strikes over Saudi Arabia, he'd gotten a taste of tanking off the KC-135 in less than optimal conditions. With most of the jets from the *Saratoga* going for the tankers, there was only one problem: There were over fifty airplanes in a small piece of dark sky, and it was hazy and very gusty with thick cloud cover. "Our tanker track took us directly through a thunderstorm." It was the first time he'd tried to tank off a KC-135 in the middle of the night in the clouds with five of his squadronmates, all flying tight formation so they didn't lose one another in the goo. "Everyone seemed to keep their cool though," he continued, "and we did the whole thing comm out—not one word—except, of course, for some chatter from the F-14 guys, but you have to expect that from them."

One by one, the fighter planes rotated into position to stick a probe into the tanker's fueling basket and fuel up. Since he had a fairly long track yet to go on his mission, Hull pulled his jet away and slipped to the back of the formation. As he did, he looked down into another pilot's cockpit. "We were at the left side of the tanker moving in," he remembered. "I came off the basket and to the right side of the tanker. I pulled my plane up twenty or thirty feet and looked down at this guy below me tanking." He didn't know who it was and couldn't ask; once again, they flew "comm out," staying off the radios to avoid adding to an airwave overload. Piecing it together later back on the ship, he realized he had been looking down into Scott Speicher's cockpit.

Hull marveled at what he saw below: the glow of the instrument panel and the green formation lights of the F/A-18 Hornet, an aircraft many thought to be the most versatile military jet yet made. "Man, that is so cool," Hull said to himself. "Think of the power."

Designed for both air-to-air combat and bombing ground targets, the F/A-18s sported a sophisticated electronic identification system and packed two Sparrow and two Sidewinder missiles for taking on enemy jets. Near the target, the pilot could flip a switch, go from air-to-air to ground-attack mode and drop a bomb. On this night Speicher and the other VFA-81 pilots were each loaded with three high-speed anti-radiation missiles, or HARMs. "The HARM missile is an extremely sophisticated, deadly weapon. I love those things; they're about a million bucks a pop," said Hull. Their job was to take out Iraqi radar, command and control centers and surface-to-air missile sites. The *Sunliners* and their sister squadron, the *Rampagers*, ten Hornets in all, would roll in on their assigned targets just seconds after a volley of cruise missiles fired from American warships. The Iraqis would detect the cruise missiles, flip on their radar, and man their SAMs (surface-to-air missiles). Just then the Hornets would launch their radar-seeking HARMs and slam Iraqi defenses. "The ten of us were like spokes on a wheel," said *Rampager* Dave "Frenchy" Renaud, "all coming toward this target, shooting off our missiles." Then a third wave of bombers would come through and hammer the targets.

The mission of suppressing enemy air defenses and ground targets was dubbed "Iron Hand," a crucial blow to Iraq to start the Gulf War. It was an intricate plan, relying on precise flight paths and accurate information from U.S. Air Force AWACS planes, airborne radar and communications stations that monitored the sky.

The pilots needed every warning that technology had to offer, because on this first night they flew straight into one of the most sophisticated integrated air defenses ever encountered, with about 500 radar installations located at roughly 100 sites. Lieutenant General Charles "Chuck" Horner, in charge of the air campaign, had told allied commander General H. Norman Schwarzkopf that one of every five of his aircraft might get shot down. That would have meant hundreds of losses.

Within minutes of leaving the tanker, Speicher and the other Hornet pilots would get a close look at what worried Horner. They crossed rugged terrain along the Saudi border, and as soon as they entered Iraq, antiaircraft fire streamed up at them. Commander Bob "Ripper" Stumpf was already anxious. Stumpf, executive officer with VFA-83—VFA-81's sister squadron—was the *Rampagers'* leader for the mission. "We proceeded solo and then rendezvoused with the tankers in western Saudi," he recalled. "They dragged us across the drop-off point, about fifty miles south of the Iraqi border." Stumpf had gotten behind an A-6E Intruder pilot at the KC-135 Stratotanker, and the pilot must have had the jitters. The Intruder crew took a long time to get fuel, and Stumpf had to head for the target without a full tank. This troubled him as the mission progressed, but there was nothing he could do about it. The tanker plane had broken off its position with the Hornets and headed for its next tanking assignment.

As he moved closer to his target track, Stumpf's radar warning devices filled his cockpit with warbles and whistles and deedle-deedles. He looked toward the horizon and saw something glowing. It pulsated, as though alive. In the clear night sky he couldn't tell how far away it was. It could have been five miles or fifty. "We didn't really expect this but pretty much as soon as we entered Iraqi airspace, there was antiaircraft fire, missiles and triple-A [antiaircraft artillery]." Stumpf had flown in the 1986 raid on Benghazi, Libya, but that was routine compared with the first night of Desert Storm. Orange balls of antiaircraft fire were shooting up at him. "Holy shit," he thought, "I think I'm going to die."

Each pilot was assigned an altitude in the twenty-five to

thirty-thousand-foot range to make sure they wouldn't collide, but Stumpf started flying up and down quickly to become a tougher target. "That was a violation of the plan because there were so many planes over Iraq that night that each person was assigned a certain route and a certain altitude. You were supposed to stick to it," he said. "If everybody did what I did, they would deconflict, kind of like the FAA does. But I figured the chances of getting hit by a missile were much greater than getting hit by some other airplane I couldn't see." The eyes and ears of Cougar, the AWACS controlling the western Iraqi skies that night, would have to keep Stumpf and the other Hornets on track. Normally, a Navy E-2C Hawkeye watched over Hornet pilots, but on this night, an Air Force AWACS was running the show.

Due to the nature of their mission, the *Saratoga's* Hornet pilots flew alone—no wingman. To make matters more complicated, the rules of engagement that night were strict, particularly those involving beyond-visual-range (BVR) friend or foe identification. With hundreds of jets in the sky, the possibility of "blue-on-blue," or a friendly fire kill, was extremely high. The Hornet pilots had to confirm an enemy fighter at least two ways before firing a missile. They had to see it with their eyes (nearly impossible at night unless the opposing aircraft got extremely close to one another), or they could identify it electronically and the controller could declare it hostile. But they had to have the approval of the AWACS controller, identified that night as tactics officer Captain Jimmy Patterson, to shoot down the bandit. In theory, the AWACS surveillance radar should've been able to distinguish friend or foe right away, but theory didn't always translate into practice—at least not at first.

Hull saw a pulsing glow ahead, too. At first he thought it must be an optical illusion. Then he thought that the Middle East

must have something akin to the Northern Lights. Soon he was
in it. It was in front of him, behind him, to both sides. "I just remember being terrified," he'd say later. The whole landscape was
lit up with an intense glow in the distance. Iraqi antiaircraft fire
shot up like Fourth of July sparklers, illuminating the night and
blanketing the ground. The realization of what it was hit Hull
like a gut punch. The glowing vat turned out to be Baghdad.
Hull's warning gear also began chirping like crazy, distracting
him. He remembered what the Vietnam pilots sometimes did,
and reached over and turned it off. "Screw it," he said, and
started using his own eyes to look for missiles. Looking into the
darkness around him, Hull pondered the old-timers' advice, occasionally glancing at his Hornet's radar homing and warning
gear that he'd just switched off. "I'm going to die looking at this
gauge," he thought.

Just then the controller aboard Cougar—the AWACS—called
out: "I've got a pop-up SA-6."

"You do not want to fly through the envelope of an SA-6. It'll
shoot you down," Hull said. The SA-6 was one of Iraq's most
feared surface-to-air missiles. A pop-up meant that the satellites
hadn't shown it. The eighteen-foot SA-6, mounted on a half-
track, could reach a jet at thirty thousand feet and explode when
it detected the metal of the aircraft. Hull waited for someone to
ask for the missile's location, but no one did. "Damn it," he said.
"Give me the coordinates!" Finally the controller rattled them
off. Hull jotted the location on his kneeboard and compared it
with where he was—and got a sinking feeling. "Oh God, no! I'm
dead over the top of an SA-6." He pushed on, however, and
never saw a missile.

The pilots kept glancing outside their cockpits for immediate
threats and down at their radars, sweeping for enemy fighters.
Cougar's controllers continually updated the air picture as the pi-

lots pushed toward Baghdad. A little over two hours into the mission, bearing north-northeast, *Sunliner* pilots heard their strike leader and Speicher's commanding officer, Spock Anderson, break into the radio frequency using his ATO (air tasking order) call sign, Quicksand 01. "I've got a fast-mover, on my nose, he's hot," Anderson called out. "This is Quicksand 01. Confirm bandit. Request permission to fire."

Anderson needed the controller to call the fast-mover a bandit, an enemy, instead of a bogey, an unknown. Anderson later estimated that he was about forty miles from his target when he picked up a MiG-25PD Foxbat E, a Soviet-made jet that could fly at nearly three times the speed of sound, approaching about 1,000 feet above him. "He was going very fast," Anderson recounted later. "He was headed west-southwest and trying to get around me." Then Anderson and the MiG starting turning toward each other, and Anderson got a good look at the Iraqi aircraft. "I got a radar contact on him first, and then I had a visual contact on him. I was very positive it was a MiG-25."[1] There was also no mistaking the identification of a MiG-25 with the onboard computer library Anderson and the other Hornets were flying with during the war. There was no anomaly where the MiG-25 was concerned, no mistaking it for an equivalent friendly aircraft.

The hair on the back of Barry Hull's neck shot up. He had been so concerned with shooting his HARMs that he had his Hornet in bombing mode instead of sweeping for enemy fighters. "Oh my God! What was I thinking?" Hull flipped the switch and started scanning for air threats. And then he saw the MiG, too. "Oh my God, oh jeez—oh shit!" Hull had always wanted to be a fighter pilot. "I just thought it would be cool." Now there were bad guys out there, and they wanted to kill him. With the MiG on radar, Hull called Cougar. "Confirm bandit?"

But the response from Cougar came back, "Negative, Negative bandit. Confirm bogey."

The call from Anderson also jolted the other squadron pilots. Albano, flying a few miles behind Anderson, knew what "hot" meant. The Iraqi fighter's nose was pointed almost directly at the nose of Anderson's Hornet. A few pilots thought they heard Anderson identify the enemy, but the MiG-25 may have concealed another surprise that no one anticipated that night—its pilot.

Post-engagement analysis and follow-up message traffic read by a source closely associated with the Speicher case suggested that the pilot going head-to-head with Spock Anderson was most likely Russian. Russian instructor pilots were acknowledged to have rotated in and out of Iraq on a regular basis before and during the Gulf War, to train Iraqi pilots in the MiG aircraft Saddam purchased from the former Soviet Union. The Russian Air Force put out a broadly disseminated comment by Lt. Col. Vladimir Vysotsky in the *Komsomolskaya Pravda* on August 7, 1991, in which a reporter asked him whether the outcome of the Gulf War would have been different if Russian pilots had flown the Iraqi aircraft. Vysotsky's answer was "Hardly"—it would be about the same. After all, the Russian pilots had trained the Iraqi pilots. When the reporter suggested that Russian pilots were not that bad, Vysotsky said: "Every pilot with a rational head on his shoulders knows that in case of war, the role reserved for him is that of cannon fodder. He also knows that the situation worries very few people in the highest command echelons." Vysotsky seemed unconcerned that he'd made such strong comments in the face of his superiors. Instead, he offered up the view that he "knew what would happen to his attack aircraft in the first days of the war."

That night, high over the pulsating glow on the fringe of Baghdad, Spock Anderson may very well have been up against an experienced Russian instructor pilot in a MiG-25 Foxbat—and the Russian wanted a fight.

The MiG pilot had flown right over Phil "Chauncey" Gardner's cockpit to get to Spock. "I was feeling some heat," Gardner would recall later. "We had the timing of our shots about a minute to two-and-a-half minutes apart. We were on the west side of the strike package." But the Hornets still had a respectable distance between them, estimated later to be between two and five miles. Chauncey was in the middle of the pack, behind Spock Anderson, to the left in the ten o'clock position, when all hell broke loose and the MiG started to converge on Spock. He heard Spock repeatedly ask permission to fire. The AWACS kept declaring a merge plot, meaning Spock and the MiG-25 were too close to one another to distinguish the two aircraft on radar. Chauncey flipped to Choctaw, one of the *Sunliners'* assigned frequencies. Then he realized there were more MiG-25s in the air around them. "Flying with lights off, the sky was so filled with planes it was the equivalent of doing it blindfolded," he said later.

Meanwhile, Albano looked around frantically for the MiG Spock was chasing on his radar. "He was either out of my radar's field of view or in what I would call a beaming maneuver, which wouldn't negate my radar but it makes it harder to find." By the time it was all over, the only chatter Bano heard on the radio was Spock and the AWACS. The only one who seemed to be oblivious to the MiG was Scott Speicher, who was flying without enemy radar warning because of a system malfunction.

Anderson kept asking Cougar for permission to fire as he and the MiG pilot roared through the dark sky at each other. Anderson didn't want to shoot down one of his own. No stain clung to an aviator more than a blue-on-blue kill. Fellow pilots would talk behind the pilot's back, ask what was wrong with him, get antsy about flying with him. Anderson wanted someone else to see what he surely saw. They'd been told dozens of times: Better to let a bad guy go than shoot down a good guy.

But how could the AWACS not see the MiG? There were several possibilities, but the most likely one was a phenomenon called a Doppler notch. Pilots call it beaming. When two aircraft are flying at or near the same speed and headed in the same direction, both aircraft can vanish from the AWACS' radar screens. The MiG-25 slipped into the notch and disappeared from Cougar's screens.

"Confirm bandit," Anderson said again, not quite yelling but emphasizing the words strongly.

"Negative bandit," the controller said. "Declare bogey."

Now sweeping, Hull spotted the enemy jet on his radar, but it wasn't coming toward him. Albano and the others desperately looked for it but couldn't find it. The AWACS controller came back at Anderson and said, "Standby, looking . . ."

Anderson asked a third time, even more firmly, "Confirm bandit."

"Negative . . . bogey. Negative . . . bogey."

Denied again, Spock Anderson said something that no one up that night is willing to confirm. He then went off the AWACS frequency. And just as he did so, Cougar called back, now seeing the MiG-25, and said: "Confirm bandit! Confirm bandit!" Setting up for their HARM runs, Hull and Gardner heard Anderson get permission to fire.

The Iraqi fighter and Anderson's Hornet zoomed past each other one last time, at a combined speed of better than Mach 2. Neither fired a missile. After three turns with Anderson, the MiG broke away and headed toward the east. Anderson proceeded toward his target. "I'm pretty sure I saw Spock's HARM missiles being launched as I was approaching the axis at a perpendicular aspect. But this was after he had already broken off the engagement with the MiG-25," said Albano. The pilots figured the jet "bugged out," just kept flying away from the Hornets, knowing they didn't have the power to catch him. Some A-6E pilots saw the massive exhaust, nearly three hundred feet long, of a MiG right over their heads. A few minutes later, at 3:49 in the morning, an intense flash startled Anderson. He noticed that it came from the east, where Scott Speicher had been headed on his HARM mission. In all the confusion, no one paid attention to who said it, but one A-6E crewmember heard a Navy pilot cry out:

"Fireball! Fireball! Somebody just got hit!"

There were four Navy Intruders in the area where Scott Speicher was last spotted. With their night vision goggles, they could see airborne threats no one else could. One of them did a left 360-degree turn looking for the MiG that had flown over their formation. The Iraqi fighter was gone, but they could see flaming wreckage careening toward the desert below.

"Who would have guessed that a MiG-25 would circle back behind us?" Hull said. "I mean, you just think about it, when you meet in the merge, when you've got over seventeen hundred knots of closure and somebody goes *whhhhhhhewwww* past you . . ." The experience of seeing the MiG-25 so close was unnerving.

Dave "Frenchy" Renaud, from VFA-83, heard Anderson say the MiG had turned "cold," flown out of firing range. "When a fighter turns away like that," said Renaud, "he takes himself out of the head-on envelope of the Sparrow missile. He's not in range anymore." Renaud was right. The MiG-25 was gone. A few minutes later, he saw a big explosion off to his right. It seemed close, maybe five or ten miles away. He didn't see the missile, just the flash, and the bright light mesmerized him. He watched it sparkle and glow all the way to the desert floor. "Must be an Iraqi jet getting knocked out by an F-15," he thought. That made sense. Air Force F-15s had launched ahead of the other jets and were to sweep the skies of Iraqi fighters. The radio frequency was still buzzing, so Renaud didn't report the explosion—there was a lot of needless radio chatter. Nor did he mark his latitude and longitude. Just in case, though, he did talk into a tape recorder running in his cockpit. He remembers saying into his HUD (Head-Up Display), "I see a big explosion off to my right. There's a secondary explosion."

Scott Speicher had also heard Spock Anderson's calls to Cougar on the MiG-25, but it never occurred to him that the MiG-25 had turned east toward him. He was still on autopilot and focused on his HUD when the MiG-25 Foxbat blew past him, creating what the AWACS controller later called another merge plot. Though there was more than one MiG-25 in the area that night, the one that Spock chased seemed the most likely guilty party. But the Foxbat kept going and cleared the area. Then a missile fired beyond visual range detonated in the proximity of Spike's Hornet. Though obviously not intentionally, a MiG sweeper had panicked and fired at a "MiG-25," a Defense Intelligence Agency (DIA) source, who asked for anonymity, confirmed.

Stumpf saw the explosion, too. The blast lit up his Hornet like a strobe. There was a pale yellow flash that some of the pilots who saw it described as like the exhaust of a missile or the jet plume of a rocket. "You knew something was there," said Stumpf, "but I didn't see a fireball. I wasn't looking directly at the flash." Pay attention, Stumpf told himself, and don't do anything stupid. He and Renaud pushed toward the targets, fired their HARMs, and then turned south toward the tankers.

Stumpf had never fired a HARM before. As his HARMs released, one by one, they made a *whoosh* sound so loud he could
hear it. The Hornet shook with each one coming off the rail. "It
takes off and it's real bright . . . white exhaust . . . big exhaust
plume coming out of this rocket, real fast and these actually start
climbing. They go out in front of the airplane and start this steep
climb," he recalled later. The HARM's proportional guidance
system causes the missile to arc as it homes in on the selected target, making appropriate in-flight corrections. "At that point
you're thinking about getting out of Dodge without getting
bagged, so you're going fast and changing altitudes, navigating
so you hit the proper exit points, which were all defined earlier,
so you look like a good guy, not a bad guy." Stumpf wanted to
haul out of there, but instead he had to chug back to conserve
fuel. It seemed to take forever to near the Saudi border.

Renaud got worried after firing his HARMs. "I think I got
most scared," said Renaud, "when I shot my third HARM and I
had to do a one-eighty . . . from the target area. It took me a
longer time than I wanted to make the turn, and I can remember
getting a little bit slow in the turn so I lit up the afterburners to
get more power." Then he thought to himself, "Now I'm going
to get myself seen."

Hull also lit his afterburners to blaze home, then remembered
that would make him an easy mark for a heat-seeking missile,
and he backed off. The Hornets all converged at the fuel tankers,
where they had to pass through a gateway, a specific location and
altitude that would let others know they were not enemy aircraft
trying to slip through. On the way back, the Hornets turned on
their IFF (identify friend or foe) so friendly aircraft could distinguish them from enemy aircraft.

About twenty miles from the Saudi border, pilots started

checking in with Cougar. Speicher—ATO call sign "Indian 502"—should have reported in before Albano but didn't. Anderson asked Albano to try to reach Speicher, so Albano tried a tactical frequency used only by VFA-81.

"Spike . . . Bano . . . You up?"

Nothing.

"Spike . . . Bano."

He switched to another frequency. "Spike . . . Bano . . . You up?"

Silence.

Albano radioed Hull and asked him to try. "Skull, can you talk to Spike?"

"Spike . . . ? Skull."

"Spike, have you got me?"

"Spike, come in! Spike, everything okay?"

"Spike! How copy?"

No response.

Hull radioed Albano and said he couldn't raise Speicher. "Bano, I haven't got him. I'm heading south. Everything's fine with me, but I can't raise him." Albano relayed the message to their skipper.

"Bano's back up."

"Any word?" Anderson asked.

"No, sir."

As they rolled off the tanker and headed back to the ship, Dave Renaud heard Albano talking to Hull: "I wish Spike would check in."

Tony Albano knew it was not a good sign that Speicher hadn't answered. He ran all the possible scenarios in his head on the way back to the *Saratoga*. First he thought Spike had had a mechanical failure, turned around and gone back to the ship. Or maybe he flew to one of the diversion airfields for an emergency landing. Bano never considered that the MiG-25 had gotten Speicher. "From what I heard," he said. "the MiG just started running toward the east, toward Baghdad, and I don't know if anyone else saw [the MiG] or anything like that. There were no reports of him later." Whatever happened, Bano never thought for a moment that Spike was dead. Speicher could have ejected and been rescued by a special operations team or, in the worst case, ejected and started evading capture. That possibility sobered Albano, and he flew in silence back to the *Saratoga*.

Waiting for them was the *Saratoga*'s E-2C Hawkeye, their usual controlling plane. It had been "in the box" all night, flying an elliptical pattern in the northeast corner of Saudi Arabia, away from the action. The crew wasn't comfortable out of the action, separated from their air wing strike package and out of the lead controller's role, but they were lucky to be there at all. Their participation in the first strike was not part of the original plan. "At the last minute, with everybody wanting a piece of the action that night, they were given a role," recalled Tony Albano. The Hawkeye crew was assigned to watch out for friendlies leaving Iraq and guard against the possibility of an Iraqi jet trying to make a break for a sneak attack on the fleet in the Red Sea.

Lieutenant Commander Mark "Shark" Cantrell, VAW-125's mission commander in the back of the Hawkeye, was tasked with trying to keep up with the combined Navy strike package off *Saratoga* and *Kennedy* with the help of his air control officers (ACO) and radar officers (RO)—Lieutenant Richard "Rick" English and Lieutenant (junior grade) David "Wavy Davey" Adams—sitting to his left and right. "Our sole job that night was to try to keep Air Force fighters under AWACS control from shooting down our guys. But there were just too many planes up that night for us to get a clear picture of anything—and we were out of range once we parted ways with the F/A-18s and A-6Es at the crossover point on the border, where we stayed back and the AWACS took over control of the strike. We did stay in contact with the AWACS, and every time we called them up they were there."

As the *Saratoga*'s F/A-18s began crossing back over the Iraq-Saudi border, Cantrell, English and Adams counted noses coming out of Iraq, checking to make sure they all made it. "I remember all of us saying at the same time, 'Where's Spike?'" said Cantrell. "We checked a couple of times, tried different frequencies and got nothing. We called the AWACS to see if they had him. Nothing. I got on the radio with the JRCC [Joint Recovery Command Center] in Riyadh via the AWACS and told them we were missing an airplane." Cantrell's call should have been enough to initiate a check of divert fields where Speicher could have landed his jet if it was crippled and let SOCCENT [Special Operations Command Central] know there was a pilot down. It wasn't. The crew went immediately to the carrier intelligence center to debrief the flight. There Cantrell told intelligence officers Speicher hadn't checked in and that he'd notified JRCC. The JRCC later claimed no record of the communication. That was the first mistake, but hardly the last, that would doom Scott Speicher to the desert of Iraq.

CHAPTER 2

Indian 502 Is Down

There was a four-hour cycle between preparing to receive the first strike and prepping the next one. "We'd gotten the first group back and were counting noses when we realized that there was one missing. The moment the rest of them got on deck," said flight deck coordinator Terry Chandler of the *Sunliner* pilots who returned from the strike, "they bolted for the ready room—except for Spock. He came over to me and said, 'Chief, I think we lost Speicher.'" The chief took four of his plane handlers and staged up on the bow for the next two hours waiting and hoping that Scott Speicher would come back. They stayed there until the air boss, Captain James "Jet" O'Hora, came on the radio on the roof and said, "*Sunliners*, breaking the deck."

"We knew then that he wasn't coming home," Chandler recounted, the emotion breaking his voice. "We waited for him as long as they'd let us stay up there. When I shook his hand, it meant something to me. It meant we'd be there for him when he came back. I promised him."

Shell-shocked, Dave Renaud strode through the passageways of the carrier *Saratoga*, his mind replaying that night's strike,

unscramble the radio calls about the MiG-25, the
seen and the other pilots trying to get a response
peicher. He couldn't believe that, of all the pilots in
the sky, he'd had the best view of the explosion. It seemed so big,
Renaud thought that no one flying over Iraq at the time could
have missed it. He chastised himself that he should have marked
his position, should have broken onto the AWACS frequency
and reported what he saw, but the radio was busy, and he had
missiles to fire. Everything had been so confusing, happening
so fast.

When he'd landed his F/A-18 back on the *Saratoga*, Renaud
had gone straight to the ship's intelligence center, where pilots
report the details of their missions. The air wing intelligence officer asked Renaud if he'd seen anything out of the ordinary. Renaud told him about the fireball, how big and bright it was and
how he watched it fall into the desert. "It didn't look to me like
that was a survivable explosion," Renaud said. "You know," the
intelligence officer told him, "Speicher did not come back. Go
straight to Spock Anderson and tell him what you know."

Renaud found Anderson in one of the ready rooms. Renaud
always flew with a tape running in his head-up display, to record
the action in front of the Hornet and in the cockpit. On a night
mission, the video would be worthless, but he'd still have the
sound—the radio communications and anything he said would
have been recorded. They listened to the tape a couple of times,
and found where Renaud was when he spoke into his micro-
phone about the explosion. They matched that against other
Hornet data that tracked Renaud's flight minute by minute.

If a surface-to-air missile or an enemy fighter had knocked
Speicher out of the sky, Anderson would have to know precisely
where to get special operations forces to search. They pulled out

Renaud's flight chart. Renaud scribbled a circle where he thought he'd seen the explosion. Next to it, he wrote, "Spike."

In the meantime, Bob Stumpf headed to the carrier's intelligence center for his post-mission debrief. As he wound his way through the ship, he ran into a *Sunliner* pilot, he doesn't recall who it was. "Hey, how'd it go?" Stumpf asked. "Speicher didn't come back," said the pilot. "Oh my gosh," said Stumpf. "I guess I thought he was probably on the ground, evading, or that there was a rescue mission in process and we'd see him in the morning." In Stumpf's mind, there were two likely scenarios: ejected and rescued, or ejected and captured. He never considered that Speicher was dead. Stumpf based this belief on the fact that in an air-to-air situation, the missiles have smaller warheads than ground-to-air missiles. Air-to-air missiles are designed to render the aircraft unflyable, not kill the pilot or totally destroy the aircraft.

"As I recall," said Stumpf in a July 2001 interview, "Spock Anderson started a personal movement . . . I mean he took it upon himself to figure this out." He remembered Anderson saying, "I got to figure out what happened to Spike. I need to make sure things are happening." Anderson stopped by Stumpf's room and asked for all the data from his flight. "We went to the airplane and dumped all the information out of the computer. I gave him a big stack of printouts that defined my flight pattern. He did a very detailed analysis trying to figure out when [Spike] went down, what happened, and I know I asked Frenchy from our squadron to be Spock's assistant if he needed any help."

Meanwhile, Albano wondered if Speicher had his survival radio, and if so, was he simply going by what they'd all been told briefing the mission: Don't turn on your radio and monitor because the Iraqis will use direction finding to locate you. "They had that capability." If he'd done everything right, Albano thought, he felt sure Spike was alive. Albano wondered where he'd landed, too. With the winds the way they were, he could have landed up to two-and-a-half miles from where his plane was thought to have gone down. Then Bano inevitably came back to the thought: "Could I have done more about the MiG-25?"

Anderson's initial effort to figure out where Scott had gone down didn't get a great deal of support from the air wing chain of command. The *Saratoga* started recovering aircraft from the first air strike at 5:38 A.M. By 7:04, the ship had completed the recovery of its planes, minus one. The petty officer of the watch wrote in the ship's deck log: "Completed recovery of aircraft with the exception of F/A-18 side #403—Pilot LCDR Speicher of VFA-81." Shortly before launching the second wave of aircraft at 11:12 that morning, the *Saratoga*'s commanding officer, Captain Joseph S. Mobley, came up on the 1MC—the shipboard address system—to announce that Speicher had not come back from the first strike. But still, no one had notified Naval Forces Central Command (NAVCENT) that they had a pilot missing. The delay of Scott's air wing in reporting his shootdown was critical. As a rule, the first four to five hours after a shootdown are when a combat search and rescue is most likely to succeed. This time frame was exceeded twice over before Lieutenant General Chuck Horner received the information and told General H. Norman Schwarzkopf that the Navy had lost an airplane.

The first news about the initial air strike that General Schwarzkopf received was completely positive. "My Air Force component commander, Chuck Horner, had told me," he recalled when interviewed on August 21, 2001, "we could expect as high as twenty percent casualties, which would have been literally in the hundreds of aircraft shot down, so I was very anxious for the first report back." He received it from the Navy at 5:50 A.M.

In his combat diary, it reads: "All 56 aircraft from the first strike are back." At 6:55 General Horner called Schwarzkopf to say, "All aircraft back."

"Again," he said, "I just assumed he was talking about all aircraft that were used in the first strike. They were going to be flying through the worst of it." The first indication that Schwarzkopf had that he had any downed aircraft was at 12:55 P.M. on January 17, "and that report stated at that time there had been two losses—Speicher and the British GR-1 Tornado crew of Flight Lieutenants John Nichol and John Peters. My God," he exclaimed, "that is an order of magnitude better than what we expected."

"I know [Anderson] was terribly frustrated," said Stumpf. "He was not happy. I got the sense that he wasn't getting the help that he needed from the hierarchy." From the combat reports, the assumption was made that Scott Speicher had gone down in a ball of flame. Adding to that perception was the fact no one had heard a call on emergency frequencies. But in all the confusion, had they just missed it? The other possibility was that Scott had experienced total electrical failure, in which case he didn't have a chance to make a radio call from the cockpit before ejecting. The deputy air wing commander [DCAG] on *Saratoga*, Dave Park, had flown in an A-6E, and he didn't know for sure about Spike until he got back on deck. "I asked them to check divert fields before I got some sleep. We were all tired—exhausted from the mission," recalled Park, now a retired captain. "I got up four hours later and no one had done it. I made them do it when I found out." By then nearly eight hours had slipped by, and Scott Speicher was still stranded on the desert floor. "We on the *Saratoga*," said Park, "never confirmed he went down."

Park and Captain Dean M. "Milo" Hendrickson, Speicher's carrier air wing commander or CAG, were in the key positions to save Spike. "As DCAG," said pilot Craig "Bert" Bertolett later,

"Park was in the prime role to be responsible for communicating between what the squadron and air wing knew—for example, the oversized radios for vest pockets, disabled seat locators, [where] Frenchy's estimated crash site [for Speicher was]—and what CENTCOM or Arthur's staff should have known to execute smart decisions about CSAR," or a combat search and rescue. Bertolett was not alone making this point. "I've often blamed the faceless 'somebody' in the organization who failed to act, communicate and decide," Bertolett said.

Hendrickson and Park had issued the order to their squadron maintenance officers to turn off the electronic transponders (ELTs) in the ejection seats, as had some of the other air wing commanders on other aircraft carriers in the Red Sea and Persian Gulf, and that helped seal Scott Speicher's fate that night. Another factor was the Motorola AN/PRC-112 radio. The new radios had arrived on the ship on January 16, just hours before departure on the first air strike. Because they had been rushed out to the *Saratoga*, they never went through the operational testing that normally takes place before a new product is introduced to the fleet. The AN/PRC-112s, which have since been improved and sold to thirty different countries, have worked fine, according to Motorola. Yet the Navy had to issue a directive that the AN/PRC-112 was to be placed in a Ziploc bag because it would short out when exposed to too much moisture. The radios were not meant for carrier aviation. They were also not designed to fit in the vest pockets of naval aviators' flight gear. Scott's paraloft chief, Ted Phagan, told Scott and his squadronmates heading out on the first strike, "There's a real good chance if you eject, this thing's not staying in your pocket." Though Phagan devised a flap to hold the radio in place for aviators on subsequent missions, that was too late to help Scott Speicher. Some aviators insisted on keeping their old radios, PRC-90s, when they found the new ones too awkward to carry. As the PRC-112 began to show its shortfalls, the PRC-90s became prize possessions to Navy pilots.

In this case the media knew more than the chain of command aboard the *Saratoga*. Less than twelve hours after Scott was shot down, Paris Antenne-2 Television Network (broadcast in French) ran a news spot at one o'clock in the afternoon Paris local time that included an Islamic Republic News Agency (IRNA) report that said an American jet was downed—pilot ejected. Less than six hours later, the Joint Chiefs of Staff sent out message traffic with a printed transcript of the news video attached. In a note scrawled in the margin, someone wrote, "Only U.S. plane lost was a Navy F-18; pilot never heard from." But no one ran down the source of the news report or passed along the information about the ejected pilot to combat search and rescue forces in Riyadh.

The initial loss report for Speicher, filed twelve hours after his disappearance, was forwarded from Rear Admiral George N. "Nick" Gee to Rear Admiral Riley Mixon, senior commander— the boss—in the Red Sea. "Riley," said Gee, "the loss of AA403 during our initial Baghdad strike is most unfortunate." He compiled the facts as they were known from aircrew debriefs and observations by Spock Anderson. Anderson reported that Scott Speicher was headed to his target—Al Taqqadum—roughly forty miles west of Baghdad. His time on target (TOT) was estimated to be 3:50 A.M. Baghdad time, and Speicher failed to show up for his tanking point along the Raisin tanker track at 4:40 A.M. A radar cut gave Speicher's last position as 29-15NE7/041-005E. The time was 3:20 A.M. and Spike was heading 015 degrees true. His launch point was 015 degrees, 268 nautical miles from his refueling point.

At 7:30 the following morning, January 18, Anderson filled out an information sheet for the Defense Intelligence Agency

(DIA), giving the agency pertinent information on Scott's crash.
He was still listed as "Duty Status, Whereabouts Unknown." Anderson referred to his own message traffic reporting the loss, sent
around first light on January 17, then added, "No firm info as to
where and when the aircraft was lost or the fate of pilot. Search
initiated." Strangely, in the blank for location of loss, Anderson
scribbled, "Classified." Yet if the loss location were unknown, why
not state the more accepted phrase "Whereabouts unknown"? Instead Anderson had marked that the location was a secret.

Stumpf thought that Anderson had gathered enough information to go look for Spike. He'd given a good appoximate location, and there was no evidence that Scott Speicher was dead, "so
it seems to me that with all our massive array of airpower and
rescue forces available—exercised just a couple of days later, that
I know of firsthand," said Stumpf, "it was all there, it was in place
and we should have gone in and looked." But Stumpf realized,
too, that the *Saratoga* was a long way from the search and rescue
forces in Riyadh. "We were seven hundred miles away from
where Spike went down. We couldn't just pick up the phone and
call Riyadh and say, 'Hey, go ahead. Launch the rescue.'"

What Stumpf and the other pilots aboard the *Saratoga* didn't
know was that when the coordinates for Scott's probable crash
site were finally reported, they were not confirmed, resulting in
another set of coordinates being reported as the shootdown site.
The erroneous coordinates were reported as 3245N/04445E,
which would turn out to be far from where he actually went
down. By then the damage was done. The wrong set of coordinates continued to be the ones put out in messages well past the
end of the war.

Twelve hours after Scott was shot down, military leaders in
Washington briefed the media about the first night of the Gulf
War. Secretary of Defense Dick Cheney and Chairman of the

Joint Chiefs of Staff Colin Powell described an incredibly successful series of air strikes. "There's been a single American aircraft lost," Cheney told reporters. "It involves a single casualty. I
don't know that we want to identify the aircraft, do we?"

Cheney looked at Powell.

"It was an F-18," Powell said.

Was that a wounding or a death? a reporter asked.

"A . . . ," Cheney hesitated, "a death."

Cheney didn't name Speicher, but the pilots back on the
Saratoga knew who he was talking about. As soon as the squadrons
returned that morning, Speicher's fate became the buzz of the
ship. Cheney's statement assumed that the blast Renaud saw was
Speicher's jet and that he couldn't have survived the explosion.
That theory would fuel assumptions of his death for years. "How
do you say something like that," said Albano recently, "without
knowing all the facts?"

Bob Stumpf, of the VFA-83 *Rampagers*, heard that Speicher
hadn't tried to contact anyone with his survival radio, but he also
heard that VFA-81's new radios wouldn't fit in their pockets.
Maybe Speicher lost his when he ejected and couldn't contact
anyone. He knew that Renaud hadn't seen a parachute after the
explosion, but it was the middle of the night. Stumpf thought
they would declare Speicher killed so quickly only if someone
had found his body. "Killed in action, that's just bullshit," said
Stumpf. "They had no business saying that because there was no
evidence he was dead. So he's missing in action at that point, but
they said 'killed' so I'm thinking, 'Well, shit, they know something we don't know.' To me, that was very decisive, absolute, to
say that he was KIA [killed in action]."

If Speicher wasn't dead, the pilots knew that what Cheney had
said could doom him. If the Iraqis captured Speicher and if President Saddam Hussein knew U.S. leaders thought he was dead,

maybe Saddam would keep him. An American pilot would be a trophy prisoner. Fellow pilots hadn't assumed Speicher was dead. If a missile had impacted Speicher's Hornet, he likely ejected, they thought. "So, you know, it was premature," said Stumpf, of the Cheney gaffe declaring Speicher killed in action. But what none of the *Saratoga*'s pilots—and much of Speicher's chain of command—didn't realize was that Cheney's public pronouncement of death was nothing more than that—a snap judgment in front of a room full of reporters. The Navy's official status for Scott Speicher was MIA.

Why had Cheney declared Scott dead? When NAVCENT Vice Admiral Stanley R. Arthur requested information about the loss incident, Milo Hendrickson told Arthur that Scott's Hornet had been blown out of the sky—with no chance of survival, no ejection. Arthur called Vice Admiral Jeremy "Mike" Boorda, then chief of naval personnel, and repeated what he'd heard from Scott's air wing commander. When Cheney came in the next morning to give his press brief, he stuck his head in Boorda's door and asked where they stood on the F/A-18 loss. "Hey, it doesn't look good," said Boorda. Cheney replied, "He's dead?" "Yes, sir, pretty much he's dead," Boorda told him.

In a war involving pilots launching bombing raids from carriers in two different seas and coordination between military leaders in Washington and Riyadh, it might take days to thoroughly search for a downed pilot. Later that day, Anderson called a meeting of his officers. Barry Hull remembers Anderson giving the news straight. "Guys, you know Spike didn't make it back last night," Anderson said, "and he did not divert, either." "That's when it hit us," said Hull. "What the hell happened? Where's Spike?" He remembered what he and others kept thinking, "Well, he must be pissed off 'cause he's walking around in the desert and he's got sand in his boots. We just never let ourselves think that he was dead."

That afternoon in Jacksonville, Florida, Navy wives and relatives anxiously wondered which Hornet pilot had been killed. A middle-class neighborhood had sprouted under the flight paths of Cecil Field Naval Air Station, and there was no ignoring the jets when they roared overhead. Many of the pilots' teenagers went to Nathan Bedford Forrest High School, Speicher's alma mater, where his wife, Joanne, had briefly taught home economics before quitting to have Meghan, then three, and Scott's namesake, Michael, nearly two.

Scott had met Joanne at Florida State University in 1977. She was a public relations and marketing major; he was a business major one year ahead of her. She would never forget the time he went to his first job interview, in his senior year at Florida State. It was for a typical nine-to-five desk job. He couldn't see himself pinned down behind a desk every day and told her so. "I want to fly," he confessed.[2] Though he'd never flown an airplane before, years of listening to his father, Wallace, a World War II fighter pilot, tell stories about his missions hooked him on the idea. The career path seemed perfectly suited for Scott, the risk-taker with the impish grin, the kid from Missouri who moved to Florida and loved to sunbathe: "You're living in Florida, man, you gotta have a tan," he'd say.

Scott Speicher loved the thrill of life on the edge. He was the guy who one-upped his Florida State buddies on the rite of passage of diving from a thirty-foot cliff into Big Dismal Sink, a sinkhole about fifteen to twenty miles south of Tallahassee. "When you got there," said David Rowe, a childhood friend, "depending on the water level, it's anywhere from a thirty- to sixty-foot sheer drop to the water." They all took turns jumping feet first off the edge of the cliff. To get out, they'd grab a rope and pull themselves out of the mud and slime at the edge of the water below. Speicher watched his friends jump in, then stood at the edge of the cliff and grinned. "C'mon, Spike," they hollered up. "Is that the best you can do? That's baby lotion!" he yelled down. "That's baby lotion" was Spike's way of saying, "That ain't nothing." Speicher climbed an oak tree on the western edge of the sinkhole and soared headfirst about sixty feet into the water. "Headfirst," his friend recalled, "then a back flip. I can see him now with his arms flying, head back, looking to spot the water." Rowe thought right then that Spike was destined to get cata-pulted from aircraft carriers for a living. "Way to go, Spike! You are the man!" There was no doubt that Scott was okay. "You had to know Spike," said Rowe.

Soon after graduation from Florida State in 1980, Scott headed for Aviation Officers' Candidate School (AOCS) in Pen-sacola. He was an excellent pilot from the start. Two-and-a-half years later Scott completed flight training and married Joanne, by then an assistant department store buyer, in a Navy wedding ceremony at Cecil Field in December 1983. From the start, the couple understood the dangers inherent in Scott's flying. He made sure she understood what to do if anything happened to him. He'd make her recite it to him every time he left for workups and deployments. "If anything happens to me, you know what to do?" Scott asked her. She'd inevitably reply yes.[3] Joanne never imagined she'd actually have to put into action any of the contingency plans they discussed.

Navy representatives drove down the street, past the yellow ribbons and red, white and blue streamers that had been tied to lampposts five months earlier when the ships first deployed for Desert Shield. They could have stopped at many homes in that neighborhood, but they knocked on the door of Joanne Speicher's battleship-gray ranch house.

She, too, had heard what Cheney said, but she didn't know who'd been killed. They told her. The Boy Scout, the kid who had balanced on the end of the diving board for a shot in the high school yearbook, the husband who sat on the floor with the four- and five-year-olds in his Sunday school class to help color and paste, would not be coming home when the war ended. Now, as Navy officers in crisp dress blues stood in Joanne's doorway to give her the news, suddenly the past worries, the fears that she'd hesitated to share with Scott, came flooding back—and so did the weeks and months that had elapsed since she last saw her husband.

Joanne thought back to when he'd left on the deployment, on August 7, 1990. She remembered that the morning was not remarkable, other than the fact that Scott was heading off to the air station to leave for six months or more. She told Kathryn Casey at *Ladies' Homes Journal* that she kissed him good-bye at the front door and off he went. The children waved. "This was part of our lives," she told Casey. "It was like a regular day."

Joanne kept to her routine, taking Meghan to her preschool three times a week and Michael to a Mothers' Day Out babysitting program held at a nearby church on Wednesdays. Casey reported in her June 1991 article, "Ten days after Scott left, his letters began arriving. They were scrawled on yellow legal paper, and he often signed them 'Spike.'" Though Joanne had not been in the habit of keeping Scott's letters in the past, she began to tuck them away in her top dresser drawer. She told Casey that she'd not wanted to burden Scott with disappointing news, but when she realized their attempt to conceive a third child hadn't worked, "I had to write and tell him that it hadn't happened. I was disappointed. He was, too. Later I felt like there was a reason it hadn't happened." In reply, he wrote back, "Don't worry about it. We'll do it. There's time."

Joanne didn't get scared until around Christmas, as tensions escalated with passage of the UN Security Council resolution permitting the use of troops against Iraq if it didn't vacate Kuwait by January 15. With the resolution, President George Bush had been given the green light to go after Saddam Hussein for his encroachment on Kuwait that fall. In the letters she and Scott exchanged during the holidays, Joanne began to express her fears of what might happen in the Persian Gulf region. "You know that I am completely proficient in this airplane," he wrote. "I'll be home. I guarantee it."[4] But there were no guarantees. Joanne just couldn't understand, she later told Casey, why he kept saying, "I guarantee it."

As the deadline for Iraq's withdrawal from Kuwait neared, Joanne was glued to her television set like the rest of America. When Saddam ignored repeated warnings on January 15, fireworks were soon to follow. She'd been almost euphoric about Scott's participation in the first strike, and it wasn't until the next morning when she heard a reporter on television talking about a downed F/A-18, according to Casey, that a dose of hard reality snapped her out of it. Yet since no one had called to tell her anything had happened to Scott, she went about her daily routine.

Joanne would remember later that all she heard when the car pulled up was the door closing. "She looked out the screen door," wrote Casey, "toward the driveway and saw the admiral of Cecil Field, the local base, the commodore, the commodore's wife and the chaplain. The men were in their dress blues." "They didn't have to say a thing," Joanne recalled. "The first thing I asked was, 'How did it happen?'" What followed after uttering those words was a blur. The Speicher house soon filled with people, as family and friends, officials from Cecil Field and well-meaning squadron wives filed in and out. Joanne, meanwhile, was slumped on a couch as she talked to them, one at a time, sometimes in small groups. It was all too much of a shock. She was overwhelmed. Then she thought about Meghan and Michael. Meghan was old enough to understand, but Michael wasn't. He played on the floor with his toys as he did every day, except for the crush of visitors in his house. When Michael's two-year-old curiosity got the best of him, he stopped playing to visit among the throngs of strangers and familiar faces, but he had no idea why they were there.

Meghan was a different story. Joanne took Meghan into her daintily decorated little girl's bedroom to tell her about her father. As they sat there together, Joanne asked her if she knew why all the people were in the house. "No," she said. "It's because they have something to tell me about Daddy," Joanne replied. "Something happened to Daddy's airplane." They were quiet for a few minutes, then Meghan said in her little voice, "My daddy?" Joanne nodded and said, "Yup."[5] Sensing her mother's grief, Meghan knew that whatever had happened to her father, it was bad. Joanne didn't have to say another word.

She didn't know for certain what had happened to her husband, but her thoughts drifted to what he might have been thinking in his last moments in the airplane. The torment was nearly unbearable. But the children kept her focused. She drove Meghan to preschool the next morning.[6] Still she didn't know exactly what had happened to Scott—and wouldn't for some time.

Casey writes that on Joanne's thirty-second birthday, the first Sunday following Scott's loss, she had a friend send President Bush a telegram. She didn't want the president to think she was angry about what had happened to Scott. Her support for U.S.

action in the Persian Gulf was unwavering. The president got the message and replied a couple of weeks later. "I am proud of your wonderful husband, and I will never forget him," he wrote. "Sometimes God acts in strange ways—ways we do not understand right away."[7]

The president's letter wasn't the only one to arrive at Joanne's door. For several weeks to come, letters Scott had mailed in the days preceding his disappearance were brought by a tearful mail carrier. Folded inside each envelope were several pages of yellow legal paper filled with Scott's thoughts. He always assured Joanne he'd come home.[8] She was numbed by each word, still unsure what had happened to her husband. Maybe he'd make it. Maybe he would come home. After all, the *Saratoga*'s captain, Joseph S. Mobley, kept personally communicating with her. "Every effort," he said, "continues to be made to locate Scott." Spock Anderson told her the same. "All, repeat, all, theater combat search and rescue efforts were mobilized." She couldn't know that this was far from the truth. She was terrified and hopeful at the same time, and it was taking its toll.

Two weeks after she'd learned about Scott's loss, Joanne finally came to grips with the feelings of loss she'd kept pent up inside her. It was late—half past two in the morning—and she'd talked for hours with friend Albert "Buddy" Harris, who'd decided it was time for Joanne to let out the emotions that she'd hidden well from everyone coming by the house, as well as from the children. She admitted her deepest thoughts, the fears she had for Scott but didn't want to hear herself say. "I didn't want Scott to know. I didn't want him to be scared for one second. I didn't want him to think, 'Oh, no, I'm going down,'" Joanne related to Kathryn Casey. "And I couldn't bear the thought of having a service and having nothing to bury."

Several days later Joanne received a large brown envelope that contained Scott Speicher's personal effects, including a red nylon wallet with his Florida driver's license, credit card and pictures of the children, his gold wings, a gold wedding ring—and one last letter, written January 16, 1991, the day before he disappeared. "All along I knew that there would be one more letter," Joanne said.[9] The content of the last letter Scott had placed with his personal effects speaks for itself.

"As I sit down to write this letter," he wrote, "things in this part of the world seem to grow more intense every hour." He continued, "I am more certain that our air wing will be called upon . . . If you are reading this letter, it will be for one of two reasons: 1) I have decided I need to personally share these thoughts with you instead of holding them inside, or 2) Something has happened to me. I hope it is number one."[10]

He wrote separate sections to Joanne, Meghan and Michael, each beginning with "I love you." To his children, he offered his heartfelt wishes for what he wanted them to do with their lives. He told them to set goals and pursue a good education. Be kind to one another, he said. Put God first in your lives. To Joanne he said, "You are the centerpiece of my life. I have lived with you in complete satisfaction. If I am gone, learn to love again." Joanne, wrote Casey, was quieted by Scott's words. But at the time she believed Scott was dead. She was ready to move on. The children would move on. "I'm at peace. I feel like it's over, and he is in a better place. I would have been angry if he died in a car crash. This was his life, and Scott wouldn't have wanted it any other way."[11] Asked what she would say to Meghan and Michael about their father when they wanted to know what kind of person he was, she told Kathryn Casey, "I'll tell them he was a good man. That he loved them very much and he didn't like to leave. That he loved his job, he loved to fly, he loved his country and he loved God. That he was doing what he had to do. That they should be very proud of him, because he's a hero."

After the family was told, Speicher's father, Wallace, kept insisting his boy would come home. "Scotty's coming home," he'd say to anyone who'd listen.

David Rowe, Speicher's friend from high school and Florida State University, had just finished a day of deer hunting in Eustis, Florida, when he turned on the television. A day after the air strikes began, war coverage still transfixed most Americans. Rowe knew many Navy pilots from living in Jacksonville, and he knew others from his job at the Naval Aviation Depot. The United States has lost its first pilot during Operation Desert Storm, CBS's Dan Rather reported. A photo of a smiling pilot in a flight suit flashed on the screen—Scott Speicher. When Rowe saw that picture on the television, nausea swept over him. He slid off the couch onto his knees, slapped the floor and cried. "God, no!"

Marine F/A-18 pilots stationed at Sheikh Isa Air Base in Bahrain heard the news about Scott Speicher almost immediately. Among them was a young captain named Patrick R. "Roller" Rink with the VMFA-333 *Fighting Shamrocks*, who had met him when Spike had given Roller instruction in the Hornet. He'd never forgotten him either. "He was a great teacher."

The base at Sheikh Isa was supposed to be a secret, but everybody knew about it. The airfield was new, so there were no Bahrainis or airport personnel entrenched at the field when the Marines flew their Hornets into the break over the new control tower and pristine fourteen-thousand-foot runway. "The potential for at least one of the gaggle of about one hundred fifty fighters to swap paint at the ninety, or to meet in the middle of the

runway after doing simultaneous approaches from opposite positions, was averted by adopting a calm and organized—though
completely spontaneous—cadence of radio calls between flights,"
he recalled recently. "Thank God there was no Fresnel lens at
the end of the runway," he said, referring to the series of lights
that help pilots land on the deck of an aircraft carrier by project-
ing a landing "ball" that pilots use to guide them down. "I don't
think any of us jarheads, and especially the Air Force Wild
Weasel Phantom drivers, remembered what the ball looked like."

The hangars were modern structures with detached office
buildings that reminded Rink of his dentist's office back in the
States. Two miles north of the airfield were the barracks, brand-
new and empty. To get there, the Marines had to travel a paved,
sand dune–lined road along the west side of the airstrip via do-
nated cars—two per squadron. Or they could take public transportation. That consisted of dilapidated buses three-quarters the
size of the ones in the U.S. "They were driven by Pakistanis and
Jordanians who secretly dreamed of Nascar careers when the war
was over," explained Rink. "They didn't dig the fact that we all
carried our nine-millimeter Berettas in shoulder holsters everywhere we went. I know of at least one occasion in which one of
those Berettas was used to persuade the madman driver to slow
his Pakistani butt down."

The mood at Sheikh Isa was often tense. Spaced along the
road roughly several hundred meters apart were twenty-foot ce-
ment guard towers. They were rarely manned, but when they
were, the Bahrainis manning them had their machine guns
pointed in at the Marines on their way to the field instead of out
toward the potential threat. "Those pistols of ours," Rink remarked, "were feeling mighty comfy [wherever] this occurred."
At the north end of the runway were fuel pits, beside which was a
Bahraini Roland mobile SAM. For a while, the crew inside the

Roland chassis thought it was amusing to track the Hornets with their targeting radar as they took off. "That nonsense stopped when we locked them up with our ground attack radar when returning from missions. I'm sure they saw the HARMs draped under our wings."

The barracks resembled two-story dormitories with rooms about twice the size of normal college dorm rooms. Unfortunately, there were too few buildings to accommodate all the American pilots. A tent city sprouted up almost immediately. The troops and aircraft maintainers stayed in the tents at the airfield while the ground officers and pilots, who would be doing the combat flying, stayed in the barracks. It sounded like a good deal to everybody until they did the math. There would be eight men to a room—but at least they had climate control.

Close quarters made for some great stories, especially after the shooting started and the nightmares kicked in. Hearing one of the boys scream "Pull up!" or "Break right" in the middle of a deep sleep put a damper on rolling over and going back to sleep. Even more remarkable, it was amazing to Rink how fast some of the pilots learned to don a gas mask while still asleep—and just as quickly, sheepishly tear it off. "We even had one guy draw his pistol, drop into a shooter's stance and do a John Belushi dance like the actor did in *Animal House*." He didn't remember anything the next morning.

When they found out about Spike, Roller and his buddies were gathered in the lobby of the barracks. They'd shoved an ottoman against one of the walls, and on top of it was their primary source of wartime intelligence: a little twelve-inch television. Cable News Network (CNN) was playing on the screen 99 percent of the time. Every day they'd swing through the lobby for the latest news. "It was not a morale booster to see our intelli-

gence people huddled there also getting updated," a bemused
Rink said. "As you can imagine, the lobby became quite popular
when the shooting started. Most of us couldn't sleep very well
from the moment we knew the shit was about to hit the fan,
which was the night prior to the commencement of festivities."

Roller was standing in the lobby watching CNN along with a
dozen other pilots when the news came about Scott's shootdown.
It was dark outside, and he was still trying to wake himself up for
his upcoming mission brief. Later that morning, Rink was scheduled to fly a sortie to bomb the Az Zubayr rail yards in the slot
between Iran and Kuwait, north of the mouth of the Tigris and
Euphrates Rivers. In a telling comment later, he described what
missile fire looked like. That mission was the first time he'd ever
encountered a SAM missile. "Huge explosion. I actually heard
the *Whumpf!* and remember thinking for sure one of us had been
hit. Being new at getting shot at, I wasn't so sure it wasn't me."
But the giant orange and white ball he saw was only the missile's
warhead—everybody was okay. "I can see how someone without
combat experience might have thought Spike's jet was blown to
bits," observed Rink.

In that lobby in the wee hours of the morning, the news of a
shootdown seemed to suck the air out of the room like a giant fist
to the gut. Hearing about the first casualty of the air war was not
what any of them needed before stepping into the cockpit for a
trip north. Yet the Marines' attitude quickly changed to anger.
"Though we didn't know who the pilot was, we were pissed and
someone was going to pay. While wondering who the unlucky
pilot was," said Rink, "we also wondered how the SAR [search
and rescue] would react. Any one of us would have fought the
first jerk who even suggested that we wouldn't go in to get the
downed pilot.

"I don't think we found out the downed pilot was Spike until later that day. That was another blow. Spike had been my instructor during initial training in the Hornet," Rink recalled. "Now here I was, still wet behind the ears with a license to carry enough ordnance to wipe out a small town, and not nearly as much knowledge and skill to effectively employ those weapons as the man who had just been shot down. You can imagine where my seat cushion quickly ended up the next time I got in the cockpit to face the SAMs and triple-A." Still, he didn't really have time to dwell on Spike, other than thinking the usual "Why haven't they found him?" Not only was he busy trying to keep his own backside from sitting in an interrogation room in downtown Baghdad, but he was also upgrading to flight lead—under combat conditions.

Back on the *Saratoga*, the pilots also had to focus on their missions. They did not yet control the skies over Iraq. But that would come soon enough. *Sunliner* pilot Lieutenant Craig Bertolett wrote his family and friends near the end of the war that he'd been confident all along that "we would own the skies within three days." The night after Speicher went down, the *Saratoga* lost an A-6E Intruder and a few days later an F-14 Tomcat. "We've had some losses as I'm sure you've heard," wrote Bertolett. "LCDR Scott Speicher did not return from his mission the first night. He was an instructor of mine when I was learning to fly the Hornet and joined our squadron just over a year ago. He was an excellent pilot and a great person."

It took several days for Speicher's loss to feel real to his squadronmates. To the other pilots, dying on a mission became a real possibility. "Spike, he's better than me and he got it," Hull kept thinking. "That means I can get it." Lieutenant Doug "Coop" Cooper was as shocked as the rest of his buddies that

Spike hadn't returned. No one could've imagined that he wouldn't make it. They figured he'd be found and later returned to the ship. "I'll never forget the night that I had the duty with the senior chief, just a few days before the shooting started. There was nobody else in the ready room and senior chief and I were sitting behind the desk doing nothing in particular. Must have been close to midnight when in walks Spike. He looks around, makes sure no one else is nearby. You could tell he wanted privacy. Next thing you know, he pops a tape in the VCR and gets comfortable in one of the ready room chairs, thinking we're not going to notice. The chief and I just smiled at each other." Spike had put in a tape of his children that Joanne had sent out to the ship. "He was quiet, then you'd hear him just having the best laugh."

For Stumpf, a seventeen-year veteran pilot, getting back into his F/A-18 for his second mission was the toughest thing he had ever done. Stumpf, Hull and the others tried to block out what had happened on that first strike and bear down on knocking out Iraqi air defenses. "There was much more running through my mind," wrote Barry Hull of the first night, "but the main emotion was fear." He also realized that all the practicing the *Sunliners* had done before the war had paid off. Pilots were drilled to keep their eyes open for threats all around them—especially from behind, what pilots called their "six." "Someone told us way back if we didn't check six in practice, we wouldn't do it in combat. Everyone on that mission came back with a sore neck from jerking our heads back and forth, checking six. The instinct of survival, I've felt it pretty good now, I think."

Anderson released the findings of his investigation on January 25, recommending that Speicher's status remain as MIA. This status was based both on the positively confirmed reports that his aircraft had been shot down and the lack, at that juncture, of an identifiable crash site. He also reported that "theater strike rescue forces have reported no visual signals or radio communications from LCDR Speicher. Strike rescue efforts will continue."

Yet a signal had been sent. One of the many tragedies associated with the Speicher case is the dismissal of a report by a former Joint Rescue Coordination Center commanding officer.[12] Two clicks were picked up on January 18, 1991, by an Air Force RC-135 collection platform and a Navy E-2C Hawkeye. The communication, heard at 8:21 P.M. local time, came in on the "404" emergency guard frequency. Department of Defense Prisoner of War/Missing Personnel Office (DPMO) analysts later dismissed the incident, correlating it to the A-6E lost off the *Saratoga* on the night of January 17. But it could not have been the Intruder crew. One of them dropped his radio on the way down in the parachute, and the other, who'd broken his collarbone, removed his flight vest with his bombardier-navigator's help. As they moved to evade potential captors, the A-6 crewmen left the pilot's vest behind, with the radio inside. They didn't have a radio to make any calls or make any clicks on 404 guard frequency.

Worse yet, Anderson's statement was misleading. No strike rescue forces were looking for Scott Speicher. No rescues were planned or mounted. Spike had been left behind.

CHAPTER 3

Blue-on-Blue

"**T**he day after he got shot down," recalled retired Vice Admiral Michael J. "Carlos" Johnson, "I told the people down at Cecil Field how he got shot down." As director of the Office of Naval Intelligence's Strike Projection Evaluation and Anti–Air Warfare Research (SPEAR) group, during Desert Storm, then-Captain Johnson provided critical analysis to support combat preparations. But he also got involved in analyzing U.S. air losses. SPEAR analysts searched data from collection platforms and AWACS aircraft for information that might tell them what had happened to Scott Speicher. Those aircraft included the AWACS in Speicher's sector, a Navy EP-3 Aries II, and several Air Force RC-135 Rivet Joints and EC-130H Rivet Fire/Compass Calls, as well as a J-STARS platform that was making its combat debut—a Grumman Boeing E-8 plane that conducted ground surveillance of the enemy from the air.

"We knew at the time that it was an attack from another aircraft," said Johnson recently. "We also knew that nothing catastrophic had happened to Speicher's aircraft," meaning that the jet hadn't blown apart in midair. They looked at infrared overheads and scanned for Speicher using electronic intelligence capabilities. Nothing turned up. Carlos discounted any missiles launched from the ground and striking Spike. An SA-6 couldn't have gotten him—none were under his flight path. And it couldn't have been an SA-2 or -3. Those weren't close enough to where Scott was last seen. Then they checked pilot reports, especially from Intruder aircrews with night vision goggles. No one saw any SAM trails.

All evidence kept pointing at the MiG-25. It had stayed at afterburner two-thirds of the time it ran hit-and-miss through the Navy's strike force. Expertly threading his Foxbat through Anderson's Hornets, the MiG's pilot knew he was running in a crowd—a crowd with enough friendlies that someone taking a shot at him seemed unlikely. In fact, the rules of engagement precluded it unless the bandit was in the clear. But the MiG-25 was the only protagonist in the immediate surroundings high over the western Iraqi desert that night.

"We realized that the MiG-25 pilot hadn't communicated with his handler on the ground. But there was also no report of a MiG-25 loss that night either," said Johnson. No enemy fighters fired on Coalition aircraft that night. Further, no Iraqi media reported a MiG-25 shooting down an American aircraft. "If an Iraqi pilot shot down an American F/A-18," Johnson continued, "it would've been in the Iraqi media by morning. It wasn't."

So who got Scott Speicher? "I personally thought it might have been a midair [collision] between Speicher and the MiG-25," Johnson speculated. The two aircraft were "on top of one another" for a few seconds, observed Johnson, so the MiG-25 wasn't able to fire at him. After-action evaluation suggested rightly that the MiG-25 had passed by Scott at breakneck speed. Plus, when his wreckage was located much later, the crash investigators saw no evidence of a midair collision. The evidence showed damage from a missile. This begged the question—whose missile? What seems more likely is that someone panicked when Anderson reported there was a MiG-25 in the area where Scott Speicher was last seen flying. The pilot fired, and Scott became a friendly-fire shootdown—he was the "MiG-25" bagged by a U.S. pilot. Tony Albano remembered, "I heard that an Eagle pilot claimed he bagged a MiG-25 just after, so maybe he got him." He added, "We were on Air Force AWACS strike frequency that night and the F-15s were on a different CAP [combat air patrol] fighter control frequency, which is where I think the confusion occurred trying to identify the MiG so Spock could shoot."

Despite Johnson's analysis of Speicher's shootdown and the lack of physical evidence indicating Scott had perished with his aircraft, then–Secretary of Defense Dick Cheney told the press that a surface-to-air missile had downed Speicher's Hornet. "There seemed to be a great deal of resistance to admit an air-to-air loss," said Johnson. The perception at the time leaned toward "total victory," a flawless performance by U.S. pilots. "We've destroyed twenty-nine Iraqi aircraft—with not one air-to-air loss on the part of the Coalition," claimed General H. Norman Schwarzkopf at a briefing in Riyadh on January 30. "The score is totally one-sided," President Bush reiterated to the media six days later. "In fact, in every engagement in the air, the Iraqi planes and pilots have gone down."[13]

The air war was not, as Mark Crispin Miller observed in his *New York Times* article "Conduct of the Persian Gulf War," "quite the shutout that the U.S. propagandists kept extolling." To him, the thought of a Soviet-made MiG-25 taking out a U.S. Navy F/A-18 ruined the pretty picture the Pentagon wanted to paint at war's end. In its final report to Congress, the Pentagon claimed, "Fortunately, all but one plane (an F/A-18 from the USS *Saratoga*) returned safely." Writes Miller, "the Speicher episode is further obfuscated by an upbeat description of another event"—a

MiG shootdown by an F/A-18 pilot, VFA-81 from USS *Saratoga*. "Our relief," the report concludes, "in having successfully completed the strike without loss to ourselves was overwhelming."

A naval officer told Mark Crispin Miller that it was primarily an ego issue that no one wanted to come clean publicly about the MiG-25. "That refusal," wrote Miller, "to acknowledge any loss, was surely hardened by the American perception of Iraqi 'backwardness'—much as in Vietnam, where U.S. officers likewise deemed the enemy too primitive to thwart our gleaming weaponry."[14]

Little did Miller or anyone else realize at that time, but no one with access to the most highly classified intelligence, including Carlos Johnson himself, believed that a MiG-25 shot down Scott Speicher. As for his squadronmates, they believed that the official version was nothing more than a convenient means of subverting the truth of who did take down Scott Speicher's Hornet that night. They knew it was a blue-on-blue, but who'd fired beyond visual range and then didn't own up?

Interdepartmental confusion points toward the answer. Back at the beginning, before the war started, the targets for the air campaign had been crafted by the U.S. Air Force, whose planners dominated Schwarzkopf's staff in Riyadh. General Chuck Horner, Central Command Air Force Commander (CENTAF) and Joint Force Air Component Commander (JFACC), and his staff maintained strict beyond-visual-range rules of engagement for fear of possible blue-on-blue kills. While there were no confirmed cases of Coalition friendly fire incidents, it didn't mean they didn't happen.

Air Force Colonel John A. Warden III had crafted the original Instant Thunder air campaign that became Operation Desert Storm. Daily missions were broken into air tasking orders (ATOs). The orders scheduled and coordinated all daily Coalition

air activity over Iraq and Saudi Arabia. The planning did not
cover Navy fleet defense sorties because, not knowing which assets would be available to him when he started writing it on August 6, 1990, Warden planned only for Air Force participation.
"We were told to build an air option, and we did it from an Air
Force perspective because of the expertise that we had and what
our tasking was," he'd write later.[15] After he had a briefing with
General Schwarzkopf on August 10 down at MacDill Air Force
Base in Florida, Schwarzkopf told his planners to ensure that they
prepared appropriately for integration of Special Forces, Army
helicopters, Marine Corps ground and aviation assets, and planning forces from the Navy, among others. To augment the air plan
and make it one that would decisively strike Saddam Hussein's
forces, Horner brought in Air Force Brigadier General Buster C.
Glosson to rewrite Warden's original strategy. The planning
team, nicknamed Checkmate and located in a Pentagon subbase-
ment, quickly expanded the plan from eighty-four targets and a
seven-day air campaign to one that kept on growing as December
arrived and more aviation assets arrived in-theater. Despite Glosson's input, the plan still leaned toward the Air Force. To Glosson's credit, he tried as much as possible to accommodate the
other services, but his was not the only hand in the planning process. The team grew exponentially as the war grew closer, and included Special Forces and intelligence assets.

The daily air tasking orders, which took their cue from the
overall air campaign plan, provided each sortie with ATO call
signs, deconfliction of airspace, friendly air defense coordination,
electronic warfare, suppression of enemy air defenses (SEAD),
and combat search and rescue. The document also gave out target assignments, weapons needed to effectively take out the target, and escort and tanker rendezvous. Each ATO, when
completed, looked like a three-hundred-page telephone book.

To avoid shooting down friendly aircraft Horner's chief air planner, Lieutenant General John A. Corder, took Horner's lead and established stringent rules of engagement. These rules required friendly fighters to make two types of independent verifications that declared bogeys as bandits before air-to-air missiles could be fired. But the Navy fighters didn't have one aircraft that could do both. The F-14 Tomcat had the capability to identify friend or foe transponders in opposition aircraft, but did not possess the more sophisticated electronic identification features of the Air Force's F-15 and F-16 aircraft. The F/A-18 Hornet had advanced electronic features but was hobbled by its inability to distinguish between friend or foe aircraft. One Marine Corps pilot stated in a postwar House Armed Services Committee report, "We need to start buying airplanes more like the Air Force, with the full set of gear. Instead, we buy Cadillacs with rollup windows, like the F/A-18 with unsatisfactory radar warning receivers, expendables such as chaff and flares, and missile and bomb racks. I would give up one of the twelve aircraft in my squadron in order to fully equip the other eleven." Corder made the comment: "My perception was the Navy thought the reason we were insisting on two independent means of verification was because we were going to take this opportunity to wrest the Top Gun medal away from these guys. It was a manhood thing."[16] But it had nothing to do with manhood and everything to do with an unyielding policy that hobbled the F-14 Tomcat for the entire war.

In his thesis on joint operations in the Gulf War air campaign, P. Mason Carpenter writes, "The [Navy] F-14 with the Phoenix could fire at targets fifty-five to sixty miles away, and the Navy wanted to be able to employ it. The Navy wanted to use AWACS to distinguish enemy aircraft from friendly, but, again, the USAF commanders were reluctant. AWACS, by itself, was unsatisfactory because AWACS-identified positions can be off by as much as five or six miles." An added difficulty was the difference in the ways the Air Force and Navy employed their fighters. Carpenter adds that the Air Force developed its tactics from "air-saturated" Central European environments in which enemy fighters were harder to identify. Because of this, "the Air Force developed and procured extensive identification systems to avoid or reduce fratricides." The Navy planned air operations in a blue-water, controlled environment.

Desert Storm more closely resembled the Air Force's experience in Central Europe, a fact understood by Vice Admiral Stanley Arthur at the Naval Forces Central Command. Yet his carrier battle group commanders were frustrated by the restrictions placed on use of the Phoenix missile. Though the degree of displeasure varied widely from one aircraft carrier to another, the unhappiness was generally shared. Arthur's commanders weren't pleased. As Carpenter notes, frustrated naval officers felt that the strict rules of engagement were designed "to optimize USAF air-to-air capabilities at the expense of the Navy." He quoted Navy representatives to the Joint Force Air Component Commander's Special Planning Cell: "This war was utilized by the USAF to prove 'USAF Air Power,' not prove that combined forces or even joint forces could force multiply and more effectively conduct the war. For example, the F-14 was originally restricted from forward combat air patrol (CAP) positions because CAP aircraft were required to have the ability to electronically identify (EID) and interrogate IFF, friendly and foe."

Horner recalled a visit from Arthur that ended in a stalemate. "Stan Arthur came to me because the F-14 guys wanted to use the Phoenix. I understood exactly where he was coming from," he said. Then he asked Arthur, "Please send your case to Schwarzkopf and let him adjudicate it. This is one area where we have an honest difference of opinion." Arthur went to Schwarzkopf, but the general didn't understand the argument so the matter was referred back to Horner. He wrote to Arthur, "I understand where you are coming from, but the trouble is, the risk is higher than the benefit."[17]

Lieutenant Commander Eddie Smith, "Fast Eddie" to his friends, had planned the mission Scott Speicher flew the night he went down. Fast Eddie was a Navy representative to the JFACC in Riyadh. He was also an F/A-18 pilot. "It should have been a benign and relatively safe sortie for all involved," he said. He was intimately familiar with the big picture over western Iraqi skies that night. The possibility of friendly fire and a missed MiG-25 elicited a pointed response from him. "There should have been no Air Force aircraft in the vicinity, or at least closer than the AWACS." But according to Fast Eddie, other friendlies could have been flying on the fringes of the HARM shooters' range— perhaps Air Force F-4 Wild Weasels, "although nothing else friendly that could have reached out and touched Scott, at least not Air Force–wise." This, however, was followed by a qualifier. He noted that, among other issues between the Navy and Air Force during the war, the Air Force F-15 pilots would flip to the Navy's portion of the ATO so they could follow the Navy's MiG-sweepers' missions closely. They knew that the Navy pilots were forbidden from firing on enemy aircraft without the proper identification capability beyond visual range, and they took advantage of it. That night F-15 pilots weren't supposed to be anywhere close to the Navy Hornets' strike force, but they were. Those pilots were waiting to jump into the fight when Spock Anderson couldn't get permission from the AWACS to fire.

A House Armed Services Committee report, released on March 30, 1992, a year after the war, noted that the air tasking orders often hindered naval pilots' ability to respond to real-time battlefield developments, and Air Force pilots would jump on a

Navy target when the Navy had the situation well in hand. The report used the real case example of two brothers, one a Navy pilot and the other an Air Force pilot. During the air campaign, the Persian Gulf Carrier Task Force came across intelligence that revealed several MiGs parked at an Iraqi airfield. The Navy passed the information repeatedly to Riyadh with an urgent request for a tasking in the ATO to attack the target. The next few orders arrived without a tasking to hit the airfield. Carrier air wing commanders again contacted Riyadh to say, according to the House document, "Hey guys, this is a great juicy target. Let us take it out." Again the order arrived without the tasking. Eventually, the Navy pilot called his brother at Al Kharj Air Base through the commercial satellite hookup and told him about the target. The next day, the Navy pilot got a message from his brother: "Mission accomplished. Thanks for the DFC!" The DFC is a Distinguished Flying Cross.

Eagle pilot Brent Beecham of the 71st Fighter Squadron, 1st Fighter Wing, didn't fly the first night of the air war, but he was briefed before his mission the next day to listen for any message from what turned out to be Scott's flight. "I do have a friend, Steve 'Tater' Tate, who was in the area the first night and shot down a [Iraqi] Mirage F-1," said Beecham. "I have since talked with other Air Force pilots, all of whom believe that an F-14 shot down Scott." He emphasized that confusion existed in the early days of the air war. In one instance a pilot in his squadron was given the order to shoot a target. The pilot was not sure about the target, so he held his fire. It turned out to be a U.S. Air Force F-111 Aardvark.

Marine Corps Hornet pilot Patrick Rink had a similar story: "I know of at least two occasions where the Marines were cleared by the AWACS and our EID display to fire on MiGs. But they turned out to be friendlies. Thank God we didn't shoot." The

F/A-18 EID software that we were using for the Gulf War would almost always identify Marine Corps AV-8 Harriers and Air Force F-4 Wild Weasels as MiGs. "Bottom line," said Rink, "that was an eye opener for everyone, and I'm really surprised we didn't have some blue-on-blues those first few missions."

Accompanying each Navy squadron on the first air strike were Navy F-14 Tomcats providing forward combat air patrol. With them as well were Navy EA-6B Prowlers, to jam enemy radar and communications. Fast Eddie remarked that the EA-6B Prowlers wreaked havoc with aircraft radars. That night, Tomcats and Prowlers were vectoring between the HARM shooters. Since the Navy and Marine Corps routinely plan and work with the EA-6B, "we would have been on the correct [directional] axis to avoid such interference. The Air Force AWACS, though, might not have been. We just weren't that well coordinated," remarked Fast Eddie. He'd heard that the AWACS missed the MiG-25, the one that everyone assumed got Scott, because of the Prowlers. He asked around, and two separate and credible sources confirmed what he'd been told. "In other words, that might be what's so secret—and the reason the Air Force won't cooperate" with inquiries into Scott Speicher's loss that night.

Scott and Joanne Speicher's friend Albert "Buddy" Harris, was a Naval F/A-18 pilot who had met Scott in Pensacola, Florida, in 1980, when they both were in Aviation Officers' Candidate School training to be fighter pilots. Harris then went on his first deployment, and his Jacksonville home caught on fire ten days before he returned. The only clothes he had were those he'd taken with him. Speicher heard what happened and showed up at the ship when Harris got back. He handed Harris a suitcase of his own clothes.

"Here you go," Speicher said. "You need these worse than I do."

Harris was now working at the Pentagon compiling a report on the Navy's role in the Gulf War air campaign, and he made comments recently that add fuel to the blue-on-blue debate in the Speicher case. Harris was frustrated by everyone involved denying responsibility. "It kept getting me angry because these people kept saying: 'It's not our fault, it's not our fault.' And it absolutely was their fault. And unfortunately, those are some of the same people now who are in a position to go forward and try to resolve . . . ," he hesitated, "to get Scott repatriated." When asked about the Air Force and Navy roles in Scott's shootdown—whether it was a fighter pilot or AWACS controller who made the error—Harris interjected quickly, "Fighter jet. That guy didn't really . . . it really wasn't his fault. It was the Navy's fault. The controller gave clearance to fire to Anderson. . . . The Air Force guy was not given clearance. He had an opportunity, but he was not given clearance. Pretty much nobody disputes that. But Spock is the only one who disputes it. Everyone else goes, 'Yeah, I heard it,' but Spock says, 'I didn't hear it.' " Spock Anderson would have heard the clearance to fire had he not gone off his assigned frequencies, possibly because he was so disgusted with the Air Force controller. As a result, Spock missed the call from the AWACS to take out the MiG-25, a call the Air Force F-15 Eagle pilot heard clearly. "But Spock had just switched frequencies," Harris said, "and went back to his squadron frequency," which was also not right, because it is possible to listen to both. "So, he was off frequency. That's why he didn't hear it. The strike leader ended up not being on the same frequency as the whole pack, which is a very unusual circumstance."

Others would disagree. Craig Bertolett remarked of Anderson recently, "Spock knew the ATO cold, so if there was a way to solve the MiG-25 problem, I'm sure he attempted it." He cited examples. "During workups back off the east coast of Florida, he'd carry a cellular phone into the cockpit. He'd call the shore detachment and supplement the comms regarding maintenance and parts. Also, during Desert Storm, he'd take NVGs [night vision goggles] into the cockpit—he'd let us do it also. These were the binocular type used by ship's company to defend against small boats at night, and not the aviation, helmet-mounted kind. We wouldn't take them into bad guy country but rather use them on combat air patrols. He was a technology guy, loved gadgets, and kept looking for ways to apply them."

The AWACS controllers aboard Cougar, including tactics officer Jimmy Patterson, may bear part of the blame. When Anderson and the MiG pilot merged the last time, hurtling toward each other at a closure rate of one thousand seven hundred knots, Anderson performed a maneuver called "the bug."

"We call it a bugout," said Barry Hull. "You point your nose . . . directly at somebody and you merge. You try to merge at 180 degrees out with no angles on either one of you and you unload and you go." For an enemy fighter to turn around and chase you down once a pilot has "unloaded," or given the jet full power, is nearly impossible at that point. "But who would have guessed," he said, "that the MiG-25 could blow through the formation like that?" The question arises: Where was the AWACS in all this? The AWACS should have been all over the merge, vectoring the fighters to an advantageous heading for a successful bug, and giving frequent situation reports on the position and aspect of the MiG. "If this isn't what happened," said former pilot Patrick Rink, "the AWACS definitely dropped the ball. The MiG was pushed to the back burner when he should have been priority one."

Barry Hull might have had part of the answer had he kept his HUD tape from that night. He replayed it for himself so many times he can recite the radio calls nearly verbatim. "I remember

listening to the audio later. I wish I hadn't done this. It embar-
rassed me because my breathing is, you know . . . I sound scared.
So I erased it. Now I wish I hadn't." At the time, says Hull, "I was
in the middle of this war. I can't sound scared." No other Hornet
pilots on Anderson's strike saved their HUD tapes from that
night. On his tape, Hull remarked, it was possible to hear all the
radio transmissions. "It recorded everything I could hear in my
headset." He added later that much of what he knew—and he
didn't know if it was still classified or not—had been top secret.
"I will tell you, on the other side I was pounding my hand against
the canopy and saying, 'Pull the fucking trigger.' But God, you
know, things happen."

"There's some other points in there I can't go into right now,"
Harris said, pointedly putting off questions about the way everybody's mission was flown that night. "I've agreed not to with the
secretary of the Navy. Some mistakes were made in the flying aspect of it. People felt very guilty about their mission and how
[the MiG-25] got past [strike combat air patrol]. There were
some people up there who were supposed to be supporting him
[Scott Speicher] and they failed miserably." No one person was
at fault, not the way Harris sees it. A series of mistakes led to
Scott Speicher's shootdown. Still, Harris observed that the tensions were high the night Scott disappeared, and any flash would
have seemed like an immense explosion, especially with darkness
as a backdrop. "They did see a secondary explosion, but they
thought it was large pieces of the aircraft impacting the ground,"
said Harris. "Turns out it appears to have been Scott's ejection."

Neither Hull nor any of the Hornet pilots with him that night
fault Spock Anderson for what happened to Scott. "We all live
with our demons," says Hull in retrospect, "and there's nothing
that can be done about it, and that's not the point."

"He's so right," added Rink. "It's easy to Monday-morning

quarterback, but having experienced the chaos with every mission, I can tell you there doesn't seem to be anything negligent here—until the government decided to try and let what happened to Spike blow away in the wind as if one life doesn't matter in the big scheme of things."

Adding to the weapon systems issue is the fact that the Air Force F-15s may have been carrying an experimental version of the AIM-120 advanced medium-range air-to-air missile (AMRAAM) that first night of the war. It was still a "black," or classified, program the first night of the air war over Iraq. The AMRAAM had surfaced briefly in the media several years before—typical of "vanishing" programs mentioned in the press before turning black. The first production AMRAAMs were delivered by Hughes (now a part of Raytheon) in 1988 to the 33rd Tactical Fighter Wing at Eglin Air Force Base, Florida, where nearly two hundred test firings occurred before Desert Storm. In its history of the Desert Storm experience, the 33rd states: "The wing distinguished itself by scoring 16 aerial kills, including the first kill of the war, the most of any single unit. In addition to the kills, the 33rd accomplished a number of firsts including: the most air-to-air kills, the most double kills and the most sorties and hours flown by any unit in the combat theater." The 33rd Fighter Wing became the only unit whose wing commander scored an air-to-air victory, plus destroying the most MiG-29 Fulcrums (he scored five). The 33rd's official history also notes that following Operations Desert Shield and Desert Storm, the Air Force restructured its forces. Under the new structure the 33rd was redesignated the 33rd Fighter Wing. "The same year, it became the first fighter wing to bring the AIM-20 AMRAAM into full combat-capable service."

Only a small number of people would have known if the AIM-120 AMRAAMs were loaded on the F-15s on the eve of

January 17. Among them were the pilot and the enlisted ordnance personnel who put them on the Eagles' racks. Though an
open source (fact files from the Air Force and Navy about the
missiles loaded on this aircraft) states that "none were used,"
Navy F/A-18 pilots who later worked in VX-4 and VX-5—two
of the Navy's experimental test squadrons—on their post–Desert
Storm tours of duty found out that might not have been the
story. The pattern of warfare in modern times has been to slip in
a few experimental weapons to test combat capabilities, and to
assess the weapons' strengths and deficiencies. Eagle pilot Brent
Beecham recalled that Eglin-based F-15s carried AMRAAMs at
the end of the war to chase down Iraqi aircraft fleeing across the
border into Iran. "We had a hard time chasing them over such a
short distance, and the AIM-7 didn't have the legs to run them
down. Though they were 'rushed' into service, they had been
tested extensively, and most F-15 units were already beginning to
receive simulators that would enable us to practice AMRAAM
employment." He added that the software had been installed for
some time prior to the war. "The only thing that held back AM-
RAAM employment earlier," said Beecham, "was that they
wanted to make it smaller to be compatible with the F-16 out-
board wing station." The Air Force completed its initial operating capability tests in September 1991 and the Navy two years
later. The AIM-120A was redeployed to the Persian Gulf in 1992
for use on F-15 and F-16 fighters. In December 1992 an F-16
pilot fired the first fully approved AIM-120A in actual combat,
shooting down a MiG-25 Foxbat during a confrontation over
southern Iraq.

The AIM-120 is a "fire-and-forget" weapon. With a warhead
classified as "blast fragmentation," the AMRAAM weighs 340
pounds and uses an advanced solid-fuel rocket motor to achieve
a speed of Mach 4 over a range in excess of thirty miles. In

long-range engagements the AMRAAM heads for the target
using inertial guidance and receives updated target information
via a data link from the launch aircraft. Air Force information on
this weapon notes that it changes to a self-guiding terminal mode
when the target is within range of its own monopulse radar set.
That frees the launch aircraft to engage other targets. The AIM-
120 also has a "home-on-jam" guidance mode to counter electronic jamming. "With its sophisticated avionics, high closing
speed, and excellent end-game maneuverability," says the Air
Force, "chances of escape from AMRAAM are minimal. Upon
intercept an active-radar proximity fuse detonates the 40-pound
high-explosive warhead to destroy the target." In a situation such
as Carlos Johnson describes, in which the two aircraft are "on top
of one another"—a merge plot—the missile could make a split-
second choice of its target. The MiG-25, at two-thirds afterburner and hauling east, was passing too quickly to get caught.
Scott Speicher, focused on his mission, had just bunted the nose
of his Hornet, lowering his jet in order to get into position at the
right altitude for his HARM run. Being radar dead, he would
never have known what was coming.

In a world of highly sophisticated weaponry, the element of
human error has been greatly lessened. Yet an entire string of errors on the first night of a new kind of war led to Scott Speicher's shootdown. As the war came to an end, and desk-bound
bureaucrats replaced top-gun fighters, the errors would only be
compounded.

CHAPTER 4

Tribute to a Hero

"The war keeps on keeping on," wrote Barry Hull in a letter home in early February. The raging fires in Kuwaiti oil fields were horrifying. The destruction in Iraq was unimaginable. The *Sunliners* reached the point that they'd call in targets over the radio based on fires or smoke from the ground caused by previous bombs. A typical call from Hull to a squadron mate reflected that: "Coop, I've got a line of trucks two miles northeast of the big black smoke just north of the original target."

For the pilots, the worst part of the war was the fear of actual combat itself. "After doing it for a month, I can now take it further before it kicks in, but once it throws itself in your face, there is no stopping the terror that sweeps through your body," wrote Hull in mid-February. "The first night, anything and everything sent me into a state of terror." As the air war wore on, that reaction decreased, but it didn't go away completely. "One night recently," he recalled, "one of our strikers had a system malfunction just before Miller time—aviator lingo for release of bombs on target—which is very unusual for a Hornet, but anyway, he dropped his bombs a couple of miles off target." In his cockpit, Hull saw one of the explosions made by the other Hornet out of the corner of his eye. In the dark of night, the explosions caused a huge flash, and for a split second Hull thought a SAM had reached out and touched him. He was terrified until he realized what it was. That first night, when Scott went down, the missile that detonated under his Hornet had seemed large enough to make them think the entire plane had exploded. By February Hull and the others knew that any missile going off at night was going to look bigger than it would seem in the daytime.

As the war dragged on, being cool under pressure came to mind more readily than being scared. Hull and the others tried to emphasize "calm" as much as possible. "I forgot about it the first night over Iraq, but it's back with me now," he wrote. "The fear is there, but so is the calm." The moods of the *Sunliner* pilots reflected mixed emotions, ranging widely in Hull's recollection: "When is this war going to end so we can go home?" Or, "Yeah! We were studs today! Did you see that ammo dump go up in flames? Secondaries for twenty minutes! What a light show!" And then there was the ubiquitous, "Listen, I'm beat. Don't call me unless you need me to brief. I'm going to sleep." One of Skull's personal favorites was "Gosh, Skull, you got another big pile of mail, and more cookies! Oh, they're from your sister Nora? Well, uh . . . I just ate, thanks anyway." Then he'd go feed them to the maintenance crew. Another common one: "Hey, Oscar, looks like my mom baked another batch of brownies. I'll throw a few toward the duty desk to create a diversion. Then you open the door and I'll see if I can get the rest up to our room." Now that he'd seen combat, Hull knew, like the others, the importance of creating a diversion. His favorite mood, he wrote, was "Hey, I'm just going to sit here and read these letters and do a little daydreaming. Unless the war breaks out, don't call me. Oh yeah, the war did break out. Well, it can wait."

Near the end of February, missions off the *Saratoga* continued to press into Iraq or Kuwait, depending on the target. After crossing the border, adrenaline pumping, they'd head for their targets, always talking continuously with the controller. The AWACS, far away from the strike group, eventually smoothed their working relationship with Navy pilots and watched over them more closely on their missions. "They have some female controllers," wrote Hull. "They are great at controlling. You know why? It's not because they do a better job, although they do just as good a job. It's because of their voice. When you hear a female voice, you instinctively listen up." The Navy loaded a female voice, in fact, into the F/A-18's computer alert system. The pilots called the female computer voice "Bitchin' Betty." "When Betty talks," the twenty-five-year-old Hull wrote home to his family in South Carolina, "we listen. Also, it has to do with a study of fighter pilots. They found we are abnormally sensitive and caring, tender, romantic, sweet thangs and thought it would be appropriate to have a female voice, since we just hate those male chauvinist stereotypes. Shucks."

Tasked to hit more difficult and precise targets, the *Sunliners* demonstrated a strength of the aircraft that was largely dismissed in postwar summations of the air war. They carried sophisticated ordnance on the Hornet, requiring exact sequences of cockpit switches to fire the weapons in the correct manner, performed in a matter of seconds or they'd miss the shot. Combine that with the pilots' thoughts of survival and the pucker factor went up tenfold. They had become combat pilots.

On February 27 a cease-fire was called. The war was over. The *Saratoga*'s pilots had hit targets all over Iraq, from Baghdad to the west on the Syrian and Jordanian borders and back to Kuwait. "There were a few occasions of blue-on-blue," wrote Hull on March 2, but he didn't think at the time there were any from the *Saratoga*. He was thinking mostly of the ordnance dropped perilously close to ground troops. "We briefed in detail. Not even counting the grief of the families, but from a pilot's point of view, it would be hard to live with yourself knowing you dropped on blue troops."

With the war over and an occasional no-fly day, footballs and joggers and suntanners replaced the hundreds of plane handlers on the flight deck. The war had drawn *Sunliner* pilots together like family. Many would soon be leaving the squadron, going on to their next assignment. "There is an unspoken commitment to each other," Hull wrote. "We sit around and complain, but if an outsider badmouths one of us—look out. I guess I can criticize family, but no one else can." He'd miss his friends and the flight time. But one thing he wouldn't miss was the fear of combat. "I sure won't miss living on this boat, trying to sleep through cat shots, trying to deal with the idiots in the post office, standing alerts at all hours of the night, spending month after month away from home, and taking showers where not only the cold hot water runs out, but all the water runs out!"

On March 4, Navy officers called Scott Speicher's roommate, Tony Albano, and instructed him to go to Riyadh, Saudi Arabia. Iraq had released its prisoners of war, and Albano was sent to see if Speicher was among the ones who walked off the plane. He wasn't overly optimistic, but there was a chance. That hope died quickly. By the time the plane touched down with twenty-one American POWs, Albano had been told Speicher wasn't among them. He flew back to the *Saratoga*. "I didn't even get to stay long enough to see my other shipmates," he mused later.

In another letter home, Barry Hull remarked that they'd

heard the POWs were released. "That's good news." But the pervasive mood aboard the *Saratoga* was the desire to go home. "There's nothing more they can do to us," he continued. "I think we've been through the worst. Now we wait and listen. Every time the captain, Smokin' Joe Mobley, gets on the horn, we hope it's to tell us we're headed west. He hasn't told us yet, but that's okay. Now that the shooting has stopped, waiting is easy."

By mid-March the *Saratoga* was headed for home. Despite the *Sunliners'* anticipation of returning to their families, reuniting with loved ones and friends, they were still short one of their own. "The one thing that will stick with the VFA-81 pilots when all else has faded is the loss of Scott Speicher," Hull wrote on March 15. "The twenty-four-hours-a-day closeness we have out here makes for such tight friendships, and that adds to our sadness. Some people you feel when they are around. With Scott, we feel him not being around. We came to expect a certain sense of humor and response out of each individual that made up our team, and we feel his loss." This was the next-to-last letter Hull wrote while on the cruise. His last was a note to himself that he never intended to mail. It was written March 27, the day of the traditional flyoff of air wing aircraft to their respective home airfields. Though he'd been scheduled to go, Hull gave his jet up to a married friend. He relished instead walking off the boat into a sea of well-wishers, a postwar homecoming that was already beginning to draw emotions from him that ranged from nervous and excited to sad.

"I'm sad," Hull said, "that the closeness the junior pilots developed will start to fade. I feel sad for the loss of Scott. I feel sad knowing I will probably never see another time like this again." What's important, he decided, is what you take with you when it's all over. For Barry Hull, these were the main things: "First of all, we lost a good friend in Scott Speicher. What a great guy he was. I still can't believe it happened to him. Second, I love my country. It used to get on my nerves to hear some old geezer preaching about how good we have it in the United States. Now I think there is a little of that in me. I won't go around being a pain about it, but it will be there in me from now on. There is one more thing" he wanted to remember, too, and it was by far the most important thing he'd learned during the cruise, "and that is how much I love my family."

Longtime buddy David Rowe and some of Speicher's college friends decided to hold a golf tournament in his honor. Even before the *Sunliners* returned, Rowe and John Webb, "Webby" to his buddies, were grieving for Scott. Webb had been in Scott and Joanne's wedding. The golf tournament seemed like a good idea, especially if they could help Joanne with money for Meghan and Michael's education. "At first," said Rowe, "Joanne said, 'Look, I'm going to take care of the kids. I don't need any help.'" Then Webb's wife, Linda, explained to her, "Look, these guys are grieving and all they're trying to do is something." Then Joanne gave her blessing.

The golf tournament wasn't scheduled until the squadron got home from the cruise. The flyoff was March 27, and the *Saratoga* pulled into Mayport the next day. Rowe went over to Spock Anderson's home one night not long after the return, and they talked about the golf outing and swapped stories about Speicher. Rowe told Anderson about the time Spike jumped from the cliff, and Anderson told Rowe about Scott's hitting the bulldozer with a kielbasa.

Anderson and Rowe had a good laugh. Then Rowe asked if Anderson didn't mind telling him what had happened to his friend. "It was a SAM that got him?" Rowe asked. Anderson's eyes filled with tears. "It was no SAM that got Spike," he said.

"Let me tell you what happened." So Anderson told Rowe about how Spike came to him begging to go on the mission, and Anderson said no. But Spike came back a second time, and Anderson changed his mind. "So we launched, we'd just refueled and we split to our targets," Anderson told Rowe. "Right after we split to the targets, I got a tone. I was locked." Then he told Rowe about the MiG, and how the rules of engagement leaned toward letting an enemy fighter go if you weren't sure. "So I locked him," continued Anderson, "but problem was I couldn't keep up with him because I was loaded down with weapons." Once Anderson locked up the MiG, he bugged out. Rowe was surprised, because for months the Pentagon had stuck to the story that Speicher had been downed by a surface-to-air missile. "I'm telling you right now, don't believe what you're being told," Rowe remembers Anderson saying. "It was that MiG that shot Spike down. I had him, Dave, and I could have taken him out."

The day of the golf tournament, John Webb and two of Spike's other college roommates flew in from Texas and South Florida. "Commander," asked Rowe, "if you wouldn't mind, please, would you tell these guys—these are some of Scott's best friends—would you mind telling them what you told me?" He said, "I don't have a problem with that at all." They staked out a large shade tree and some privacy, and Spock told them what had happened to their buddy.

John "JR" Stevenson, an A-7E Corsair II driver aboard USS *John F. Kennedy*, got back from his deployment at the end of March. The *Kennedy* had sent its air wing home the same day as the *Saratoga*, and the ship berthed the next day in Norfolk. Two weeks later, Stevenson ran into Joanne Speicher outside the Rocket 17—the Cecil Field officers' club—and told her about the MiG-25. Joanne had known nothing about the MiG until JR said something. He told her they should've been able to find some sign of Scott's wreckage because the MiG's flight path that night was known not only from surveillance aircraft but also from any number of *Saratoga* and *Kennedy* pilots who got electronic identification or visuals on the MiG's distinctive afterburner trail. The MiG-25 lit up the *Kennedy's* strike leader and VA-46 *Clansmen* commanding officer, Commander Mark "Lobster" Fitzgerald, in his A-7E as the MiG pilot streaked off to the east.

Joanne thought about what JR had said and soon after went to see Dean "Milo" Hendrickson, Speicher's CAG, to ask some questions about the MiG, but he told her to go home and stop asking about it. Agitated by Joanne Speicher's visit, Hendrickson's office called Stevenson. Milo wanted JR front and center. When he got there, Hendrickson closed the door and proceeded to chew him out for telling Joanne about the Foxbat. He was told to never mention it again. "I wasn't even in Milo's air wing, so I had no idea what he wanted when I got there," Stevenson recalled later. "It was unsettling." With that, the official story of what happened to Scott Speicher started to come unglued.

There were two buglers, one echoing the other, as a low-altitude missing man formation swooped over the chapel at Cecil Field at the end of Scott Speicher's morning memorial service on May 22. The service for Spike was emotionally charged, packed with his family, friends and squadronmates. Lieutenant Ron Craddock, Light Attack Wing One chaplain, started with reading Psalms 104:33–34. "I will sing to the Lord all my life; I will sing praise to my God while I live," he read somberly. "Pleasing to him be my theme; I will be glad in the Lord." That fitted Scott well. He'd held God close to him every day, and like many of his friends on the ship, he'd read the Bible more frequently as war grew closer and he was reminded daily of its inherent dangers. After Tony Albano eulogized Scott, Mike Anderson gave his remarks. As he readied himself to speak, tears filled his eyes and he began to sob. "The man was devastated," said David Rowe. "When you look in a man's eyes, especially a warrior, and you see the tears, the pain in their eyes . . . These guys compartmentalize. They put it away."

After the presentation of awards by Vice Admiral John K. Ready, Commander in Chief, Naval Air Force Atlantic Fleet, Commander Bill McKee, Scott's executive officer, read from Deuteronomy 6:6–9: "Take to heart these words which I enjoin on you today. Drill them into your children. Speak of them at home and abroad, whether you are busy or at rest. Bind them at your wrist as a sign and let them be as a pendant on your forehead. Write them on the doorposts of your houses and on your gates." He also read from the much-used passage about the strength and endurance of love from I Corinthians 13:4–8a. Aviators sobbed quietly in the pews.

After Chaplain Craddock's reflections, the chapel filled with choked voices singing "Eternal Father Strong to Save": "Lord, guard and guide the men who fly/ Thro' the great spaces of the sky/ Be with them traversing the air/ In darkening storms or sunshine fair/ O God, protect the men who fly/ Thro' lonely ways beneath the sky."

Scott Speicher was mourned for the brave pilot and good man that he was. Little did his family and his friends know that Scott was still alive, stranded in a remote desert region of Iraq. The truth was enmeshed in a confused tangle of military bureaucrats who became increasingly involved in covering up what had gone wrong.

CHAPTER 5

Left Behind

few days after the war ended, Marine Corps Captains Patrick "Roller" Rink and Frederick W. "CJ" Sturckow hopped into one of the base's Toyota pickup trucks and made the forty-minute drive to Manama at the north end of the island. "We went to the port and finagled our way on board the USNS *Mercy* (T-AH 19), where the recently repatriated POWs were marshaling before going home. CJ had been Bob Wetzel's best man at his wedding. It was during this visit that I talked to many of the POWs," said Rink. (Lieutenant Robert "Smilin' Bob" Wetzel was the pilot of the A-6E Intruder shot down off the *Saratoga*.) He noticed that Spike wasn't one of the POWs and asked the pilots as well as Major Rhonda L. Cornum, the U.S. Army flight surgeon captured after her helicopter was shot down en route to pick up a downed F-16 pilot, if they'd heard anything. "All but one of them hadn't. But remember," Rink cautioned, "at the time we thought Spike was dead." Everyone in the squadron echoed Tony Albano's disappointment that Scott was still missing. But they didn't realize then that Scott Speicher's name had not been placed on the International Committee of the Red Cross (ICRC) list requesting repatriation of Coalition personnel from the Iraqis. How could this happen?

In a postwar evaluation of United States Central Command (CENTCOM) problems, evaluators took umbrage with the way the Riyadh staff had reported casualties. The problem arose because casualty information was provided to the Joint Chiefs of Staff by CENTCOM and the individual armed services. Although parallel reporting channels existed, data requirements and submission times varied widely. As a result, JCS received inconsistent reports and CENTCOM was constantly required to divert resources to resolve discrepancies, detracting from other wartime responsibilities. Another casualty reporting problem was the impact that requests for detailed information had on headquarters. Prior to offensive operations, CENTCOM's priority had been reporting non–battle-related casualties. When offensive operations kicked into high gear, its priority shifted to MIAs. As a result of constant requests for detailed information on other than MIAs, CENTCOM had to refocus the reporting effort, giving greater emphasis to fratricide-related casualties. Requirements for detailed information exceeded CENTCOM's capability, and at that point CENTCOM mostly passed responsibility for providing accurate data on MIAs to the individual services.

This issue was high on General Schwarzkopf's agenda the day of the cease-fire agreement. He and Joint Forces Commander General Prince Khalid bin Sultan bin Abdul Aziz met with seven Iraqi military officials, headed by Deputy Chief of Staff Lieutenant General Sultan Hashim Ahmad Al-Jabburi Al-Tay, at Safwan Airfield in occupied Iraq on March 3. After a two-hour meeting, the Iraqi military formally accepted all demands for a permanent cease-fire. "When I went to the tables with the Iraqis to negotiate the continuation of the cease-fire," recalled

Schwarzkopf recently, "one of the first questions I put to them is that I wanted all of our POWs returned, and in addition to that, I wanted all of the bodies of anybody who had been killed returned to us. That was one of the first conditions that I put on the Iraqis for the continuation of the cease-fire." General Ahmad agreed to the immediate release of a small number of prisoners of war as a show of good faith from an undefeated enemy.

The next day, the Iraqis released ten prisoners of war, six of whom were Americans. They were turned over to U.S. officials by the International Committee of the Red Cross near the Jordanian border station of Ruwayshid, then transferred to the *Mercy* for medical evaluation and treatment. The following day, March 5, the Iraqis released another thirty-five prisoners, fifteen Americans among them, to the Red Cross. "At the end of the war," continued Schwarzkopf, "I was assured one hundred percent that everyone was fully accounted for and that there was no MIA situation."

In actuality, several aviators still were missing. The Red Cross concluded later that several names were left off the list—names that the U.S. military had not accounted for at war's end. But by then it was too late. "If he wasn't a POW," said Schwarzkopf of Speicher, "he wouldn't be on the list. Again, it doesn't make sense that the Iraqis would have listed everybody except one person on a POW list that they give to the Red Cross. Why, if they're going to withhold one name, why that specific name, and the only logical explanation if he was alive, is the fact that they didn't know that he was captured. But that doesn't make any sense either, because knowing how centralized the Iraqi military was, they would certainly know something like that."

In fact, the United States had not accounted for all of its MIAs. The Iraqis received at least two lists from the Red Cross with the names of Coalition personnel—by nationality—that their respective countries wanted returned immediately. The Iraqis waited each time to see whose names appeared on the list. Thus, if a service member was not asked for, Saddam was essentially handed a trophy prisoner because of that prisoner's omission from the list. In a reply to a message sent to the Iraqis on October 21, 2001, specifically addressing Scott Speicher, Dr. Fahmi El-Qaisy, the head of legal affairs in the Iraqi Ministry of Foreign Affairs, wrote on November 6 that "the American authorities did not claim for him within the lists of the POWs in 1991, nor did it include his name as missing."

The U.S. government didn't report any pilots or ground troops falling into Iraqi hands in the opening days of the war. On CNN, Iraq's minister of information, Latif Nassif Jasim, stated emphatically that American and British aircrews had been captured, but the Pentagon issued a complete denial. Lieutenant General Thomas Kelly, then director of operations to the Joint Chiefs of Staff, stood before a packed press room and told reporters that no Americans had been taken into custody by Iraqi forces. Kelly and others in the Pentagon didn't back off from their denial until Iraq made tapes of the POWs it had captured and played them for the public via major news media. Among the most memorable of those was Lieutenant Jeffrey Zaun, the bruised and battered A-6E Intruder bombardier-navigator off the *Saratoga*, whom the Iraqis picked up with his pilot, Lieutenant Robert Wetzel.

In another case, it took a concerned parent to recover an MIA. Army Specialist Melissa Rathbun-Nealy's father, Leo Rathbun, was concerned enough about his daughter's disappearance on January 30, 1991, to go public. He was afraid if the war ended, his daughter would be left behind. Specialist Rathbun-Nealy, part of the 233rd Transportation Company, was the driver in one of two heavy equipment transport (HET) vehicles delivering a repaired truck back to troops when she and Specialist David Lockett came under fire. The tank carrier in front of them managed to turn around and speed away, but as it did so, the other 233rd team saw Rathbun-Nealy and Lockett stuck in the sand and the Iraqis moving in. Both Rathbun-Nealy and Lockett were surrounded and captured. Despite eyewitness accounts of the event and reports by captured Iraqi soldiers that they'd transported two American soldiers, whom they'd described as a white female (Rathbun-Nealy) and black male (Lockett), to Al Bashrah, Kuwait, the Pentagon carried Rathbun-Nealy and Lockett as "whereabouts unknown" for two weeks before finally declaring them "missing."

In a pointed letter by North Carolina Senator Jesse Helms dated May 23, 1991, introducing an examination of U.S. policy toward POW/MIAs conducted by the U.S. Senate Committee on Foreign Relations Republican (Minority) Staff, Helms remarked that on February 12, 1991, the chief of the Special Office for Prisoners of War and Missing in Action (POW/MIA) resigned. "Colonel Millard A. Peck felt that he could no longer fulfill the demands of duty, honor, and integrity under the policies which he was asked to implement," said Helms. "In a detailed and forthright letter, which did not become public until May, Colonel Peck confirmed that a 'cover up' has been in progress. He spoke of a 'mindset to debunk.' He said that there was no effort to pursue 'live sightings.'" Helms attached Peck's entire report to the letter and forwarded it to committee members and staff. "The fact," continued Helms, "that Colonel Peck's conclusions were so similar to the conclusions of the Minority Staff is a matter of regret, rather than a vindication. I had hoped that the Minority Staff investigators would be able to alter their preliminary findings, because the implications of a deliberate effort by the U.S. government to deceive the American people is a matter that all of us would prefer to believe unthinkable." Helms sent the Minority Staff looking for historical precedents, and there were lots of them. Three cases from the past show the differing outcomes that shed insight into Scott Speicher's circumstances. The first was that of John H. Noble, a Detroit native taken prisoner by the Russians at the end of World War II in 1945, and shuttled from prison to prison—Dresden, Muhlberg and Buchenwald—before finally ending up in Vorkuta, fifty miles from the Arctic Circle. He was so close to the North Pole that it was too cold for bacteria to survive, yet *he* did. He labored in mines, pushing two-ton coal cars, even after his body weight dropped from 155 to 95 pounds. He was kept totally incommunicado. The Russians kept his name out of their files and refused to acknowledge his existence for more than seven years. If not for a postcard sent by a trusted friend in the Vorkuta prison system—and courageous people in the State Department who believed the card had been written by him, John Noble would never have made it back. He was eventually released after a telephone call from President Dwight D. Eisenhower to the Kremlin. While it was obvious that the Russians could have gotten rid of any evidence that Noble was alive, they didn't.

Massachusetts textbook salesman Newcomb Mott wasn't so lucky. Mott traveled to Scandinavia in late summer of 1965 and took a walk across the Russian border with Norway to get a Soviet "red" stamp in his passport. It was a walk from which he never returned. Five months later, accused as a spy, Mott endured a violent death at Boris Gleb, a Russian village just inside the former Soviet Union's border with Norway. He was failed by the State Department, which handled his case poorly and could not muster the resources or argument to gain his release.

The third case, that of Navy Commander Columbus Darwin "CD" Smith, concerned a naval officer the Japanese couldn't seem to capture and keep. Even after they confined Smith to an escape-proof facility at Shanghai, he escaped and began his walk of more than six hundred miles—behind enemy lines—with Chinese assistance to avoid further capture by the Japanese. The U.S. government intentionally declared him "officially dead" in order to get the Japanese to believe he was dead, too, and not look for Smith while he was on the run. As a result, the Japanese never pursued him. Smith made it to his contact points, was recovered and came home, where, comically, he had a hard time getting his status changed back to "living."

"I felt that these precedents were absolutely necessary to an understanding of the present problems," Helms wrote. "Of course, this fundamental historical research required a massive undertaking to find the original documents, most of them formerly classified, in the National Archives and in the issuing agencies. Accordingly, readers will find in the report something which has never before been attempted: a historical analysis of the fate of U.S. POW/MIAs in the hands of the Bolshevik regime after World War I, the Soviet regime after World War II, the North Korean regime after the Korean War, and the Vietnamese regime after the Vietnam War." Doubters, Helms said, should examine more compelling evidence cited in the report that illustrates the massive problems the U.S. government has had in handling the POW/MIA issue. Within the Peck report was the bizarre case of Melissa Rathbun-Nealy and David Lockett.

After their capture by hostile forces, the two were never listed as MIA or POW. Why? "The reason lies with U.S. Army regulation," stated Colonel Peck. "Missing" by U.S. Army definition is very distinct from MIA. "Missing" is reserved for personnel unaccounted for in noncombatant operations. From the Army's point of view, the convoy was a noncombatant operation, even though it came under enemy fire. Therefore, Rathbun-Nealy and Lockett were never listed as MIA or POW, even though the Army had information that they had been captured under fire. "This distinction," concluded Peck, "is an important illustration of how the Department of Defense uses technical distinctions to avoid a finding of POW/MIA."

In his letter to Melissa Rathbun-Nealy's parents, Lieutenant Colonel J. G. Cole, Chief of POW/MIA Affairs, demonstrated for Senate investigators that the Department of Defense knew a great deal about what had happened. "There were no signs of fighting or blood," wrote Cole, "but personal gear had been scattered around the area, and weapons were missing. As the Marines were searching around the vehicle shouting for the soldiers, they were confronted by several Iraqi foot soldiers at the HET and an armored personnel carrier [APC] approximately fifty meters north, headed in their direction. No shots were exchanged by the Marines, who departed the area and called in attack helicopter support, which destroyed the APC within thirty meters of the HET . . . The Marines returned to the area the following morning, where they collected some of the personal equipment and found the vehicle running but found no trace of Melissa or SPC Lockett . . . During the battle in and around Khafji several Iraqi soldiers were captured." Presumably, these captured soldiers could positively identify Rathbun-Nealy and Lockett by looking at photographs, but they weren't shown any.

Iraqi soldiers did give witness statements. "Following interrogation of enemy prisoners of war by Saudi forces," according to Peck's report, "two reports were received. One concerned information provided by an Iraqi lieutenant who witnessed the capture of an American male and female. He further stated that both had been injured and that the white female had sustained an injury to her arm. The second report received from Saudi forces concerned two other Iraqi prisoners of war from a captured patrol who indicated they had seen a white female and a black male near the city of Al Bashrah, Kuwait," not far from where their HET was abandoned. When Leo Rathbun asked Cole why his daughter was not listed as an MIA with these sightings on record, Cole replied that the Iraqi lieutenant had not made "a positive identification"—as though, stated the Senate report, "there were hundreds of pairs of white female and black male soldiers captured in the area." Cole went on to state that U.S. interrogators had no current picture of SPC Rathbun-Nealy to show the Iraqi officer—even though her photograph was by then showing up in every newspaper in the Western Hemisphere. (The same was true of Scott Speicher, whose picture appeared for days on the front pages of newspapers and in weekly magazines.)

Without positive identification, Rathbun-Nealy and Lockett could not be listed as POW/MIA—and never were. "Had there been an extended war and extended negotiations to secure the return of prisoners, the name of neither one," stated Peck, "would have appeared on any list of POW/MIAs being sought. They were listed only as 'missing,' that is, unaccounted for but not known to be in enemy hands. Had a difficult negotiation been required to secure a return of listed POW/MIAs, Iraq need never have returned Rathbun-Nealy and Lockett because they were not on the list." This is what Colonel Millard Peck reported as a "vivid illustration" to remember when pondering "the bureaucratic mindset that refused to go outside of artificial restrictions in order to find real people. If the case had been prolonged, if the report had come months or even years later, if the vivid memories of the event had gathered dust in DoD files, the same facts would have rung true."

The second error in the omission of Scott Speicher from the Red Cross list occurred because they assumed he was killed. Among the second group of Coalition prisoners returned by Iraq were two probable killed in actions (PKIAs). Marine Corps Captain Craig Berryman and Air Force Captain Dale Storr had been put on the list even though the U.S. government was pretty certain they were dead. So American officials were floored when they saw Berryman and Storr among the released prisoners of war.

The case of Navy Lieutenant Bob Wetzel had a different twist. Vice Admiral Carlos Johnson came up to Bob after a post–Gulf War Tailhook Association symposium and told him that the Office of Naval Intelligence (ONI) had known Bob was alive and captured within an hour of his shootdown. But they couldn't say so, declare him a POW, without giving away how they knew. Bob was lucky. At least his and the others' names ended up on the Red Cross list and they'd been given a fighting chance of coming home.

By March 6, the Department of Defense had revised its casualty data to twenty-six MIAs and no POWs, believing the Iraqis had returned all captives. Schwarzkopf insisted, "I can tell you absolutely without qualification that by the time the war was over, and certainly before we ever came home, that I had been told that one hundred percent had been accounted for. That was the report that was given to me because I asked over and over again. I am absolutely convinced," he went on, "that there was no neglect on the part of anybody in my command with regard to the sensitivity of this matter or effort we made to recover bodies or prisoners of war."

To the best of his knowledge, General Schwarzkopf was right. He'd been guaranteed by his staff that they'd done their jobs and accounted properly for all U.S. service personnel. But they were anxious to get everything over with. At the end of the war, it was far easier to declare MIAs killed in action, with the body not recovered, than to resolve the thornier issues of their precise whereabouts.

"From day one," Carlos Johnson insisted, "he should never have been anything but an MIA. We didn't have a game plan for pilots like Scott Speicher." CENTCOM in Riyadh didn't have the names of a half-dozen unaccounted for Navy aviators on the Red Cross list. The names conspicuously missing were Speicher, Lieutenants Patrick Connor, Robert J. Dwyer, William T. Costen and Charles Turner, and Lieutenant Commander Barry T. Cooke. The status of these flyers had not been determined when the war ended and Coalition prisoners were released. Their cases hung in limbo, for the simple reason that no one had put their names on the list. As it turned out later, nobody did much to look for them either. No search and rescue forces had been deployed to make a physical assessment of the loss of any of them.

Only Turner's, Costen's and Connor's remains turned up later. Connor's body washed up in the mud of Faylaka Island on March 31. His VA-36 *Roadrunner* A-6E Intruder had taken a shoulder-fired SAM missile up the tailpipe on February 2. Connor and his bombardier-navigator, Barry Cooke, had actually been placed on the Department of Defense's missing-in-action list but not the ICRC's list. Nine days later, the Navy retrieved the tail section of their aircraft. Barry Cooke remains unaccounted for today, a distinction he shares with Robert J. Dwyer.

As for Scott Speicher, without his name on the Red Cross list, "we lost leverage with Iraq and support in the international community for getting him back," Carlos Johnson observed. "The political cowardice was unconscionable. We had the mentality that had there been some glimmer that he survived, we would've gone to find him, but we didn't look at it close enough to make that determination." Johnson made the point that Speicher's whole case went back to the argument, "Do you risk hundreds for one? We'd crossed the line to say no, you don't. We had policies of convenience, not conviction."

Ambassador Richard Butler, former executive chairman of the United Nations Special Commission (UNSCOM) for Iraq, offered his expert opinion of Scott's situation: "There is a tendency on their [the Iraqis'] part to lie, hector and play games. This reached its height on biological weapons. You'll probably recall my big showdown meeting on August 3, 1998, in which the Iraqis asked me to declare them biological/chemical and arms free. I refused. They had four tons of VX. We could tell them this, prove it with pictures and documentation." When they lie, Butler indicated, they lie big. The Iraqis had accused former Marine Corps intelligence officer Scott Ritter, one of Butler's weapons inspectors, of spying for the CIA. "When the Iraqis say you're a spy, that you've been seeking one of your aviators, they are vociferously covering up. When they cover up loudly, they are most guilty and diabolical. This means Speicher is probably still alive. Otherwise, why accuse us of searching for him?"

Some of the blame for Scott's circumstance, Butler believed, lay with CNN and their coverage of the war. "I have personally seen [Foreign Minister] Tariq Aziz watching CNN," said Butler. "I walked into his office during one of the inspection meetings, and when he saw I noticed, he immediately turned off the television set." CNN, in Butler's opinion, "has a heavy responsibility in all this. I have been to the network's top executives to tell them just that—and to caution them about how heavily CNN is patronized by the Iraqis." Saddam likes the coverage he gets from CNN. The Iraqis gleaned many details about Scott that they would later use to identify and hunt him down once CNN began to report that Scott may not have died the night he went down.

But from his initial shootdown, all they knew was that a pilot named Michael Scott Speicher was missing.

Vice Admiral Thomas R. Wilson, director of the DIA, concurs that the cable network CNN bore some of the blame. "We created the circumstance for [the Iraqis] to keep him when we declared him gone so quickly after the shootdown and didn't ask for him after the war," said Wilson in 2001. "There was a public perception of Scott's loss via CNN that preempted an official one on May 20, 1991, but even that declaration of his death was without clear evidence that a death had occurred. We should never have classified him anything but MIA based on what we knew at that time," Wilson added.

Why hold Scott? Butler offers this view. "The Iraqis would exact a terrible price for him. They have a ten-year investment in keeping him. If he's still alive—and they would keep him going to use him—it means they've kept him against a rainy day, for a tremendous thunderstorm." This means that when the time comes, they'll put it all on the line for something of enormous value such as renewal of relations with the United States. "There is a terrible price on his head." While the Iraqis could have used Scott to stop bombings, sanctions or as leverage in a regional dispute, they haven't done so because the "tremendous thunderstorm" has not yet come. Butler pointed to the thousands of Iranian prisoners in Iraqi jails since Saddam's eight-year war with the ayatollah in the eighties, and to Kuwaiti citizens taken captive by Iraqi forces during the Gulf War who remain in Iraqi prisons to this day. "When I observed that there were hundreds or thousands involved in this respect," Butler offered, "what I've continued to hear from other diplomatic sources is this: The Iraqis know for the United States, it only takes one."

Everything seems to lead to the same question: Why didn't

anyone ever go and look for Scott Speicher? A memorandum issued on July 19, 1999, by Deputy Assistant Secretary of Defense (POW/Missing Personnel Affairs) Robert L. Jones, stated, "Search and rescue forces were alerted and possible divert airfields were contacted with negative results." It went on to say, "LCDR Speicher's crash site was not located prior to termination of Operation Desert Storm."

Neither of these statements is true. No rescue forces were ever contacted to search for Scott Speicher. While the chain of command from the Joint Chiefs of Staff to theater commanders in Riyadh to his commanding officer on the *Saratoga* knew that Speicher was down, information that indicated he might have ejected was not passed up to Special Operations Command Central (SOCCENT)/J2, in charge of search and rescue. Nor was an accurate coordinate for the crash site given. SOCCENT got a message about the radio clicks reported on January 18, but didn't pursue it further. Also, according to Bob Stumpf, within twenty-four hours of the shootdown, pilots on the *Saratoga* calculated exactly where they had seen Speicher's "fireball" by comparing notes and reviewing data from aircraft and voice recorders. During their intelligence debriefings on the ship, Lieutenant David Renaud, who for a long time was thought to have been the closest pilot to Scott Speicher, reported seeing explosions five miles away, in Spike's direction, at the same time Stumpf had witnessed a blast in the sky. Renaud even drew a little circle on his map where he calculated he had last seen the fireball. "This information," says Stumpf, "was relayed up the chain of command. Years later, when the wreckage was actually located, it was in the precise spot they had identified."[18] But, as has been previously noted, an erroneous coordinate was run up the chain of command. "His commanding officer [Mike Anderson] and his CAG [Dean M. "Milo" Hendrickson] should have been more involved, and they should have grabbed the torch and run with it," said Buddy Harris of the lack of a search on Speicher's behalf, "and they just didn't do that."

Vice Admiral Stanley R. Arthur, then commander of all allied naval forces in the Persian Gulf, has gone on record regarding this incident. "The first report was 'airplane disintegrated on impact; no contact with the pilot; we really don't believe that anyone was able to survive the impact.'" Yet when it comes to combat, time and again the amazing has happened. During Operation Homecoming in 1973, Major Douglas B. "Pete" Peterson, shot down in September 1966, was debriefed. A few weeks before he was shot down, Peterson had been engaged in air combat over North Vietnam. He returned from the mission to report his wingman was dead. A missile hit him, and the aircraft was engulfed in a massive explosion. No parachute was seen, no beepers heard—just hundreds of small parts flew through the air. They even had a funeral service. When Peterson was shot down not too long after, he was captured and taken to Hanoi, where the first American he saw in prison was his "dead" wingman. It was almost too much for Peterson to comprehend, but there he was—in the flesh. Peterson's story is hardly the only one like this. There have been many.

The reason given why no one looked for Scott Speicher was the fear of losing the rescue parties. During Desert Storm, General Schwarzkopf put Army Colonel Jesse Johnson in charge of search and rescue efforts, and Johnson set up strict guidelines for launching a search. The teams would have to hear from a downed pilot, find out his location and assess the risk before going into Iraq. "We had a very, very sophisticated search and rescue plan made up, so that in the event that anybody went down, we could dispatch search and rescue if they were alive on the ground. We could hopefully rescue them—a very dangerous mission—I'm sure you can understand," said Schwarzkopf.

Technically, all reported downed aircrew were considered "actionable" events for search and rescue. But not all of them could be carried out because of shootdown location, lack of precise coordinates (such as the erroneous set submitted for Scott Speicher) and lack of confirmation of life. Timothy G. Connolly, the former Army Ranger and later principal undersecretary of defense for special operations and low-intensity conflict, commented recently on the low number of rescue missions actually executed during the war, where he was assigned as part of a group working with the Iraqi resistance. "We did virtually no SAR for anyone. Jesse Johnson, head of special operations for Central Command, was responsible for combat SAR forces. His rule was, we're not launching unless there's somebody on the ground waving their arms for us. He didn't want to risk casualties."

That was a drastic change of policy from Vietnam, where teams would head out and search when they heard that a pilot had gone down. Seventy-one search and rescue team members were killed, but Air Force rescuers saved more than four thousand Americans, and the Navy picked up hundreds of others.

In the Persian Gulf War, thirty-seven fixed-wing aircraft were lost in combat, but Johnson launched search teams for only seven of them. They ended up rescuing three pilots. Kuwaiti resistance also made at least three attempts, possibly more, to get downed aviators in Kuwait. Either the pilot got picked up or the rescue route was so flooded with Iraqi troops that Kuwaitis were not able to get the aircrew.

General Schwarzkopf was taken aback recently that no search and rescue was done for Scott Speicher. "I would be very surprised at that," he stated, "unless the reports were so specific as to say that there could not have been life or that he could not have survived the crash." Then he said something that raises the question of how well informed he'd been regarding this theater of operations. "I do know we did run many search and rescue missions," he continued. "If there was any chance at all that there would have been a survivor, they would have gone out and attempted to recover him." Yet the math is simple. Seven searches out of thirty-seven, with only three recoveries, none inside the four to five hours rescue forces like to work, left upward of thirty aircrews without rescue attempts.

The breakdown of communication between CENTCOM and SOCCENT/J2 began even before the first shot was fired. In September 1990, an article in the *Arab News*, Saudi Arabia's English-language daily, reported statements by a Jordanian-based tribal leader of the Unezyh or Shamariah tribe, one of the many tribes in that region of the Middle East, that their tribe should support Coalition efforts against Saddam Hussein. Further, the SOCCENT/J2's Kuwaiti contacts said those tribes would assist their Coalition partners. The two tribes were native to western Iraq and routinely traveled across the international borders of Jordan and Saudi Arabia. At that time, a member of the J2 staff, Major James Gregory Eanes, Evasion and Escape Officer for SOCCENT, an Air Force reservist called to active duty during Desert Shield, submitted a memorandum to Army Lieutenant Colonel John P. Grace, the SOCJ2—his boss. In the memo, Eanes suggested that SOCCENT/J2 initiate a campaign to actively solicit the support of those tribes as well as establish communications with their leaders in an effort to begin an escape and evasion network.

Grace effectively nixed the idea. He stated to his staff that such networks were a CIA operation and it was not SOCCENT/

J2's responsibility to initiate that kind of program. In truth, the CIA had stated at a personnel recovery conference in 1983—seven years earlier—that it did not establish these networks anymore. But apparently Grace didn't know it. The CIA was instead interested in cultivating among the indigenous population political and paramilitary organizations who could supplant Saddam. Grace indicated almost indignantly that it was SOCCENT/J2's job to wait for orders, not initiate operational concepts. Eanes gasped and wondered what the hell they were then doing. "I was really steamed at the time, feeling our job was to prepare for the coming conflict, but Grace and others somehow thought we were strictly there as a deterrent rather than a liberation force."

Grace was a by-product of the Vietnam era, a veteran who survived the politics of the post-Vietnam period by not taking a proactive position on issues that might be career busters. Unbeknownst to his staff at that time, he suffered from severe asthma and remained heavily medicated during his tenure as SOCJ2. Lieutenant Commander Michael Williams, deputy SOCJ2, found Grace on the floor of his room comatose on one occasion. The second time, Grace nearly died, and this led to his return to the United States in late September or early October. Eanes's memo never went beyond Grace, though it had been tagged for the SOCJ3, Army Colonel James Fletcher. Fletcher told Eanes in November that he was never shown the memo.

By that time Saddam Hussein had begun to offer cash rewards for downed aircrew captured by Bedouins, Biduns or Iraqi civilians. Saddam offered $35,000 for each aircrew taken into custody. The SOCCENT/J2 policy was not to get into a bidding war, so there was—and is—no price tag placed on friendly assistance. They preferred instead to reward the assistor with whatever they wanted in return such as sheep, goats and so on. In the past, the practice had worked. But it became readily apparent after the first Coalition air losses in January 1991 that Saddam was winning the reward game—sheep and goats weren't as tempting as cold, hard cash. This came to pass despite the fact that considerable amounts are set aside each year to support the program.

This was a missed opportunity. SOCCENT/J2 had a chance to establish an indigenous resistance force that could have aided in the recovery of downed aircrews. Time was of the essence and Saddam acted; the U.S. didn't.

Eanes and others back in Riyadh also found that the Navy offered up little information on its downed aircrews. The U.S. Naval Forces Central Command (NAVCENT) rescue coordination center (NRCC) was located with Vice Admiral Arthur aboard the command ship USS *Blue Ridge*. The center was responsible for all over-water combat search and rescue for both the Red Sea and the Persian Gulf. NAVCENT appointed two regional search and rescue controllers—Combined Task Force (CTF) 151 in the Persian Gulf area and CTF 155 in the Red Sea. CTF 151 was responsible for assigning units and developing plans to support search and rescue operations and coordinate with SOCCENT and the multinational forces. But neither CTF 151 nor 155 was supposed to handle over-land losses—and this is another place where the responsibility for rescues became muddied.

"NAVCENT could have tried its own recovery operation," said Eanes. "Each service component was responsible for its own SAR. Technically, SOCCENT was only to be called for denied areas [such as inaccessible areas behind enemy lines] because we had the specialized assets to get into the denied areas." The Navy has a file with Scott's name on it marked NRCC N001—the first

Navy case run through the rescue coordination center on the
Blue Ridge. The file contains messages pertaining to Scott Speicher's loss and information as it dribbled in during the war. The
telling content is what was not done for Scott Speicher—a physical search—and the two sets of coordinates, one of them erroneous. In any case, the Navy was unlikely to launch a mission
from the Red Sea, over seven hundred miles from where Scott
Speicher went down.

As for SOCCENT, their policy was simple, observed Eanes:
"If we could not verify a man on the ground, we weren't going
after him. The risk posed to the assets and Special Operations
Force crew did not outweigh the gain. With our limited assets
and guidelines to avoid casualties, we could not take a chance on
a recovery without verifiable contact." If SOCCENT rejected
the mission, it would go back to the Joint Recovery Command
Center to ask if anyone—such as the Kuwaiti resistance or
British Special Air Service (SAS)—could take the mission. Eanes
went on to say that SOCCENT turned down at least one rescue
mission because of the enemy threat. "An Army team picked up
that mission, was predictably shot down and lost its helicopter."

This was Flight Surgeon Major Rhonda L. Cornum's flight.
Her commander dispatched Cornum and her crew to pick up
downed F-16 pilot Major William Andrews. The threat was particularly high in his circumstance. They did not do a pre-mission
analysis, and several crew members on Cornum's flight were
killed and the rest captured. Meanwhile, Major Andrews had
been captured the moment his boots hit the desert floor. In other
cases SOCCENT teams made attempts to rescue helicopter
crews but with negative results, even when, in one case, they
continued to make radio contact for two days. "I find this interesting," said a source familiar with the cases, "because they tried
so hard on this case but made no attempts for many others."

Eanes, whose forces were closest, never received any communication from NRCC aboard the USS *Blue Ridge*, and never dispatched a search and rescue team to recover Scott Speicher. The tragedy in this respect was that Eanes had assets who could've scooped up Speicher within forty-five minutes in and out of his crash location.

The first shots of the war were fired at 2:38 A.M. on January 17 by 101st Airborne Division (Air Assault) pilots who took out two key early warning radar sites in western Iraq. Code-named "Normandy," their mission was one of the most dangerous combat assignments that night. Each of the two Tall King long-range radar sites, about thirty-five miles apart, was struck by a team of two Special Forces MH-53J Pave Lows and four AH-64A Apache helicopters. The teams infiltrated and exfiltrated from a forward airfield in northwestern Saudi Arabia—Al Jouf. Reaching the targets, they released twenty-seven Hellfire missiles that took out between sixteen and eighteen targets at each location. The facilities were laid waste in roughly four-and-a-half minutes. Another Apache and a UH-60 Blackhawk helicopter waited south of the border, ready to jump into the action if a search and rescue mission was needed. Yet no U.S. Air Force or Army aircraft was lost along the corridor the Apaches opened up that night. "We owned the airspace," said Eanes later. "The 101st Airborne's assets remained on the border, and I could've contacted them on the ground for assistance. I didn't know Scott Speicher was down." The Navy had not reported his loss.

As for Schwarzkopf, Eanes remarked that he had to depend on his staff to report accurate information to him. "Schwarzkopf and Horner had a war to run; one downed pilot is just part of the breaks of the game and was not something that could have or should have consumed their thoughts at that time. They had more important things to focus on, and they had staffs and commands responsible for taking appropriate actions. A commander has to depend on those staffs and the people at the commands to do their jobs correctly and, if an error is made, to be mature and responsible enough to admit the mistake so corrective actions could be initiated."

What Eanes didn't realize at the time was that he coordinated the drop of British SAS teams on Speicher's correct loss coordinates on the night of January 20. In order to better explain his point, Eanes spread out the evasion chart Scott would've been carrying with him on his mission and smoothed it down to his kitchen table. The consternation on his face made it painfully obvious he still felt responsible for Scott Speicher as an operator on the ground who needed his help. He put his finger on the intersect point for 3300N/4200E on the map, and said affirmatively, "I had a British SAS team *here*." Bravo One Zero and Bravo Three Zero were dropped in the area to hunt SCUD missiles and disrupt enemy operations. Chris Ryan writes in his Gulf War memoirs that his team, Bravo Two Zero, which later went in behind the other teams on January 22, should've paid closer attention to their cover story—a search and rescue team sent to recover downed airmen.[19] The Bravo teams all operated under this cover story, ironic since a downed airman was in the very area in which they'd been inserted.

Bravo Two Zero's experience could not have been unlike Scott's own as he unfastened his parachute harness and assessed his surroundings. The landscape was not what they'd been briefed it would be—all around them was dirt and rocks. There was no sand readily available for the team to fill their sandbags to make machine gun nests. Goatherders' dogs barked at the commandos in the night, and young Bedouin boys called out to quiet them. Their voices reverberated in the vastness of the wadi. But the dogs kept barking. The men on Ryan's team watched the wadi for any sign of enemy troop movements. "It was so cold," Ryan recounted, "that several of them struggled into their NBC (nuclear, biological and chemical) suits and lay around in them."

More recently, in late 2001, it became known through retired Vice Admiral Michael L. Bowman, former commander of Naval Air Forces, Pacific Fleet, that a classified message made the rounds among the carrier air wings in the Red Sea that a Special Operations team had possibly located Scott Speicher's wreckage while the war was still being fought. Bowman was air wing commander aboard the USS *America* in the Red Sea during the war, and though he couldn't recall much detail about its content, he prompted a search for the message itself.

General Schwarzkopf also had a recollection of the information to which Bowman refers. "As I recall at that time," Schwarzkopf said, "I was asking Chuck Horner the status of search and rescue on the two pilots that were down." As Schwarzkopf remembered it, he heard that a combination of information sent back through "a fellow pilot" who'd witnessed the explosion was part of the reason no one looked. But the rest hinged on the fact that "search and rescue people went out and reported back no visible life at the scene of the crash. Again, that's my recollection, but I can't be specific."

Though not the message Bowman read, Captain Bernie Smith at NAVCENT sent a message to Rear Admiral S. Frank Gallo, Deputy Chief of Naval Personnel, on March 10, 1991, that addressed a conversation that had taken place the day before, March 9, between Captain Steve Loeffler and Smith's department. "The information is the best we can obtain from aircrew debriefs and radio communications relayed up the chain," wrote Smith to Gallo. "We have intentionally made this a classified message in order to give you as much detail as possible." The following personnel were still listed as MIA, in addition to

Scott Speicher: Lieutenants Charles J. Turner, William T. Costen, Patrick K. Connor, Lieutenant Commander Barry T. Cooke, and Marine Corps Captain Reginald C. Underwood. Of Speicher, the message basically states that wreckage had been located in the area the *Saratoga*'s Hornet pilots had indicated in their own investigation. But Smith's evaluation of this is: "It was not possible to determine if the aircraft was Speicher's, but no other aircraft were lost. There were no communications or beacons reported." Smith writes at the end of the message that he "hopes this information will assist in dealing with the families. A concern is that we raise no false hopes."

As for the message Bowman saw, the only detail he recalled was that the Special Forces team had picked up a flight helmet and a few items of pilot gear found near smoldering wreckage. The team could not get close enough to the aircraft to identify it. Was this Scott Speicher's Hornet? It seemed so. Was it an SAS team who grabbed up his gear and thought nothing else of it? No one knows, but they had teams in-country and SOCCENT did not. "I can state without reservation," said Greg Eanes, "that no SOCCENT–associated Special Forces teams found pilot gear immediately after the event. My recollection is that we didn't even have any teams in Iraq at that point, though the British had several."

It is possible to re-create what Scott went through after his plane was hit. A post-combat search and rescue scenario documenting the loss of VF-103's Tomcat on January 21 states that during his descent, pilot Lieutenant Devon "Boots" Jones saw his backseater, Lieutenant Lawrence R. "Rat" Slade, in his parachute about four hundred feet away, but received no response to his shouts. In the predawn darkness, Jones sighted the exploding wreckage of his aircraft below the cloud layer about five nautical miles away, but lost visual contact with Larry Slade. Jones suffered loss of manual dexterity during his descent because of extreme cold at the high altitudes. Once on the ground, his initial communications were somewhat garbled due to difficulty in operating his survival radio. His initial estimate of the crash site location was also inaccurate, delaying the response by rescue forces. He also found the desert hardpan so tough he was unable to dig a hole large enough to bury his parachute and seat pan. At dawn, Jones regained his bearings and moved about two nautical miles to the pickup site, an area in which he was able to use his survival knife to dig a hole deep enough to hide in until the rescue team came. He was recovered in a daring daytime extraction.

But for Scott Speicher there would be no daring rescue. The determination that he was dead was simply a perception that began with Defense Secretary Cheney's misstatement to the press, not the military's official determination of Speicher's status. The U.S. Navy and the Department of Defense (DoD) had determined that Speicher was MIA. But on May 22, 1991, in part thanks to actions taken by Chief of Naval Personnel Vice Admiral Jeremy M. "Mike" Boorda, the Navy changed him to KIA/BNR. Despite this designation, the case remains open until a body is recovered. "You never give up looking for a KIA/BNR any more than you would an MIA," says Harris. It was also easier for Joanne Speicher to get on with her life if Scott was listed as killed. She was told Scott's demise was obvious: no radio contact, no ejection and, most damning of all, there had been an unsurvivable fireball. Even though no one was ever put on the ground to go look, in the minds of Scott's air wing commanders and Arthur's NAVCENT staff, he blew up.

"Joanne," said Buddy Harris, "said, 'He's dead, he's gone' and she put it behind her as best she could. She tried to steer her children's lives in the most normal way possible. That was her goal from day five or so after he was shot down." Harris remembers her saying, "Hey, you know, I'm freaking here, but these children need me. They need a normal life." She put off the media—with the exception of the *Ladies' Home Journal* feature in June 1991. But as soon as she clammed up, Scott Speicher's name fell away from the front page and the chances of anyone pressing for his return faded with every day that passed.

CHAPTER 6

The Falcon Hunter

In 1993, a little over two years after Scott was officially declared KIA/BNR, Robert Dussault, then deputy director of the Joint Services Survival, Evasion, Resistance, and Escape (SERE) Agency, received a call that took him completely by surprise. A friend in the Navy said he had reliable indicators that Scott was alive and being held by friendly Bedouins. Dussault's friend, Steven Collins, was a "handler" or case officer whose man operated in Iraq whenever needed. Collins was very concerned, as he was certain that his clandestine operator's information was, indeed, accurate. Up until that point, the Department of Defense's Prisoner of War/Missing in Action Office, which became DPMO the following year, held the staunch opinion that Speicher was KIA/BNR. Armed with Collins's new information, Dussault's office found themselves in the tenuous position where they felt they had to challenge Speicher's KIA status. It was a status that grew ever more complicated.

On November 19, 1993, almost a year into President William J. Clinton's presidency, the International Committee of the Red Cross (ICRC) provided a note from an Iraqi delegation dated

October 14 of that year that stated "no additional information is available" concerning Lieutenant Commander Speicher. The note read, "Regarding the Lt. Commander (Captain Pilot?) Michael S. Speicher. His name was reported by his colleague pilot Robert James who repatriated home through your esteemed delegation on March 5, 1991. No additional information is available about him in spite of [our] investigation and tracing." First Lieutenant Robert James Sweet, USAF, was an A-10 pilot captured on February 2, 1991, and released on March 5. But interestingly, Sweet is said to have made no statements about Scott Speicher to the Iraqis during his internment.

"[The U.S.] played some games with Iraq from the political aspect to try to find out if they would acknowledge information," stated Buddy Harris, who ended up investigating the Speicher case while assigned to the Pentagon. The State Department had apparently provided some teasers to the Iraqis, but they didn't jump at them. Because Iraq held fast and didn't appear responsive, Harris remarked that the State Department concluded, "There's no way Iraq has any knowledge of him. He's definitely dead. They were pretty well convinced he blew up in his plane because nothing was found." The Iraqis continued to put off U.S. officials who communicated with Saddam's representatives through the ICRC.

Lieutenant Jeffrey D. Brown remembers the debate over Speicher from the start of the Clinton presidency. Brown was an A-6E Intruder pilot assigned to a military internship in the office of the secretary of defense when he came across the Speicher case. "I was there from 1992 to 1994," said Brown, now a commissioner for the Virginia Department of Labor and Industry. "We were starting the transition between the departing Bush administration and the Clinton inauguration that January. The push in late 1992 from President Bush's staff was to get out of the White

House and out of Washington ahead of the Clinton team." This was problematic for the investigation because the Bush national security team had done a lot of data collecting about the war—and about Scott Speicher. "Unfortunately, most of the data that might have helped Scott wasn't pouring in until after Bush lost the White House in the November presidential election," says Brown. By that time, no one was ready to pick up the torch again and carry it for a missing Navy pilot who had already fallen off everybody's radar screen. The intelligence gathered since the war was simply put aside.

After Bill Clinton took office in January, Les Aspin became his secretary of defense. Les Aspin had served as an adviser to Clinton on defense matters during the 1992 presidential campaign, and because of his leadership position in the House of Representatives, Aspin's views on defense issues were well known.

Not long after taking office, Aspin discussed dangers that had emerged with the end of the Cold War: the uncertainty that reform could succeed in the former Soviet Union; the enhanced possibility that terrorists or terrorist states could acquire nuclear weapons; the likely proliferation of regional conflicts; and the failure to take adequate account of the impact of the state of the domestic economy on U.S. national security interests. Given these conditions and the end of the Cold War, it seemed clear that the Pentagon was entering a period of potentially profound change.

"It was clear from day one we weren't supposed to ask questions about Scott Speicher," Brown recalled. Aspin's agenda was clear—and Scott Speicher wasn't on it. "Les Aspin told us all we had were three issues to deal with—gays in the military, force drawdowns from a six hundred–ship Navy and base closures. He didn't want to deal with Scott Speicher," Brown emphasized. "These were, of course, all political issues between OSD (the Office of the Secretary of Defense) and the joint services." The schism with the military—particularly the joint side and OSD—was a political morass. "It was not an accidental breach of the warrior's code where Scott Speicher was concerned," according to Brown. "Speicher was ignored." While Brown didn't know if it was a conscious, directed act to ignore Scott, the attitude was that there were more important fish to fry and Speicher wasn't one of them. "The lack of respect for the military during the Clinton administration was exemplified by the Scott Speicher case," said Brown.

The Joint Service SERE Agency (JSSA) was the DoD's lead for Operation Yellow Ribbon, the individual debriefings of repatriated POWs. Robert Dussault was the senior member of the team that went through POW debriefs and also published the captivity summary for the Department of Defense. There were particular cases that got Bob Dussault's attention when the circumstances of the loss didn't marry up to what was being reported through intelligence channels. "During Desert Storm, my people had to provide briefings and their assessments to generals in the Pentagon on a regular basis, and for these we were getting intelligence from all sources. But just in my short and quick exposure to these cases, certain things that did not fit sort of stuck in my head," said Dussault. "I do recall reports of guys going down and being treated a certain way in [the] reporting that did not happen to match any of the handling received by the returnees." The returnees to which Dussault refers are the POW/MIAs repatriated at war's end. From what he saw and heard in that time frame, "either the reporting was bad, or we did not get everyone back who was captured."

One of those Operation Yellow Ribbon reports caught Dussault's attention right away. It belonged to Lieutenant Lawrence R. Slade, the F-14A+ radar intercept officer who was shot down January 21 on a mission near Al Asad Airfield, and held as a prisoner of war. The Iraqis repatriated him on March 4 in the first group of aviators sent back through the ICRC. Message traffic from the Joint Chiefs of Staff dated April 2, 1991, and passed throughout the intelligence community via Combined Task Group (CTG) 168, provided pointed information pertaining to comments made by an Iraqi interrogator concerning the status of a U.S. Navy F/A-18 pilot—Scott Speicher. At one of Slade's interrogations, he was told by his captors that an F/A-18 pilot off the *Saratoga* was dead. The statement seemed to have been made in the context of an attempt to elicit information concerning U.S. air wing personnel. Slade was asked if the *Saratoga* had lost any other aircraft. When he said yes, "an F/A-18 and an A-6," Slade was asked if he knew the pilot of the F/A-18. He replied no. The interrogator became visibly upset. He believed that the air wing was a tight-knit family and that Slade would know the pilot. Frustrated, the interrogator replied, "Well, he's dead." But Slade was given no substantive information to suggest how or when Scott Speicher might have died.

The field comment attached to Slade's debrief stated, "This may correlate to Lieutenant Commander Speicher, USN. The source [Slade] does not recall which interrogator, nor at which site and session this comment was made." In addition, Lieutenant Commander Henry Corscadden and Lieutenant Raymond Lagamasino, who debriefed Slade, noted that in retrospect, based on the interrogation's "superficiality" and the widespread publication of Speicher's status, "Slade believes the interrogator obtained the information from the press." The Iraqis were on a fishing expedition with Slade. They didn't seem to have Scott Speicher and they didn't know where he was. Was he dead? No one knew exactly. "I got information daily and helped make the debriefs more comprehensive" said Dussault. "However, there were some things that fell through the cracks until questions about Scott came up a couple of years later." These questions started with telephone calls from a Navy case officer who handled an asset known as the Falcon Hunter.

In the fall of 1993, a local tribe of Bedouins had found the wreckage of Scott's Hornet, and had begun picking up the broken pieces that had fallen away from the fuselage and selling them in a black market souk. CIA agents were tipped off that the parts to an American jet were being sold by a source nicknamed the Falcon Hunter. A member of the Qatari royal family with strong ties to the Iraqis, the Falcon Hunter happened upon locals bartering the parts in a marketplace and inquired of the sellers about the crash site. It was December 1993 and the sheikh had come to the western Iraqi desert to hunt with his falcons, as he did regularly that time of year. He wanted to see the site for himself. Led to the wreckage by Bedouin shepherds, the Falcon Hunter immediately knew what they had found—a U.S. Navy jet off the USS *Saratoga*, downed during the Persian Gulf War. It was a stunning, almost miraculous find.

The Falcon Hunter reported the incident to his handler in the Office of Naval Intelligence (ONI), who requested that he return to the site to take photographs and collect a serial number from some part of the aircraft that might facilitate its proper identification. By this time the CIA was fully involved in the case, arranging a second visit with Qatari officials to the crash location. The Falcon Hunter entered the Iraqi desert again under the cover of his hunting party to investigate the site as anxious American officials waited to see what he turned up. On December 19, 1993, during a meeting with a U.S. liaison officer in Doha, the Falcon Hunter, accompanied by Qatar's assistant chief of staff of operations, training and planning to Iraq, turned over a stack of photographs and a piece of the wreckage itself. The pictures included shots of the Hornet's canopy and large sections of the aircraft, including its relatively intact engines, the cockpit and part of the tail with the word "Saratoga" clearly visible. The ejection seat lay nearby. And more important, the Falcon Hunter had secured a metal plate stamped with identification numbers. Those numbers were traced to a Hornet flown in the Gulf War, identified by the number 163470—and the last man to fly that jet was Michael Scott Speicher.

Or so they initially thought. The Navy assigns each of its aircraft a specific, unique bureau number (BuNo). Scott Speicher was lost in AA403 BuNo 163484, which had been stricken from the Navy record back on January 17, 1991. BuNo 163470, the aircraft number that was then listed on each of Speicher's reports after 1993, is wrong. Though this aircraft did fly with VFA-81 and was still with them in July 1994 as AA400, it has since been seen flying at China Lake with the Naval Weapons Test Squadron, and with VFA-115 squadron in January 2001.

Indeed, what the Falcon Hunter had retrieved was a shard of metal from the radar mount pulled out of the *Sunliners'* cannibalized aircraft, BuNo 163470, and placed in Speicher's Hornet, BuNo 163484, before he launched for his mission the first night of the Gulf War air strikes. To explain, when dealing with malfunctioning parts on a sophisticated, multimillion-dollar jet, Navy squadrons will cannibalize parts from another jet, or a "can bird," to repair otherwise functional jets, especially on carriers that are far removed from available new plane parts. Any operational jet on board a carrier could thus have parts from many different airplanes of the same type. This was the case with Speicher's Hornet the night he went down. The radar mount that was found in the desert was later identified as coming from an F/A-18C by Lieutenant Commander "Fast" Eddie Smith. Since his stint on the ATO planning staff at Riyadh during the

war, Smith had become the Pentagon's resident expert on the F/
A-18 Hornet. But Fast Eddie wasn't asked to track down the
parts trail from one BuNo to another. He was only asked to confirm that the part was from an -18C. And Scott's Hornet was the
only -C lost during the war. The part swap never made it into the
Navy maintenance system register, so the last aircraft in which
the component was recorded is BuNo 163470, which was not the
aircraft Speicher flew that night, but another jet in the *Sunliners'*
inventory. The error was never caught by crash investigators.

The Falcon Hunter was also able to take a camera with him to
the crash site and turned over to his handlers a stack of three-by-
five photographs. There were two different sets, one for each of
the sheikh's visits to the crash site, each showing that the aircraft
was totally intact and inverted. The cockpit was still with the aircraft, the nose cone was in good condition and the engines were
still encased within the body of the aircraft. Fast Eddie only saw
the first set of photographs—not the second. He saw no ejection
seat in his set, but from what he could tell, there was a canopy,
separated some distance from the aircraft. Eddie also noted that
shortly after he got the pictures, he received a cryptic telephone
call telling him that the photographs "don't exist." Disturbed by
the call, he gave them back to officials. Shortly after finishing his
analysis of the photographs and radar mount, Fast Eddie was
pushed out of the loop. Scott's case remained closed.

Lieutenant Commander Jeffrey S. Manor, then special assistant for POW/MIA Affairs at the Bureau of Naval Personnel and
a naval aviator, received a secure telephone call from a lieutenant
in the Office of Naval Intelligence late one Friday afternoon in
1994, the subject of which was Scott Speicher and the loss reports contained in his casualty file. Manor and his assistant, Lieu-

tenant Geoffrey G. Stothard, a P-3C Orion pilot, were interested enough by the call to begin researching what they had thought was a closed case. Both knew that there were still three naval aviators whose remains did not return from Desert Storm (Speicher, Lieutenant Commander Barry Cooke, and Lieutenant Robert J. Dwyer). But it had been several years since the war, and most of their efforts had turned to Vietnam-era investigations.

As they began reinvestigating, Manor became aware of some extremely unsettling facts concerning Scott's case. "I haven't seen anyone make a big deal that public law was violated by having Scott declared deceased early," said Manor. "To me, it's one of the key elements to him being 'forgotten.'"

Public law as defined by Title 37 of the United States Code (USC) Section 555 Chapter 10, the Payments to Missing Persons Act—as it also applies to the others' cases who were declared KIA/BNR prematurely, like Speicher, Cooke and Dwyer—required that a person carried in a missing status could not be declared deceased until one year and one day after his or her loss. According to information contained in his casualty file, even though Scott Speicher was lost in mid-January of 1991, he was declared deceased on May 22 of that same year.

"This is a clear violation of the public law to which I'm referring," said Manor. "Scott's case is not the only one in which public law was violated. The Desert Storm missing individual [Lieutenant Commander Barry Cooke] was an A-6E aviator whose case is not as controversial as Scott's, who should have been carried in a missing status for at least a year also." Manor and his assistant found it extremely strange that these and other cases were closed as KIA/BNR so quickly, since public law was very clear in this matter. "There are no gray areas," asserts Manor.

As their investigation on behalf of the chief of Naval Operations' office continued, Manor discovered even more disconcerting elements. The Missing Persons Act, which then applied to noncombat as well as combat cases, required that only the secretary of the Navy or his designee could declare a person deceased. "It was clear from paperwork in LCDR Speicher's file that [Vice] Admiral Jeremy M. "Mike" Boorda (then chief of naval personnel) was the driving force behind both aviators being declared deceased. We discovered a memo from Admiral Boorda to the secretary of the Navy announcing his 'decision' to declare LCDR Speicher and his fellow missing aviator deceased. The memo predates the so-called missing person boards that were held to determine the cases," wrote Manor. "I say 'so-called' because we interviewed two of the three members of the boards, and despite it being less than three years after they were held, neither member could tell us much about how they came to their decision."

Neither member interviewed could recall being briefed on the requirements of the Missing Persons Act, which would have clearly rung bells in their heads when they discovered that there was a year requirement before a finding of death could be declared. And more important, none of the three board members who sat in on Scott's determination hearing had the special compartmentalized information clearance to hear or read information that might have raised reasonable doubt as to Scott's status. The more Manor and Stothard researched the case, the more both became incensed at how everything was handled back in 1991. "I'll never forget my assistant saying, 'That SOB, he just left him behind.' That 'SOB' referred to the CNO at that time—Admiral Boorda."

Manor still believes that the reason Scott Speicher's case was swept under the carpet and not pressured from above was Admiral Boorda's involvement. The only proof he has of that is the memorandums from Boorda as chief of naval personnel in 1991 to Chief of Naval Operations Frank B. Kelso II and to Secretary of the Navy H. Lawrence Garrett III, Manor's discussions with his predecessor, and his interview of Admiral Boorda's personal envoy to Joanne Speicher, Captain Dale V. Raebel, a Navy captain who had been a short-time Vietnam POW.

"Our review of the file itself revealed Admiral Boorda's own personal touch on everything [having] to do with the case," Manor said. Boorda had the propensity to do the unusual, follow what Manor described as the admiral's "feel" of how things should be. "I don't believe that he was being pressured from above, not from what I saw, because there were no communiqués from the top down, only Admiral Boorda's memos discussing how he was controlling the case." From what Manor and others observed, it appeared that Boorda believed that the best thing to do was help the family put it behind them. "This meant convincing Mrs. Speicher that there was no hope."

On April 29, 1991, about a month before Scott Speicher's memorial service, then–Vice Admiral Boorda notified Joanne Speicher's casualty assistance calls officer (CACO), Lieutenant Commander Tony Salazar—an F/A-18 pilot at Cecil Field—that the Navy was ready to change Scott Speicher's status to KIA, and shortly thereafter he amended this to a request for KIA/BNR. Boorda wanted to dispatch his personal emissary, Captain Raebel, down to Jacksonville to talk to Joanne about the efforts the Navy had taken to date, and to discuss the plan for a May memorial service at Arlington National Cemetery. Raebel was a good choice—he had been shot down while flying off the USS *Saratoga* in August 1972. He was captured and spent about seven months as a POW in Hanoi. Raebel's visit turned out to be unnecessary, however. Captain John W. Curtin, commander of the light attack wing (COMLATWING), intervened and personally visited Joanne Speicher. The next day, April 30, Lieutenant Commander Salazar called to confirm with Vice Admiral Boorda's office that there was definitely no need for Captain Raebel to visit. Everything was taken care of—Joanne Speicher had agreed to Scott's change in status.

"Apparently, they gave her the option of leaving him MIA or declare him officially dead. She chose to move on with her life," said John Webb, one of Scott's best friends from college. "That's my understanding."

Soon after Joanne made her decision, a quick board was held on May 20, 1991, recommending that Scott be declared deceased. Manor and Stothard were distressed by what happened to Scott Speicher. "We just couldn't believe that making the family feel good came before finding out exactly what happened to one of our aviators," said Manor. "It would have been so easy to find his wreckage. We could have demanded anything we wanted. Iraq would have had to acquiesce and the American public would have supported the effort 100 percent."

Everything Manor came across in the file had Boorda's fingerprints all over it. Boorda seemed to have predetermined Scott's change of status—even the date of his service on May 22 was hastily arranged to take advantage of burying remains purported to be Speicher's. On March 20, 1991, the Iraqis had turned over to the ICRC the remains of someone they claimed was a "U.S. pilot by the name of Mickel"—meaning Michael Scott Speicher. They even supplied a death certificate along with the remains, which amounted to approximately a pound and a half of desiccated flesh. The remains were received at the Dover Point Mortuary, in Dover Delaware, on March 23, 1991, and issued the case number DS1-256.

Eight days later, on March 28, the Iraqi delegation to the
third session of the postwar Tripartite Commission agreed to
provide a witness statement concerning the questionable identification of what were reportedly the partial remains of Lieutenant
Commander Speicher. The remains consisted of partially de-
composed portions of upper torso tissue, mainly skin. Dr. Victor
W. Weedn, a major in the Army medical corps who'd set up the
Armed Forces Institute of Pathology (AFIP) DNA typing capabilities and remained the program's director, was not hesitant to
reflect on his examination of the remains. "So here is this pound
of tissue or so, two major fragments. I think it was really less than
a pound. It was clear that you could see that it was skin with
some hair on it." But, Weedn continued, "the skin was olive colored; it was Caucasian but it was dark. There was some subcuta-
neous fat and it was old, and it was dried out. This is not like
somebody who died and the remains were quickly recovered and
sent to us." There was also a fragment of metal, originally thought
to have been bone. No additional information was available from
the Iraqi government as to why they thought the remains were
Speicher's, and they weren't willing to answer questions either.

"We did a Western Blot test on site at Dover Air Force Base
mortuary," Weedn recalled. The Western Blot analysis was the
first of three types of tests Weedn tried first to identify the remains of DS1-256, and it is standard procedure when the AFIP
receives remains through their Dover facility. Forensic patholo-
gists use dot blots and reverse dot blots where polymerase chain
reaction (PCR) products are hybridized with allele-specific
oligonucleotides (ASOs) for the purpose of scanning for muta-
tions, detecting RNA, cancer or pathogens in a specimen. It's a
"game-opener" in a repertoire of genetic testing, to provide
some basic analysis on the remains forwarded to Dover from
Riyadh. But in the case of what Weedn had in hand to test, the

sample of tissue didn't give him enough to be highly discriminatory, and he had to go to outside laboratories in order to perform more conclusive tests.

The PCR is, by definition, a technique for amplifying a specific region of DNA, in order to identify a specific trait or traits in a person's genetic makeup. The regions amplified are usually between 150 and 3,000 base pairs in length. The DNA results obtained by Weedn were later crucial in permitting him to exclude Speicher as the origin of DS1-256.

Because Weedn needed to get the DNA analysis done quickly, he arranged corroboration from colleagues with credible capability. "In this case, I basically sent it to the contract laboratory we used. It was LabCorp [LabCorp/Roche Biomedical Laboratories, located in Research Triangle Park, North Carolina]. Dr. Marcia Eisenberg did the testing." But it was taking too long to get the results back from Eisenberg, so Weedn opted to do his own mitochondrial DNA (mtDNA) testing to see what it turned up. "We really pioneered that kind of testing. We worked with some people at the National Institutes of Health. I think it was Lloyd Mitchell." Mitochondrial DNA was possible with the DS1-256 remains. Though Weedn didn't have much to work with, mtDNA can be done on bone, muscle tissue, skin and hair, as well as blood and other body fluids, even if environmental factors or time degrades the samples. The remains must provide enough material for the testing to provide conclusive results. In addition, mtDNA is inherited from the mother only, so that in situations where an individual is not available for a direct comparison with a biological sample, any maternally related individual may provide a reference sample. "Essentially, this is a reverse parentage test, so we looked at the wife and the two children and we asked the question: Could the tissue that's returned to us from the Iraqis be the father?" Weedn was also looking to compare the DNA of the remains to that of Scott's mother—Barbara Speicher. Speicher's parents, Wallace and Barbara Speicher, were still living, but she was in a long-term care facility with Alzheimer's disease.

Weedn then contacted Joanne Speicher in Jacksonville to see about getting specimens from her and the children. "The first thing she said was, 'You can have my blood, but you can't have it from my children because they're only one and two years of age and I'm not going to let you stick them for blood.'" Though surprised, Weedn relented. He tried other avenues to get samples of Scott Speicher's DNA, "like [from a] toothbrush. We got to where we would ask for various things trying to get at real samples," he said. Real samples sufficient to conduct the test eventually turned up from Scott's personal effects on the ship, but in the first go-around with Joanne, Weedn clearly remembers that he was told, "No, we don't have anything." According to Weedn, there are also difficult questions you have to ask as an investigator in order to make accurate determinations. "There are issues of parentage," he recounted. "Is the person really the father of the children? That's what led me to eventually call for a [DNA] sample on all service members and that's what we do now—just for these kinds of [situations]. It's used far more than what people realize, for what I consider to be a very humanitarian purpose—the return of remains to their families. This case alone tells you how important that function is."

After being told no about the children's blood the first time, Weedn said, "Well, not a problem. We can use oral swabs and that's what was done. We got our first set of swabs and they were absolutely clean. I mean it looked like somebody gave us the wrong swabs," said Weedn. "It looked like they were fresh out of a package without anything on them, without saliva, without cells." There was no discernible DNA on the swabs provided. Undeterred, Weedn asked for a second set, and his laboratory took the care to dispatch them by military jet. The Navy took this "very seriously," he recalls. "That day I asked for the second set, I had them. So it was a big deal and I think that shows the seriousness of the military."

After all the samples were taken, comparison of DNA tests from the tissue sample of DS1-256 were made with DNA results obtained from sera of Lieutenant Commander Speicher drawn in July 1990 and stored in the Department of Defense HIV repository. Comparison tests were also made with hair clippings from his electric shaver and hair from a deodorant bar belonging to Speicher that Weedn had obtained in the interim. The results of these tests were further compared with DNA tests run on the oral swabs and plucked hairs from Joanne Speicher and the children—Meghan and Michael Scott Speicher, Jr. The HIV serum test, having already been processed to remove white blood cells that have to be present for the DNA analysis, proved useless. After analyzing the second set of oral swabs from Scott's wife and children, and making a comparison to the remains of DS1-256, "We showed that the sample that we had [from the Speicher children] was inconsistent with [DS1-256] being the father of those children, so we wrote it up as the report. Based on that information, assuming he was the biological father, this tissue, states our report, was not that of LCDR Speicher."

Then came the surprise that arose over the DNA comparison between Scott and his mother. When results were inconclusive, Wallace Speicher finally confessed to investigators that Scott was not his or Barbara's biological son. They had adopted Scott as an infant directly from his biological parents, a young college couple who'd brought Scott to the house themselves back in the summer of 1957. It was a private adoption, so his biological parents were able to meet the Speichers. His name at birth had been Gregory. The Speichers quickly changed it to Michael Scott.

Since mtDNA comes from the biological mother, this meant the samples became useless to Weedn for comparison. That's when hair from the electric shaver and the deodorant that Weedn had obtained from Scott's personal effects on the ship came into play. Though the DNA sequence was very poor, it was enough to say conclusively that the DNA from specimen DS1-256 did not match that of Scott Speicher.

To be certain, Weedn had also done a genomic test (a genetic typing test). Though initially difficult to obtain genomic DNA test results from DS1-256 because of the sample's degradation, hair pulled from the tissue eventually gave Weedn enough to go on. It was possible to do only limited genomic system analysis, but in the end, the DNA tests Weedn conducted definitely excluded Lieutenant Commander Speicher as the origin of the remains identified as DS1-256, leading to the conclusion that "the remains are conclusively not LCDR Speicher. They are a negative match with strong conviction. A positive result would not be easy to state so strongly." The negative results of Weedn's DNA testing were passed to Captain Curtin and Lieutenant Commander Salazar. The Armed Forces Institute of Pathology Office of the Armed Forces Medical Examiner also issued a memorandum to the Department of the Navy, Bureau of Medicine and Surgery, on May 6, 1991, that read, "Results confirm that those remains are not those of LCDR Michael Scott Speicher."

In the file's conclusion, Boorda's note at the bottom of the page read: "They are running results for more evidence, but he [Weedn] docsn't really need them. It's just good lab practice and helps demonstrate the conclusion to other people." Dr. Richard C. Froede, the Armed Forces medical examiner, had signed off on Weedn's findings and forwarded them to the Navy.

In conducting his own research for the CNO's office, Jeff Manor's task was to determine if CENTCOM and the Navy front office knew for sure that Lieutenant Commander Speicher's remains were not returned. "It was clear from the file that everyone from CNP up to SECNAV knew," he said, "and I believed that the anecdotal evidence made it irrefutable that CENTCOM knew." Though he never found the answer in Scott Speicher's casualty file as to why the U.S. government did not pursue his case further, Manor did speak to a reserve lieutenant working in the Navy casualty office during Desert Storm. "He told me that he relayed to CENTCOM—Major Bagley, I seem to recall was the CENTCOM POC [point of contact] and involved in the Speicher case from day one—that the remains that the Iraqis turned over as being Speicher's were determined not to be his. Major Bagley told the lieutenant, 'Those son of a bitches, they sat across the table and swore up and down that they were Speicher's remains.'"

Manor briefed his boss—a GS-13 (department head) named Timothy Trant. "He ordered me not to relay the conversation I had with the reserve lieutenant. When I strenuously objected, my boss made the decision to accompany me to brief the CNO's office." As Manor entered Boorda's offices with his boss, he knew he would not be permitted to pass on the information he had because of his "escort." He had the occasion later, however, to update one of Vice Chief of Naval Operations Admiral Stanley R. Arthur's captains who worked in operations. The captain listened to Manor's findings, including what the reserve lieutenant had told him about the remains the Iraqis tried to pass off as Speicher's, but did not relay their conversation back to Trant. From where Manor was sitting, "It was not right" that he could not provide information to the CNO's office. Trant wanted to paint the picture that it was CENTCOM's fault because, according to Manor, "they didn't try to find out if the remains were Scott's after they were repatriated." The implication was that CENT-COM didn't press the Iraqis any further and let the matter drop. When Manor tried to explain to Trant that CENTCOM did know that the remains were not Speicher's, because of the conversation he had had with one of the reserve lieutenants who worked in the casualty office during the war, Trant prevented him from entering the information in the record. The information was corroboration between BUPERS (Bureau of Naval Personnel) and CENTCOM that they knew the 1.5 pounds of flesh was not Scott Speicher's before the board met to declare him KIA/BNR. "I felt this information was critical to their [staff's] briefing to Admirals Boorda and Arthur and was worth the risk of being disciplined." But Manor also believes that had the Navy leadership pressed the matter further, it would have remained open. The board that convened May 20 was under the impression that CENTCOM wasn't aware the remains were not Speicher's—but CENTCOM did know and did nothing to dispel the board's impression. "I'm not sure why Admiral Boorda was not opposed vigorously. The personnel dynamics were certainly a factor," said Manor.

Scott Speicher's case was the first time DNA was actually used for identity purposes as opposed to just helping put human pieces together. "We did a fair number of cases where we attached this arm to that body based on DNA," says Weedn, but Speicher's case was the first in which DNA was used to establish a person's identity from almost nothing.

Weedn was also perplexed that the Navy declared Speicher dead. The Navy's attitude was "Well, we're declaring him KIA

and he's dead," said Weedn. The whole issue of trying to recover
Speicher's body was no more an issue to Weedn at that time than
it was to the Navy. While it wasn't Weedn's job to sort out the issues of Scott's status, he made the assumption that because there
was no body, the Navy must have held out no hope of finding
Speicher's remains. He had no idea of the politics swirling
around behind closed doors in Washington. He was just as surprised as everyone else when the decision was made to declare a
pilot dead without conclusive evidence of death—without even a
crash site. The sample itself—DS1-256—had raised questions.
While he evaluated it as "Caucasian, but very dark," a conclusive
evaluation of the remains was never done beyond trying to determine whether they belonged to Scott Speicher. But Weedn had
his suspicions. From the beginning, Weedn and his staff were
convinced that the remains were those of an Iraqi soldier. "This
may be the difference," Weedn observed, "between a missing in
action and a killed in action. What I'm implying when I say that
is that maybe the Iraqis are trying to cover up the fact that they
are holding somebody hostage."

A few years later, when it was Jeffrey Manor's job to investigate the actions and determinations of those involved early on in
the Speicher case, Manor read the DNA analyses that Victor
Weedn entered into Scott's file. "To me," said Manor, "the fact
that the Iraqis turned over remains trying to palm them off as
Speicher's was important. They knew they had to do something.
[Doing] nothing would have aroused more suspicion and caused
more intensive investigation. However, given my experience with
Southeast Asia, turning over the remains that weren't even Caucasian would have caused me some pause if I was on the board."

Overall, Manor was chagrined at all the missed opportunities
Speicher's case file contained. Manor's casualty office predecessor, who handled Scott's case from the beginning, was capable,

but she was not a carrier aviator. Nor had she flown ejection seat aircraft. Perhaps more telling, she was also brand-new in her job when Scott's very complicated missing person's case came across her desk. "As you are well aware, the Missing Persons Act can be somewhat complicated, although very clear on the declaration of death requirements," Manor said. There was, however, enough clear evidence in Scott Speicher's casualty file to cause the previous casualty officer to oppose the Navy declaring Scott dead, even if the officer's statements were simply registered as a complaint laid in Speicher's record. "We had a more formal board for a Navy lieutenant who committed suicide by jumping out of a Cessna north of San Diego than was conducted for Lieutenant Commander Speicher," remarked Manor. Without anyone questioning Boorda's determination, on May 22, 1991, Secretary Garrett changed Scott Speicher's casualty status from MIA to KIA/BNR for administrative purposes. His date of death was established as January 17, 1991.

Scott Speicher's casualty file, which contains little classified information, at least between his loss date in January 1991 and Manor's involvement with it in 1994, and which was largely releasable during Manor's tenure in the Navy POW/MIA office, is now in 2002 by and large inaccessible. "I spent three years at the Defense Intelligence Agency and am fully aware of the requirement of sources and methods to be protected long after the information is gathered," wrote Manor in a letter to the author of this book. "However, the classified information from 1994 and prior is none of that. It pertains primarily to the operational nature of the war at the time it was being fought." The information in Scott Speicher's casualty record provides the behind-the-scenes decisions by Boorda (the chief of naval personnel), the Status Review Board's results and the lack of involvement of the people who really knew public law—"or should have," according to Manor. Yet in order to avoid blame, politicking arose even where the access to Scott Speicher's casualty file was concerned. "Hopefully," Manor continued, "you'll be able to impress upon the Navy leadership that politics, whether well intentioned or not, should never supersede the goal of obtaining a reasonable accounting of our lost servicemen and servicewomen." Hesitant to turn over much of what might be revealed in the file, the Navy stamped a good portion of it classified. "I was afraid that you were going to make some people nervous by asking for the casualty file," Manor said. "It's pretty damning to the Navy leadership."

Timothy G. Connolly, now principal deputy assistant secretary of defense for special operations and low-intensity conflict, had been at his Pentagon job for just a few months when in 1994 a staffer came back from a meeting with a curious question: "Do you know anything about a downed pilot from Desert Storm?"

Tim Connolly quickly jumped into the case. As a former Army Ranger, he knew that if Speicher had been left behind, perhaps it was simply a fog-of-war mistake. Wartime lapses were usually forgiven. But the war was long over. He went over to talk to the Department of Defense POW/MIA officer, and while he was getting briefed on Speicher, Connolly said to them, "Well, let me tell you the story I've got."

His story involved a Kuwaiti Army colonel who claimed to have been in a hospital with an American pilot during the last days of the war. And what a story it was. "I was with a special operations unit that was attached to the 83rd Brigade of the 82nd Airborne Division," recalled Connolly. "We ended up spending the thirty-day cease-fire interval in March outside a town in Iraq called An Nasiriyah. It's on the Euphrates. In fact, it was the

82nd Airborne Brigade that blew up what turned out to be the
nerve-gas complexes up there." One of the brigade's other roles
was to liaison with the Iraqi resistance and, more important, the
people that the Iraqi resistance freed from the prisons where they
had been jailed, both Iraqis and Kuwaitis taken out of their country during the Iraqi occupation.

Many of the people Connolly worked with had been thrown
into abominable prisons inside Iraq. "I got called over to where
my unit was, and we had an individual who identified himself as a
colonel in the Kuwait Ministry of the Interior." The colonel,
along with others, had escaped a prison in An Nasiriyah after an
insurrection against their jailers. With so many of them anxious
to get out of Iraq, makeshift camps were set up by resistance
leaders to house and feed them. Camp Mercy was one of the res-
idential tent cities established for just that purpose. These
refugee camps were full of pain and misery, the sights and smells
unforgettable for those who were there.

The Kuwaitis in Camp Mercy had had a very rough time in
Iraqi hands. There were also Egyptians, Palestinians and Oma-
nis, all of whom had been snatched from their homes in Kuwait.
"When the Iraqis took prisoners in Kuwait," recalled Sergeant
Major John Thomas, who'd been with Connolly during the war,
"they took not only the person they were after but the whole
family—old people and children, too." The camp had a four-lane
highway leading up to it. "I'll never forget this father," said
Thomas, "who brought his little girl over to a medic from the
82nd Airborne treating refugees out of the back of a little white
pickup truck." The little girl had big brown pools for eyes. Her
arm was badly burned, as she had been standing near a round
that went off. "I watched as the medic started to cut away dead,
burned flesh. While it must have been extremely painful, there

was no emotion on her face, no expression of her agony. Her brown eyes just stared." These people had seen Hell inside Iraq and wanted to go home.

But getting them back home wasn't going to be so easy. Lieutenant Colonel King Davis, commanding officer of the 450th Civil Affairs Brigade, responded to a call from G-5 (Civil Affairs Office). While he had G-5 on the line, he wanted to know Army Central Command (ARCENT) policy on the transport of refugees and general dislocated civilian policy in Iraq. He learned that his unit was authorized to use Iraqi military vehicles to move toward Kuwait as soon as possible. "The American embassy in Kuwait City didn't want to deal with refugees or help us," remembered Thomas. "We wouldn't have been able to get those people back into the city from Camp Mercy if Mr. Connolly hadn't known how to navigate narrow backroads and short-cuts. His Ranger training, his ability to follow the maps, got us there before the deadline [to return Kuwaiti citizens to their country and] to cross the border into Kuwait."

Thomas and another sergeant commandeered a couple of trucks at gunpoint from Iraqis to transport the wounded, disabled and sick. "You remember the movie *Three Kings*?" asked Thomas. "The scene at the end with the refugees trying to get through the fence—that was us." The analogy is apt—Lieutenant Colonel Davis was a technical advisor and script consultant on the 1999 movie starring George Clooney. "The story is loosely based on our mission to Iraq during the war," said Connolly, "minus the gold, unfortunately."

Major Kenneth H. Pritchard, USAR, and Captain Connolly also informed G-2—army intelligence—of the Kuwaiti secret-police colonel, Abdullah al-Jairan, who claimed he was with a U.S. pilot in a military hospital in the vicinity of An Nasiriyah in mid-February. The colonel was willing to assist the U.S. Army in any way, including looking through photographs to identify the pilot. "G-2 suggested we inform CW2 Sullens (chief warrant officer in military intelligence) to interview since Captain Smith (another intell officer), who was to come that day, did not show up." Pritchard recorded this in the log kept by a special detachment of the 450th Civil Affairs Brigade attached for combat operations to the 3rd Brigade of the 82nd Airborne Division, on the 4th of March. "He told us that he had been in An Nasiriyah, in a hospital, like three days prior to this, next to an American pilot," recalled Connolly. Connolly's unit found this very interesting because the time frame was so critical—it occurred right after the prisoner exchange. The colonel was still offering to look at a lineup, much like one would do for the police. He wanted nothing in return for the information, as he had already been accorded respectful treatment. "We radioed back to the 18th Airborne Corps headquarters in Saudi Arabia," Connolly continued, "our higher headquarters, and said to the G-2, the intell people, 'Here's what we got.'" The response Connolly received is one he'd not forget: "The prisoner exchange has taken place. We're not missing anybody. We have one hundred percent accountability, therefore this guy is blowing smoke at you—it can't be true." The Kuwaiti colonel was sent back to Kuwait City, and Connolly would never hear from him again.

While Jeff Manor continued to meet resistance in relaying information he had found in Speicher's casualty report, Timothy Connolly continued to be plagued by memories of his conversation with the Kuwaiti colonel who claimed to have seen an American pilot in an Iraqi military hospital. Knowing now that the wreckage of an F/A-18 Hornet had been discovered in the Iraqi desert, the "what ifs" began to race through Tim Connolly's mind.

The DoD POW/MIA Office had brought him up to date on

what they knew about pieces of an F/A-18 for sale on the black market in the Middle East. Working with the Defense Intelligence Agency, the JSSA—Bob Dussault's command—tasked a satellite to search for the wreckage and pinpoint its location. But they ran into a problem. "When the Qataris pointed out the location on the map and we sent the imagery overhead to look at it, there wasn't anything there," recalled Connolly. "These guys were 150 kilometers from where they actually thought they were. So rather than say, 'Okay, these guys don't know shit,' the DoD POW/MIA guys came up with the idea of going back through the infrared imagery and the archives to identify every single instance in which there was an IR event, meaning there was some heat source that had suddenly appeared on the desert floor. They correlated those heat flashes against what they identified as SCUD launches and discovered that there was one heat flash that didn't correspond to a SCUD." And when they imaged that latitude/longitude, they found Speicher's plane.

The new satellite shots clearly showed the crash site, something that could be an ejection seat and, near that, an unidentified manmade object. The F/A-18 site looked largely undisturbed. The DoD POW/MIA Office said they'd look into it. "They looked back at all the after-action interviews of every POW who was brought back, including the Special Air Service guys from the UK, to see if anyone had any stories about anyone else who was unaccounted for," said Connolly. "They also traced where they were found and how they got to Baghdad, to see if there was any evidence any of them had been taken on a circuitous route." Then, of course, they sent an investigator overseas to talk to somebody, and Connolly wished they could have talked with the Kuwaiti colonel. But the colonel, after all, could not be found. Colonel Abdullah al-Jairan had simply disappeared. Despite the DoD POW/MIA Office's attempts to confirm or refute Connolly's information regarding the colonel's claims, in Connolly's word, "the bottom line was . . . they didn't think it was true."

Albert "Buddy" Harris was also in the Pentagon looking into the case. Harris was working for an assistant chief of naval operations, and was helping to compile a report of all the Navy's missions—every strike flown, every bomb dropped—during the Gulf War. One day in late 1993, he came across a CIA report stating that Speicher had been shot down by a surface-to-air missile. He called the CIA to straighten that out.

Harris told the CIA that the Department of Defense had changed its finding about Speicher being shot down by a SAM. The DoD determined that Speicher had been, as his squadron commander said, knocked from the sky by a MiG-25, but arguably this was still not fact. The phone conversation shifted to the story about Speicher's Hornet being found. The Qataris' photographs had just come in. Harris had become one of the Navy's experts on Desert Storm and was asked to help. When Harris stated that the photographs of the Hornet and the canopy made it look like Speicher ejected, he was told to find out what information originally led the Navy to conclude that Speicher didn't eject.

Harris, who remained close to Speicher's family after Scott disappeared, was angered to see so much evidence that had not been shared with Joanne Speicher. "The family wasn't told anything," he noted. They received one letter after another from admirals and captains saying no stone would be left unturned. The Navy claimed they would search until they had conclusive evidence that Scott was either dead or alive. They told Joanne, and Scott's father and sister, not to give up on him after then–Secretary of Defense Cheney's gaff during the press conference. "'We haven't given up on him,' they told the Speicher family

repeatedly. 'Everything available will be used to get Scott back.'"
But the claims to be looking for Scott were far from the truth.
"Cheney jumped the gun," remarked Harris. "That wasn't
Boorda's intention; that wasn't Colin Powell's intention. Basi-
cally, he just misspoke. Basically, everybody just assumed, 'Okay,
[Cheney has] got more information than I do. He's gone. Let's
press on.'" But the information that surrounded the case seemed
to point more and more toward Scott having survived.

The idea that Speicher might have ejected was enough to give
any service member chills. On any battlefield, in any war, the
American code is the same—no man is left behind. Could Speicher have parachuted into Iraq? Could he have landed safely, sat
in the barren desert and looked to the horizon, expecting rescuers to pick him up?

Like all pilots in-theater during Desert Storm, Scott had been
given survival training. Before his mission that night, he'd filled
out a DD Form 1833, an authentication card, which contained
various information that he could use to identify himself, and
that the DoD could use for verification purposes. Pilots also received command codes or letters and short words to be used by
them for identification purposes in the event they became
evaders, escapees or POWs. The letters or words also give a
pilot's chain of command a time frame of when the pilot was lost.
The procedure for this process can be found in two unclassified
joint-service manuals: one on combat search and rescue and the
other on survival.

The clearest evidence of Speicher's probable survival came
from a ground-to-air signal evaluated by the JSSA in 1994.
Evaders understand that they will have to persevere to survive
and succeed at getting themselves help. They know that ground
signals may be the only means to get the message out that they
survived and want to come home. They also know that weather

has a tremendous impact on the arranged signal itself—including the shifting sands and storms prevalent in the Iraqi desert. Some signals, if made with logs and rocks and even some constructed of more permanent landmarks for sections of the signal, can still be affected by the elements. Some, if in depressions in the ground, can even become much better signals if the depressions fill with water. However, none of these scenarios apply directly to Scott's case.

As an evader once on the ground, Scott, like all evaders, would have appreciated what could be seen from different collection platforms, which would have helped him decide how large to make a signal in order for it to be seen. Some signals in sand and dirt do not require much to be effective. Camera angle and shadows are critical. This means that a shot taken from directly above the signal may not be best, but it also depends on where the sun is at the time the satellite, aircraft or drone is overhead. If the sun and the collection platform are directly overhead at the same time, the signal can become invisible. In Scott's case, once all the satellite imagery was assessed, there would be absolutely no doubt that he had built his signal many times—almost to the point where he had to question whether anyone was looking for the signal or that he was possibly not using the right one.

Besides the imagery analysis by the JSSA, the National Imagery and Mapping Agency (NIMA), in response to a FOIA request, stated that it had imagery for three different dates between 1993 and 1995 at the crash site and a ten-mile radius around it—including the area of the first-detected ground-to-air signal. Tonnette K. Fleming, the NIMA FOIA specialist, also remarked that debriefs from pilots from the night Scott Speicher was lost "would have been useful to planning an imagery search for LCDR Speicher in January 1991. However, no such information was provided to the imagery community in either 1991 nor at any other date. "Information of this type," said Fleming, "would reside with the U.S. Navy, possibly USCENTCOM [U.S. Central Command], the Joint Personnel Recovery Agency, DPMO, or the flying squadrons' or ships' records."

Scott had two signals to use—the letter of the day or the word for the week—based on what he recalled of his special instructions (SPINS) before leaving the *Saratoga* the night of January 17, 1991. Using the letter of the day for his evasion signal, possibly many times over without a response, he may have begun to wonder why no one came. Did no one see it? Was it not clear enough? Or was he using the wrong letter? To avoid the latter problem, he might have decided to vary his signals. One time he might put out the letter of the day, and at other times he might spell out the short word. The only signal ever detected from that area via satellite and recorded on film for analysis was not his letter of the day, but it was the first letter of his word for the week— the letter *M*. This letter was seen very clearly by the JSSA Director Colonel Robert Bonn, Jr., on films held by the DPMO. Bonn subsequently certified his analysis that either the letter of the day or any part of Scott's word for the week was acceptable as strong evidence in light of all else that Scott was alive, and that the benefit of the doubt should be accorded to him. Bonn also included in his memorandum a statement in which he told his superiors that everything in the U.S. intelligence inventory should be used to confirm or deny Scott Speicher being alive.

A confidential source, recognized as a longtime expert in signals interpretation, who saw the Speicher ground-to-air signal, said Bonn was absolutely positive about what he'd seen. But curiously, about two months after certifying Scott's signal, Bonn came back to the source and ordered him not to find any more signals on the imagery. "He had gone uptown to see some generals and came back shaking like a leaf. He shortly thereafter wrote and sealed a document marked to be opened only upon his death. He kept it in his safe." The source continued, "He [Bonn] also got his butt chewed by C3I (Command, Control Communications, and Intelligence) Duane Andrews's gofer, Ron Knecht, [and] a hanger-on from Acting Deputy Assistant Secretary of Defense Edward W. Ross." Both Knecht and Ross worked with Duane Andrews to persuade Pentagon leadership that none of what they were seeing on overhead imagery was a legitimate ground-to-air signal, including the one belonging to Scott Speicher. "I was rather down," said the source. "If they won't do anything for about 6,800 MIAs [through all twentieth-century wars], why would they bother with one?"

Bonn left JSSA on August 4, 1994. His successor, Colonel John Chapman, then came onto the scene. The source, at that time the best in the business of photographic interpretation, had seen Scott's ground-to-air signal and affirmed it as his marker. "I scrounged a quality print," he said. "There are more than one potential man-made marks" that could have been made by Scott Speicher. With his level of frustration peaking at not being seen, Scott had apparently begun to try anything. Looking at the situation from Scott's perspective, he was desperate and unable to get anyone's attention. So he modified and varied his approach, and sometimes got very blatant in his efforts to draw the picture for collection platforms. He had nothing to lose and everything to gain—his life was on the line. There was one ground signal that was very consistent with Scott's mission, and JSSA took that position officially—the agency had no knowledge of any signals being seen in that area before they requested coverage in 1993–94, but once they did, the evidence on the ground was very clear. Buddy Harris answered affirmatively when asked recently if the symbol belonged to Scott. "It was in an area away from the crash site and the best they could determine [was that] it was a symbol to communicate."

Actions behind the scenes also cut deeply into progress on Scott's case for investigators in possession of credible evidence that Scott Speicher was alive and wanted to come home. One of the major impediments was the movement of the POW/MIA intelligence analysts from DIA to DPMO, and the Senate Select Committee hearings on the status of POW/MIAs. There was a conflict within the DoD that rose to a slow boil between the DPMO and DIA analysts who didn't believe Scott was alive, and the Joint Services SERE Agency, which had resources in the field and back at Fort Belvoir that emphatically stated that Scott should be given the benefit of the doubt. This conflict alone, begun in late 1993 with the discovery of Scott's Hornet in the Iraqi desert, dramatically affected what was and wasn't done for Scott. He became a pawn in the battle between those who believed he was alive and those who had him prematurely buried under his jet. Unfortunately, those who vehemently argued that Scott Speicher was dead were the people most in a position to help had they given Scott the benefit of the doubt—Frederick C. Smith (principal deputy assistant secretary of defense for international security affairs), J. Alan Liotta (DPMO deputy director) and Franklin Kramer (assistant secretary of defense for international security affairs). It was more important to them to be proven right—that Scott was dead—in order to avoid being painted into a corner thanks to their own mistakes.

JSSA's information was dismissed as unreliable when high-level discussions took place. Eventually, JSSA got its orders from the Joint Chiefs of Staff to leave the case alone. "[The JCS] wanted State and CIA to handle it. That is what we did," said Bob Dussault. Dussault's assessment is substantiated by Buddy

Harris, who has since remarked that in 1995 and 1996 in particular, a great deal of inconsistent information was released on Scott. The information that came out, observed Harris, always pointed to the fact that "they wanted him to be dead."

Mitigating the fact that Scott's ground-to-air marker was discounted by the DIA, the National Photographic Interpretation Center (NPIC) at the Navy Yard, and even the CIA, is that these agencies already had a poor track record where photographic and satellite analyses were concerned. To test their ability, Dussault's office put out twenty-four perfectly good signals in West Virginia in 1994. He told them the outside coordinates for all the signals and said, "Go find them."

Of the twenty-four signals, they found only four. Then they came back to Dussault and asked him to describe the others they did not find. JSSA provided descriptions of each one, and they eventually found six more—"That's a total of ten out of twenty-four," Dussault reported. "Real sad. I lost total faith in photo interpreters at that point," he continued, "and had solid evidence for my position and they all knew it. Empirical evidence is a matter of record."

JSSA personnel had put out big and obvious symbols and signals, just as they trained aviators to do. Dussault's people meticulously recorded and took pictures of their signals and took the coordinates of each one. "We knew the ground truth." Then JSSA instructed the DIA and CIA to take satellite shots of the area and provide JSSA the photos under the belief that these would be used to build a training package for all new photographic interpreters in both intelligence agencies to help them locate evader and POW symbols in the future.

The Senate Select Committee on POW/MIA Affairs was already disheartened by what it had discovered pertaining to the CIA's and DIA's respective abilities to read evader symbols. In its report published January 13, 1993, the year before the West Virginia test that Dussault ran and the agencies failed, the Senate committee was rather surprised to find that neither CIA nor DIA imagery analysts were familiar with Vietnam-era pilot distress symbols, or had a requirement to look for possible symbols prior to the committee's inquiry. Imagery analysts from both agencies confirmed this under oath. Chuck Knapper, a DIA imagery analyst, had already stated that he was unfamiliar with distress symbols before committee investigators asked him about symbols in an interview in April of 1992. Knapper was the DIA's principal imagery analyst, one of two dedicated to the DIA's POW imagery task. In a response to the question of whether he had been looking for evader symbols in the photography before he met with Dussault's analysts at JSSA, he replied, "I was not." Roger Eggert, a CIA imagery analyst, had no knowledge of pilot distress symbols either. A senator queried, "Were pilot distress symbols something that you had ever studied before spring of this year [1992]?" Eggert answered, "No."

Though JSSA had provided a plausible assessment of Scott's situation based on the signals found in the Iraqi desert, the friction between JSSA and DPMO only increased. JSSA obtained what it could from the Joint Chiefs of Staff and other DoD agencies, but nothing came over from DPMO. Using friendly sources in other outlets, as well as its direct lines of communication elsewhere, JSSA was able to stay close to the Speicher case. It was in this manner that JSSA began to collect credible evidence that, after attempts to signal U.S. forces as to his whereabouts, Speicher had joined with a group of nomadic Bedouins. The JSSA also gained access to the one person who could corroborate that Scott Speicher had been picked up by the Bedouins—the Falcon Hunter. The Falcon Hunter's Navy handler, Steven Collins, met with JSSA between 1994 and 1998 to discuss Scott Speicher's sit-

The Speicher family, pictured in their church bulletin in 1989. *From left:* Michael Scott Jr., Scott, Joanne, and Meghan. (File photo, *The Virginian-Pilot*)

The Sunliners VFA-81 squadron's patch. This patch is affixed to a Velcro pad, the shape of which is identical to a pad found on the flight suit later found at Speicher's crash site. (Steve Earley / *The Virginian-Pilot*)

Officers of the VFA-81 squadron during Desert Storm, winter 1990. Included in the photo are (*front row, left to right*) Tony "Bano" Albano, Mark "MRT" Fox, Bill "Maggot" McKee, Michael "Spock" Anderson, Scott "Spike" Speicher, Steve "Ammo" Minnis, (*middle row, seventh from left*) Craig "Bert" Bertolett, and (*back row, fifth from left*) Barry "Skull" Hull. (Photo courtesy of Craig Bertolett)

The wives of several of the Sunliner pilots gather for a photograph in fall 1990. Joanne Speicher is in the bottom row, first from the left. (Copyright © Carriage House Studio, Inc. Photo taken by James L. Abrisch)

On liberty in Istanbul, Turkey. *From left:* Nick Mongillo, Scott Speicher, and Tony Albano. (Photo courtesy of Craig Bertolett)

The Speicher family home in Jacksonville, prior to Scott's leaving for the Gulf War. (Steve Earley / *The Virginian-Pilot*)

Commander Mike Anderson and Commander Bill McKee aboard the deck of the USS *Saratoga*. Anderson would later worry whether he could have prevented a MiG from shooting down Scott Speicher. (Photo courtesy of Craig Bertolett)

Two Sunliner F/A-18 Hornets taking fuel from a KC-135 over Saudi Arabia. (Photo courtesy of Barry Hull)

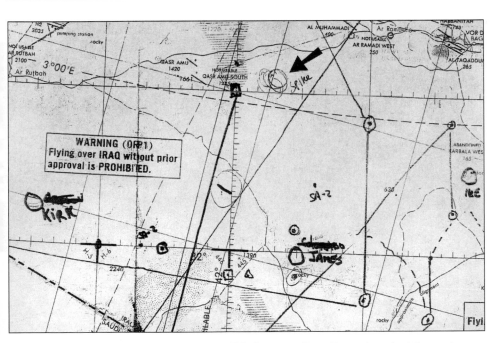

Upon his immediate return to the USS *Saratoga*, Dave Renaud marked the position on his flight chart where he saw Speicher's jet go down. The wreckage of the plane was found in that vicinity two years later. (Photo courtesy of Dave Renaud)

An unnumbered blood chit. "I am an American and do not speak your language. I will not harm you! I bear no malice towards your people. My friend, please provide me food, water, shelter, clothing, and necessary medical attention. Also, please provide me safe passage to the nearest friendly forces of any country supporting the Americans and their allies. You will be rewarded for assisting me when you present this number and my name to American authorities."

Barry Hull, a squadronmate of Speicher's who remained adamant that Scott would have survived his ejection over Iraq. (Steve Earley / *The Virginian-Pilot*)

Tim Connolly, who worked on the Speicher case from inside the Pentagon. Never satisfied with the official answers, he probed deeper. (Steve Earley / *The Virginian-Pilot*)

On May 22, 1991, a funeral service was held for Scott Speicher. This gravestone was erected in Arlington National Cemetery soon after. (Steve Earley / *The Virginian-Pilot*)

Operation "Promise Kept"
Iraq '95

Members of the ICRC's Operation Promise Kept, taken while in Iraq investigating the crash site. Pictured are Bruce Trenholm (*kneeling, far right*), Mike Buran (*kneeling, second from right*), and Dr. Thomas Holland (*standing, far right*), among others. (Photo courtesy of Mike Buran)

The ICRC team methodically staked out the crash site in order to perform a thorough investigative excavation. (Department of Defense)

The Promise Kept team sifts carefully through the wreckage. A flight suit similar to Scott's was later discovered near the site. (Department of Defense)

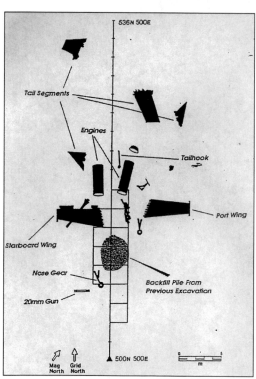

This detailed map of the crash site, detailing the position of major portions of wreckage, was included in the ICRC's final report. Note the area of backfill from a previous excavation—someone had gotten to the site first. (Department of Defense)

The starboard engine of Speicher's F/A-18 Hornet as photographed by Mike Buran, whose shadow appears in the foreground. (Department of Defense)

The canopy to Scott's Hornet was found standing on end. Studying the evenly spaced burn marks around the canopy's edge, investigators were able to prove conclusively that Speicher had ejected safely from his craft. (Department of Defense)

A HARM missile from Speicher's jet was found some distance from the main crash site. (Department of Defense)

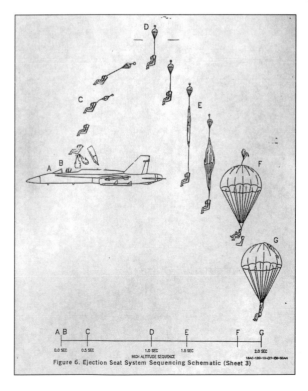

A schematic of a high altitude ejection sequence in an F/A-18 Hornet. (US Navy NATOPS Manual)

Figure 6. Ejection Seat System Sequencing Schematic (Sheet 3)

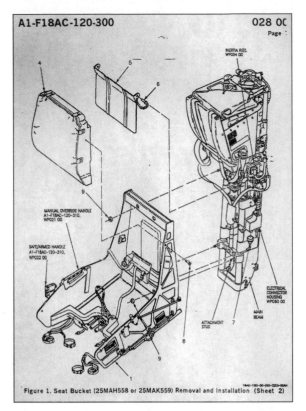

A1-F18AC-120-300

028 0C
Page

INERTIA REEL
WP054 00

4
5
6

MANUAL OVERRIDE HANDLE
A1-F18AC-120-310,
WP021 00

SAFE/ARMED HANDLE
A1-F18AC-120-310,
WP022 00

ELECTRICAL
CONNECTOR
HOUSING
WP050 00

MAIN
BEAM

ATTACHMENT
STUD

7

9

8

1

Figure 1. Seat Bucket (25MAH558 or 25MAK559) Removal and Installation (Sheet 2)

A schematic of the SJU/5A Martin-Baker ejection system. The system had an impeccable success rate in the field. (US Navy NATOPS Manual)

Senator Robert C. Smith (R-N.H.), who, along with other senators such as Pat Roberts (R-Kans.) and Richard C. Shelby (R-Ala.), worked tirelessly to resolve Scott's case. (Steve Earley / *The Virginian-Pilot*)

A special memorial was erected at Nathan Bedford Forrest High School in Jacksonville, Scott's alma mater. (Steve Earley / *The Virginian-Pilot*)

uation. "I was told at that time that the Falcon Hunter could go into the area almost anytime and meet with the Bedouins," said Dussault. "He was the first to give us word that Scott was okay. We never talked about [his] treatment because they were assisting him, keeping him alive, and would soon want to turn him over to the U.S. in a manner secure for Scott and for them. They did not want Saddam to learn about their efforts."

Three-quarters of the Iraqi people are members of the country's 150 tribes, joined by family ties and a strict code of honor dictated by their respective sheikhs. Saddam is widely known for having caused widespread unrest among the indigenous clans, particularly among the Kurd and Shi'a groups since Desert Storm, executing entire tribal factions or otherwise replacing clan leadership with a sheikh loyal to his regime. Extermination of tribal groups comes at a high price for clans Saddam has targeted—men, women and children are usually shot execution style for not cooperating.

It is plausible that the Bedouins, seeing Scott as a valuable commodity to barter, would want to ensure that he survived and was well taken care of until the opportunity arose to return him in exchange for money or other considerations. The U.S. blood chit program is one way that Scott could have proved his value to the Bedouins and thus ensured his safety with them. Blood chits are documents issued by CENTCOM to airmen in its various commands—Army, Navy, Air Force, Marines—each one specifically numbered and reported to JSSA (now called the Joint Personnel Recovery Agency or JPRA) who can account for every blood chit issued since World War II. If an aviator is captured, he can present his blood chit to his captors, which allows them to exchange their prisoner for a reward once a transfer with American forces can be arranged.

Once he was assured that the Bedouins would protect him

and feed him until it could be arranged to deliver him back to the Americans, Scott's SERE training told him what to do, explained Dussault: "Do whatever they say, following their instruction because their lives are at stake as well. Do not offend them. Stay away from their women. The latter will offend them more than almost anything else."

After a period of time passed, it is known that the Bedouins passed word through the Falcon Hunter that they wanted to turn Scott over to the U.S. They made these attempts repeatedly for two to three years without an affirmative response from the Clinton administration or U.S. intelligence positioned in the region. The Bedouins' entreaties grew more plaintive as Saddam began to suspect an American pilot was alive and with one of the indigenous western Iraqi tribes. The Bedouins were willing to talk and willing to help—as long as they did not get caught helping. But no response from the U.S. government ever resolved the situation.

The position that Scott Speicher was alive and in Bedouin protection is corroborated by two Joint Chiefs of Staff sources—CIA and Navy intelligence—who revealed in mid-1994 and 1995 that he was still with the indigenous people who had scooped him up the night he was shot down and had nursed him back to health.

The Falcon Hunter's statements were corroborated by a second independent credible source in the CIA. Still another corroborating witness was a part of the Falcon Hunter's Qatari hunting party, a Saudi prince who knew the Bedouin tribes of the western Iraqi desert quite well.

This Saudi prince made frequent trips over the Iraqi border to the Bedouin camps and was willing to continue them for the United States, offering, in fact, to get Scott Speicher out if the U.S. wanted him to do so. He was waiting for instructions when the Joint Chiefs of Staff was told by JCS Chairman General John

M. Shalikashvili to stand down. Why? The Clinton administration had apparently made the decision that bringing Scott Speicher home at that time would reveal that they had known he was in trouble since taking office. Scott was a live witness, as were the Falcon Hunter and the prince. Scott, the two hunters and the CIA agent who had visited the camps all knew the timing of the discovery of Scott's whereabouts and circumstances. The embarrassment was a political bombshell, a hit the administration was unwilling to take.

Once in Bedouin control, Scott Speicher may have shown his blood chit to his assistors. The Bedouin chieftain would not have been interested in turning Scott over for nothing. His blood chit said the U.S. would reward anyone who helped him. That is probably what the Bedouins had in mind, and therefore they wanted to maintain control of Scott until the reward had been received. To poor people, even a few camels or a few dogs and water bags are valuable—better to get something than have Scott Speicher walk away scot-free. Scott also owed his life to them and he would want the promise of recompense honored. He would be reluctant to leave the tribe without them getting something in return. The fact that he would do the latter spoke volumes about his indebtedness to the Bedouins who cared for him and helped heal his wounds. To protect him, the Bedouins would have dressed him in their clothing—the traditional Arab *dishdasha*—and taught him what he needed to do to blend with them, kept him in their tents to hide his identity, and thus reduced the threat of his being discovered by Saddam's forces. Indigenous tribes discovered aiding an American or British pilot were signing their own death warrants—not just adult male assistors, but every man, woman and child in the group. Scott, to survive, followed their instructions, as he had been instructed to do during his SERE training.

Sadly, Saddam's agents spotted the Bedouins with Scott around the time that Operation Promise Kept (an ICRC-sponsored humanitarian mission) was due at the crash site area in mid-December 1995, almost four years after Scott's Hornet fell to the desert floor. The attention stirred by the U.S. diplomatic mission, which was delayed at least three times by Saddam Hussein while his agents scoured the Bedouin camps, had drawn the enemy to Scott and his protectors, and the results were devastating. Scott was reportedly taken away and the Bedouins were slaughtered— every man, woman and child in the tribe. Saddam now had his prize pilot. Two separate sources independently reported the executions—one, an Iraqi reservist driver who claims to have delivered Scott to Baghdad, and the other the Falcon Hunter, who continued to make several visits to check on the Bedouin camps.

CHAPTER 7

Promise Kept

Back at the Fort Belvoir headquarters of JSSA, both Air Force Colonel John Chapman and Bob Dussault were devastated by the turn of events in the Iraqi desert. Both men had had dealings with the Joint Chiefs of Staff/Joint Special Operations Center (JCS/JSOC), hoping for a rescue operation. They'd lost Scott to Saddam, and any chance to make contact with Speicher and get him home had been lost. But thanks to sources such as the Falcon Hunter, at least the position of Speicher's downed Hornet was known.

The first interagency meeting on what to do about the site where the aircraft was located did not take place until April 1994. Initially, nothing was decided. The task sheet to the Joint Chiefs of Staff requesting a feasibility study on a military covert operation was not given to the interagency committee until May. It took a few months for the Joint Chiefs of Staff to finally send a planning order to the commander of Special Operations Command, who in turn sent the order to the JSOC in Fort Bragg, North Carolina, on July 5, 1994, at 1400 hours Greenwich Mean

Time (GMT). This order started the planning process for a military covert option. As it was relayed, the wording of the order was changed. The original order read:

> "When directed by the NCA, USCINCCENT [United States Commander in-Chief Central] will conduct military operations to investigate a Desert Storm F/A-18 crash site in western Iraq to retrieve information and/or recover designated pieces of wreckage to assist in determining the fate of the pilot whose remains are unaccounted for."

The National Command Authority (NCA) is defined by law as the president of the United States and the secretary of defense. Contrary to popular belief, both are required to make decisions such as the release of nuclear weapons on a target or the initiation of covert operations inside another nation's sovereign borders.

Upon receiving the message, special operations planners immediately started mapping out a feasible insertion. But the message received by U.S. Central Command (USCENTCOM), General J. H. Binford Peay III, USA, which was then conveyed to his staff, included important changes to the original memorandum. The order stated:

> "When directed, COMSOCCENT [Commander, Special Operations Command, Central] deploys a JSOTF [Joint Special Operations Task Force] to USCENTCOM AOR [area of responsibility] & conducts intrusive military operations in conjunction with JTF-SWA [Joint Task Force-Southwest Asia] assets to investigate a Desert Storm F/A-18 crash site in western Iraq. Mission is to retrieve information and/or recover designated pieces of wreckage to

assist in determining the fate of the pilot, and if possible recover his remains."

The JTF-SWA are the special operations forces that were already in the region in support of operations relating to U.S. involvement in enforcing the no-fly zone in Iraq. The change in wording from "whose remains are unaccounted for" to "if possible recover his remains" is telling. The first version points to the fact that Speicher's fate is unknown. The second is a clear indication of the command's mindset that Speicher was dead, and that his remains would be located near the wreckage. The planners seemed to have condemned Scott to death in the very investigative order enabling the task force to learn more about what had happened to him from the crash site.

Four covert teams were assembled at Hurlburt Air Force Base in Florida, under the order issued by the Joint Chiefs of Staff to the JSOC. The teams were comprised of the elite U.S. Delta Force (familiarly called "snakeaters"), experts from the Army's Central Identification Laboratory in Hawaii (CILHI) and the Naval Air Warfare Center Weapons Division (NAWCWD), also referred to as China Lake, and one investigator from Naval Safety Center Norfolk (NAVSAFECEN), Lieutenant Commander Michael Buran, an aircraft-mishap expert and Navy helicopter pilot. Buran was originally not contemplated as part of the team, but then neither was anyone from NAVSAFECEN until China Lake parachute expert Bruce W. Trenholm insisted that someone from the center be on tap to go.

Buran later became the only active-duty Navy member on the team who eventually went into the desert under the cover of the International Committee of the Red Cross in December 1995. A short time later, JCS Chairman General John Shalikashvili called prospective team members together.

The entire Joint Special Operations Task Force assembled for the briefing consisted of seventy-four Delta and Army Special Forces experts; forty-two Navy staffers, including background and field investigators and uniformed active-duty personnel; and ten Defense Intelligence Agency analysts and field officers. Investigators were trained as commandos by their respective Delta mirrors (a mirror is assigned to a specific member of an insert team and is responsible for their training and action in the field).

Some of the Delta Force assigned to the Speicher covert mission had been at Mogadishu, Somalia, in 1993; others had been behind enemy lines during Desert Storm. "When they handed you a Colt CAR-15 automatic rifle, these guys told us, even with its laser scope, not to fire unless they were standing right in front of us," recalled Buran. Delta Force, the serious shooters, did all the planning. It was their expertise that would get the team in and out of the country intact.

As a seasoned aircraft mishap investigator, Buran made a few calls and got an F/A-18 airframe shipped from San Diego to the desert environment of Fort Bliss, Texas. There, the teams practiced taking apart the cockpit for its vital components before blowing it up. Lieutenant Commander James Otto Stutz, Jr., on his joint tour in the Pentagon, was the team's background source on the F/A-18, but he did not go with the team to the desert.

As the dog days of August 1994 came and went, Michael E. Brock, an aerospace engineer at Naval Aviation Depot Norfolk, received a request through Naval Air Systems Command in Washington for photographic, dimensional and operational information regarding the Martin-Baker SJU-5A ejection seat used in earlier versions of the F/A-18 Hornet. Brock was to reply with the information directly to J. Alan Liotta, deputy director of DPMO. Brock wrote Liotta in early September, "I presume this information involves a mishap of some sort; however, since I have not spoken to you directly I cannot ascertain exactly what type of information you truly need." Brock attached basic information on the Martin-Baker's ejection sequence. After discussing Liotta's request with Peter Yost at the Naval Air Warfare Center in Warminster, Pennsylvania, Brock told Liotta that Yost could also supply some basic ejection seat dimensional information.

While Brock and Yost were providing information on the seat itself, back at China Lake, Bruce Trenholm had gotten word that the Joint Special Operations Command needed a preliminary ejection event analysis for an F/A-18 mishap. Covert planners wanted to know where to look and what to expect when they got into the desert to recover important parts of Speicher's downed jet.

Bruce submitted his report, dated September 7, 1994, in which he ran the descent path an ejected seat would have taken, as well as evaluating other key factors in the ejection event. He told Major J. Pryor at the JSOC that to evaluate an ejection, he used three factors: location of the aircraft canopy, the type of seat in the aircraft and the pilot's size. "The location of the aircraft impact site is less critical," Trenholm wrote, "since the aircraft lift surfaces may divert its flight path away from the original course and heading after the ejection event. The canopy, on the other hand, has a more predictable trajectory based on the ejection airspeed, and it generally maintains the original aircraft heading at the point of ejection." To be more responsive to the JSOC request, Bruce loaded test data on the canopy travel distance versus airspeed. The tests were conducted at the facilities of the Supersonic Naval Ordnance Research Track (SNORT), where the trajectory of an ejected seat was measured from film analysis. Bruce's document walked the JSOC through the entire ejection analysis and simulation model.

Even JSSA was tapped by Liotta's office to provide ejection seat information. A former JSSA analyst and confidential source divulged that within two months of Colonel Bonn ordering him to cease his analysis of Speicher's ground-to-air signal, he got a call from DPMO. "They asked if I could scrounge an F/A-18 ejection seat. I knew what they were up to," he said, "but they wouldn't tell me. They learned that they couldn't find something they hadn't seen before. It was quite clear that I was persona non grata for any old stuff, but new—they were interested to learn all they could. I was getting images and new tests with simple phone calls." Bottom line: Recovery of the ejection seat was a major focus for covert planners. For whatever secrets it held, the seat had to be found at all costs.

The location of Scott Speicher's aircraft canopy was calculated based on ejection altitude and windage, and then confirmed by JSSA and the Joint Chiefs of Staff after viewing satellite photographs. Bob Dussault, JSSA's deputy director, felt that the existence of the canopy in the exact location it should have been after a successful ejection was extremely pointed. "This sign alone, even before the ICRC trip, convinced us he [Scott] had ejected successfully," Dussault said. Based on his background and experience with SERE training and recovery operations, Dussault had always believed that Speicher should have been considered alive until proof of death, not the other way around. But DPMO's view continues to be the opposite: that there must be proof of life before they do anything to offer assistance. Without putting themselves in the pilot's situation, DPMO continued to state that there was no proof that Scott Speicher was alive.

"Like I told General [Harry E.] Soyster and international security affairs [in the Pentagon]," recalled Dussault of a conversation with the general in September 1991, "if John Noble's case depended on them, he would still be in Russia." Noble was the benchmark case of a missing person held incommunicado, who had been returned to U.S. custody thanks to a telephone call from President Eisenhower to the Kremlin. The DPMO has been rightly accused of focusing too much on the wrong end of operations. Recovery of downed airmen is about getting them back, not about some complex analysis of whether the aircrew is alive or dead. "That rests with the CINC [commander in chief] who lost the guy," stated Dussault. "But is this how it happened? Nope—DPMO decided on the case. Scott was dead. Drop it, CINC. They even have this tendency today, and many CINCs are pointedly stressing this concern with DPMO." DPMO seemed to have spent an excessive amount of time—much of it wasted—doing nothing on Scott Speicher's case, despite repeated signs that demanded they take a closer look.

Satellite photos confirmed that Speicher's Hornet had pancaked onto the desert floor about one hundred miles northeast of a Saudi border town named Ar Ar. U.S. forces had operated out of Ar Ar during the war, which made it a convenient base from which to insert the covert team. MH-6J Little Bird Special Operations helicopters could fly in from Ar Ar with a team of experts to examine the wreckage. Also aboard would be specialists from the Navy's mishap investigation command in China Lake and Naval Safety Center Norfolk, as well as someone from CILHI. Each would be heavily armed in the event that the team became embroiled in a firefight with the Iraqis, a prospect no one wanted to talk about at the time. They rehearsed the mission endlessly down at Fort Bliss, Texas, and memorized their tasks once at the site using information analysts provided. Still, sneaking across the Iraqi border would be sticky.

After the Gulf War, Saddam Hussein had ordered the construction of a series of radar watchtowers strung along the border with Saudi Arabia. U.S. intelligence learned to predict which ones were occupied simply by the manner in which the Iraqis

manned the towers, tossing down their gear at the base of the occupied radar site. Iraqi communications were monitored and car-
dinal headings taken between the towers, enabling covert
mission planners to tell where the high-risk areas were along the
Iraq/Saudi Arabia border. Planners determined the manning status of the towers at different times of day down to the last detail,
and found a corridor over the border near Ar Ar that solidified
the town as the best option for the team's ingress and egress of
the western Iraqi desert.

They figured they could reach Speicher's wreckage in an hour,
excavate it overnight and get back to Saudi Arabia by the next
morning. The crash site, isolated by miles of endless sand dunes,
was one reason to believe the mission profile was fairly low risk.
Demolition experts assigned to each team carried fuses, plastique
and a posthole digger to place charges and blow up what remained of the aircraft cockpit when they left. If they were discovered and had to get out in a hurry, they could be back in Ar Ar in
forty-five minutes.

But the covert mission wasn't a sure thing. At the Pentagon,
Tim Connolly felt that time was wasting. The Iraqis could happen upon the site any day, especially given the number of questions now being raised about the Speicher wreckage on both
sides. Iraqi intelligence was never certain of Scott's whereabouts
during the war, despite repeated efforts to extract information
about him from American POWs. They remained even more
uncertain now as to whether he was dead or not. But with all the
attention Scott's crash site was getting, the Iraqis had certainly
begun to contemplate the possibilities.

And a second group in the Pentagon was now suggesting a
diplomatic route to the site. The U.S. government could go to
the ICRC and ask it to contact Baghdad. The ICRC would tell
Iraqi leaders about the crash site and ask for permission to take a

team to visit it. The diplomatic proposal posed no risk of lives, and many political and military leaders were still shaken over a failed military reserve mission just a year earlier in Somalia in which two Blackhawk helicopters had been shot down and eighteen special operations soldiers killed. The ICRC path also offered the added benefit of showing the Iraqis that the United States was playing by the rules.

Military planners thought the diplomatic plan must be a ghost option, a backup for appearance's sake. Connolly didn't like it. If the United States went in undercover, intelligence agents could be certain that the information gathered was untainted and then use what they found to investigate further. He also didn't want to tell Iraq exactly where the site was, which is what a diplomatic mission of the ICRC would have to do in order to gain access. Even if they only gave Iraq the general vicinity at first, Saddam Hussein would certainly try to get his hands on a downed American jet. And Connolly was worried over how much time had passed. He tried to speed things along by warning those involved: "If it were to become known that we had identified the potential remains of a service member who had potentially died in combat and we were not immediately going in there to assure they wouldn't fall into the hands of the enemy, we would be crucified politically."

Meanwhile, Buddy Harris and a couple of other investigators kept examining the Qatari photographs and the satellite images of the wreckage. The F/A-18's canopy appeared to be a couple of miles away from the crash site. When a pilot ejects, small explosives ignite and blast off the canopy. It appeared as if that's exactly what had happened with Speicher's jet. Those who had looked into Speicher's disappearance early on didn't have wreckage to examine, but they had determined that he did not eject because no one had heard his emergency locator transmitter (ELT).

A downed pilot's ELT normally emits a distinct whooping signal that surveilling aircraft and other pilots would hear on a UHF frequency.

Being a pilot, Harris knew that some aviators liked to have their ELTs disconnected when they flew over hostile territory. They thought that the signals made it easy for everyone to find them, including the enemy. Harris asked a couple of people from Speicher's squadron, VFA-81, but they claimed they had not disconnected their ELTs that night. Maybe the ELT had malfunctioned, Harris thought. When he checked into that hypothesis, he learned that the beacons have several electronic backups that make them extremely reliable.

Finally, he tracked down VFA-81's maintenance officer, Lieutenant Commander Steve "Ammo" Minnis. If the ELTs were disconnected, he would have to have known about it. Yes, Minnis affirmed, the beacons had been disconnected. It appeared as if Harris had been misled. "Did you know they didn't go after Scott and look for him because they didn't know this and got no signal?" Harris queried Minnis. The maintenance officer was stunned. The higher-ups knew that the ELTs had been turned off, Minnis said. That message should have been relayed to those in charge of search and rescue. "There's just no way," he told Harris. That piece of information had to have been known by Minnis's superiors.

The investigators, too, were shocked. They had already been told about the new Motorola survival radios—the AN/PRC-112s—that were too large to fit into the pilots' vest pockets. Those monitoring the airwaves during the war would have been listening for some communication from Speicher, but maybe he had no way to signal. His ELT was disconnected. His radio might have tumbled out of his vest pocket, or had malfunctioned. The reasons given why they hadn't searched for Speicher when he went down had been shown to be flimsy, at best. From what they gleaned interviewing those involved with early military decisions, particularly the missteps, military planners could make an almost-perfect case for the covert mission.

Connolly left his office and walked through the Pentagon halls to the secretary of defense's conference room, located in the E-ring. This briefing, which would decide whether to go in as a special military operation or as a diplomatic mission, had been a long time coming. It was now December 23, 1994, a year since Speicher's F/A-18 had been found in the Iraqi desert. General John Shalikashvili, chairman of the Joint Chiefs of Staff, took a seat at the head of a long table. To his left sat his top planner, the director of operations for the Joint Chiefs of Staff, Air Force Lieutenant General Howell M. Estes III. Beside Estes was the deputy principal secretary of defense for international security affairs, Frederick C. Smith. Secretary of Defense William F. Perry sat to the right of Shalikashvili, along with Perry's undersecretary of defense for policy, Walter B. "Walt" Slocombe. Down the table was Colonel William G. "Jerry" Boykin, who was head of J33/Special Operations Division. (Boykin was later outed by Attorney General Janet Reno for having been one of two Delta Force officers the FBI asked for, by name, for their expertise when the FBI sought to storm the Branch Davidian complex at Waco, Texas.) Aides holding briefing packets, transparencies and flip charts stood against the walls. There was no one else in the room from Connolly's office, but many from Smith's office.

Connolly thought that was odd, but he decided to take his seat and see where the meeting's direction would take them. At no time was Connolly's boss, the assistant secretary of defense for special operations and low-intensity conflict, H. Allen Holmes, ever involved in any of the planning. If the chairman or secretary had a pointed question, Pentagon protocol was that only someone directly involved in the planning could answer it, but none of the planners who had worked out the details of the covert mission was there. "This thing's been preloaded," Connolly thought. As staffers projected the presentation onto the wall, page by page, those around the table followed along in their handouts. Connolly's counterpart, Fred Smith, talked about the diplomatic approach.

One of Shalikashvili's staff laid out the military option. They had done a threat analysis of the covert mission, breaking it down into infiltration (getting to the crash site), actions on objective (working at the site) and exfiltration (getting back to the base). In each case, chances for success were rated high, and threats were rated low.

Though the staffer made the operation look smooth, controlled and effective, Connolly knew it wouldn't be that fluid. When he was an Army Ranger, a dozen people, including the battalion commander, died just while training for a special op. Military missions are inherently dangerous, but the odds for this one looked as promising as any other. Yet the longer the meeting went, the more Connolly felt support for the covert mission slipping away. Finally, he addressed Perry and Shalikashvili directly: "This country has an obligation to go in and find out what happened to this pilot," he said. Then he quoted the fifth stanza of the Army Ranger creed: "I shall never leave a fallen comrade to fall into the hands of the enemy." He paused, still sensing the group's hesitation to again expose special operations forces to danger so soon after the disaster in Somalia. He took one more shot.

"Mr. Secretary," Connolly said, "I will go out the door of this conference room, I will stand in the hallway and I will stop the first five people who walk by in military uniform, regardless of their gender. I will explain to them what the mission is, I will ask them if they will volunteer to get on the helicopters, and I guarantee you that all five of them will volunteer."

Secretary of Defense Perry thanked him for his impassioned comments, then turned to General Shalikashvili. "Mr. Chairman, what do you think?" "Well, Mr. Secretary," Connolly remembers Shalikashvili saying, "I don't want to be the one to write letters home to the parents telling them that their son or daughter died looking for old bones." Shalikashvili was not necessarily speaking for the majority, but his opinion pulled more weight.

"Sorry thing," said Bob Dussault, "was [that] all the Joint Staff wanted to do something—made plans, encouraged others to make plans—and in the end it was all called off by the famous Shalikashvili speech, thus turning it all over to State and the CIA."

Dussault, although not present for the briefing, also knew that Shalikashvili had made the claim that no one soldier was important enough to do a military action. "I don't know," he observed, "if he said it because that is how he felt or because he was told by higher-ups that was the case and he and DoD were going to have to live with it."

Perry wanted to think about what had been presented in the briefing. He directed the military to keep the covert plan viable. But Connolly knew Shalikashvili's feelings had derailed the military option. Neither Perry nor Shalikashvili had the mettle "for putting any forces in jeopardy for this mission," said Connolly.

A month later, Connolly got a letter from the deputy secretary of defense. Perry had chosen the diplomatic path. Two weeks later, on January 4, 1995, Perry informed Secretary of State Warren M. Christopher that the United States required the services of the International Committee of the Red Cross to approach the Iraqis for a humanitarian mission to look at Scott Speicher's wreckage. Over another month passed before the Red

Cross agreed to the plan and sent Michel Cageneaux, its director of Middle East operations, to meet with Iraqi officials in Baghdad. Their February 14 meeting went smoothly, but Deputy Principal Secretary of Defense Frederick Smith remarked after discussions with the Red Cross that the Iraqis had taken detailed notes and hung on every word said. The Iraqis still did not have coordinates for the crash site, but once approached by the ICRC on behalf of the U.S., they knew that the Americans' original suspicions about Scott Speicher's having survived his crash were now seen as a distinct possibility. This put Scott Speicher more at risk than ever.

As Speicher lost the cover of his perceived demise when the investigative team announced it was going into the western Iraqi desert under the auspices of the ICRC, all kinds of questions were raised among the Iraqi leadership. No doubt these questions begged investigation of their own. If Scott was confirmed dead by the U.S. because of the remains Iraq provided them at the end of the conflict, what was the U.S. trying to discover now? Maybe the U.S. thought he was not dead. Maybe they had proven that the remains were not his. Perhaps there was something of value to national security buried among the jet's ruins? Recall that neither Schwarzkopf nor his staff went back to the Iraqis to demand answers after DNA analysis proved that the remains the Iraqis had forwarded and certified as Scott Speicher's were not his. Pentagon officials were presumptive in their findings and were not willing to consider the possibility that Scott had gotten out of his jet and was in assisted-evasion mode. One of the principal reasons the U.S. government conceded to the ICRC mission was the insistence of Frederick Smith, whose office held the line that Speicher was dead and that his remains were under the aircraft.

Though the negotiation had gone well in Baghdad, the U.S.

didn't achieve results right away. Saddam wanted time to think it over. Meanwhile, covert teams went through a complete dry run of the mission at Fort Bliss, which they code-named "Isolated Ivory," a veiled reference to Shalikashvili's comment about Speicher's "old bones" at the Pentagon briefing. On March 1, 1995, the U.S. was notified through diplomatic channels that the Iraqis were amenable to the ICRC team coming to investigate the crash site, as long as the team was accompanied by Iraqi officials. March is still cold in the desert, and no one who ventured out to the crash site would last long in the bitter cold. The desert hardpan was still frozen solid, a fact that Coalition airmen had learned the hard way when forced to eject over the same desolate, cold desert back in the winter months of 1991.

The diplomatic mission was on. But what Connolly could not have known is that despite the rapid quashing of the military option in Secretary Perry's conference room, a covert plan still moved forward to retrieve the cockpit and ejection seat, both of which held valuable information that some around the table that December day did not want the Iraqis to find. Of the four covert teams formed in the summer of 1994, one secretly broke away and ended up training at the Naval Strike Warfare Center at Fallon, Nevada.

"I was out there in late spring, early summer 1995," said a Navy commander who asked for anonymity. He noted that he engaged one of the Delta Force members in conversation off and on. "They had been out here for a short time when one day he said, 'Yeah, man, we're going out to the desert to get some guy's cockpit and bring it back.' One day they were gone. But a few days later they'd returned from the mission."

Halfway around the world, in Riyadh, Lieutenant Commander Alan "Zoomie" Baker (who was on the Joint Staff in 1994 and 1995), recalls that the Delta Force snakeaters were going in to investigate the site as well. They checked in with operations and moved out to the site using the planned insertion point from Ar Ar. They knew what they were looking for. The Qataris' photographs had shown military planners that the cockpit was intact. Satellite imagery had detected the hundred-pound shell of the Martin-Baker SJU-5A ejection seat, leaving the distinctive outline of a chair resting on the desert floor. Better to take the cockpit and ejection seat before the ICRC mission than to leave the Iraqis too much room to scavenge the site themselves, possibly gaining valuable components from the Hornet. Inside the cockpit were Speicher's black boxes—the command launch computer that controls and monitors the high-speed anti-radiation missile (HARM); the KY-58 secure encrypted radio; and the head-up display (HUD). Curiously, the plane's data storage unit (DSU), which would have recorded Speicher's final minutes over the western Iraqi desert, was left for the ICRC team to find.

The ICRC convoy rolled out of Baghdad the morning of December 10, 1995, and headed toward the crash site. Nine months had passed since Iraq had initially agreed to allow a visit to the wreckage of Scott Speicher's F/A-18. From overhead films of the crash site shot at intervals right before the ICRC team's departure for the Iraqi desert, Pentagon officials could see truck trails to and from the site, and questions about the integrity of the site arose from the ICRC team. After all, they knew nothing of a breakaway covert team and could not be sure that any damage to the site did not involve the Iraqis.

The ICRC team, having reached Baghdad, had waited until the night before they were to go into the desert to give the Iraqis the latitude and longitude of the crash site—3300125N/0421528E, the erroneously reported coordinate, in Speicher's file. But as the team neared the given coordinates, they saw nothing but desolate landscape. Bedouins, knowing the team was in the area, stood along the sandy path and waved their arms, directing the vehicles to the site. With a little help from the Bedouins' directions the team actually located the wreckage at 3300114N/0421528E, a full 150 statute miles away from the coordinates they were given by the message traffic during the war.

The United States had sent investigators from CILHI, including its chief anthropologist, Dr. Thomas D. Holland, to help examine human remains, if there were any. Experts from the Navy's crash-investigation unit in China Lake, California, and the Naval Safety Center Norfolk also went to the site, along with a medic, an explosive-disposal expert and three linguists. The ICRC sent four people. The Republic of Iraq (ROI) sent two people—aircraft investigators—and ordered soldiers to encircle the perimeter of the camp for protection. The ICRC/ROI humanitarian recovery effort was dubbed Operation Promise Kept. But as Lieutenant Commander Buran of the Naval Safety Center would observe years later, "Each person on the mission had his own agenda—his own objectives in being there." Some had agendas predetermined by their bosses back in Washington, others were given tasks outside their expertise and understanding. "I knew that the agenda of the ICRC trip was to find the body," said Bob Dussault. "My guys trained everyone who went on the trip from the U.S. on two different occasions. I know what went into preparing the team. Liotta was also much involved; but the focus was not to gather all the possible evidence, just that which supported his death." The investigation had two possible endings— the truth, or the truth as those inside the Pentagon wanted it to be. Scott Speicher was not going to come out on the positive end of the debate, but investigators like Buran, for one, were at a disadvantage to argue the point. He took his orders from the chain of command that sent him into the desert to find out anything he could about what had happened to Scott Speicher.

The group had left the fertile flatlands and lakes surrounding Baghdad and, just three hours later, stood on a moonlike surface southwest of the city in the vicinity of Tulul ad Dulaym, Wadi Thumayl. They were 1,080 feet above sea level, in the desert, less than thirty kilometers to the south of a major east-west highway in a region with no substantial natural landmarks. The Saudi border was about two hundred kilometers to the northeast. Several Bedouin camps were visible to the north and northwest of the crash site, with numerous dirt trails radiating out from the camps to nearby paved roads. Otherwise, as far as they looked, all they could see was light brown sand comprised of weathered rock particles less than half a millimeter in diameter, and a few scattered clumps of grass, shrubs and vines.

As team investigators climbed out of their Land Rovers and trucks, they could see Speicher's wreckage and they knew exactly what had happened without shoveling the first spade of dirt or examining one piece of the aircraft. Speicher's Hornet was right side up. Big chunks of it, easily recognizable parts like its engines, lay in a circle no more than sixty feet in diameter. There was no significant crash crater and the aircraft wreckage showed minimal fragmentation—it was determined to be consistent with terminal velocity, high angle and low-power impact. Military experts knew what that meant. The jet had lost power, and had dropped like a falling leaf straight to the desert floor. Speicher's jet had not, as first thought, been blown to bits in the sky. Investigators quickly noticed one other thing: The cockpit was missing. The entire cockpit and instrument-bay section, from forward of the wings to just aft of the gun, had been sheared cleanly from the rest of the fuselage. Obviously, others had gotten to the crash site ahead of them.

"It was like a car in the junkyard that you'd decided you wanted just the part from the front windshield to the bumper, and cut it off," observed Mike Buran. "The Iraqis couldn't afford *batteries* in that country because of the embargo. We brought our own. Yet the cockpit of the aircraft was cut off clean and quickly." He was incredulous at the precision. The Iraqis didn't have the equipment or remote power source to do what had been done to Scott's jet.

Whoever had been to the site first would have had to sidestep gingerly around Speicher's ordnance, much of which was scattered about the axis of the aircraft. The Bedouins, though normally anxious to take down an aircraft site such as Scott's for its saleable parts and scrap, kept their distance because of the missiles half-buried in the sand. In the past they'd only scavenged pieces that had been thrown clear of the main fuselage. The idea that anyone unfamiliar with the missiles would stray into the debris field was not impossible, but certainly not likely for the local people.

"I would not be surprised," said Tim Connolly, "if it turned out the U.S. government went in covertly at some point." In his final report, dated February 15, 1996, Buran states: "From the evidence of the crash site before the ICRC team arrived, it is likely that another force . . . examined the wreckage and removed major portions of the cockpit and instrument-bay section."

The American members of the ICRC team would later comment in their reports on how professionally the cockpit area had been dug out: It was as if whoever had done it was looking for Scott Speicher's body under the aircraft. The ejection seat, visible on satellite imagery roughly two miles from the aircraft wreckage, was taken away prior to the ICRC's arrival as well.

The wreckage that the ICRC found lying around the craft on the desert floor consisted of the nose gear and twenty-millimeter M61A1 Vulcan cannon, representing the nose of the aircraft; the wings; the engines; and the tail rudders and stabilizers. The ord-

nance located at the crash site consisted of everything Scott's
Hornet was carrying minus one HARM. Speicher had three
HARMs, two Sparrows and two Sidewinders when he left the
Saratoga's deck on his mission. "Can't remember if we had two
drop tanks [versus] one," said Tony Albano. "We always carried
the ubiquitous centerline drop tank. Except, of course, Banker,
who had only two HARMs so he could recover with both still
on." (Recall that Banker Caldwell had been the airborne spare
the night of Scott Speicher's disappearance.) Albano noted that if
a three-HARM bird had problems that required recovery, the
pilot would have to jettison one or head for a divert field. Investigators carefully moved the ordnance away from the wreckage
and roped it off. "We had people familiar with armament to take
care of this," said Bruce Trenholm of China Lake. The armament specialists buried the ordnance before leaving the desert,
but not before the members of Operation Promise Kept took the
fins off Speicher's HARMs as souvenirs.

The team further observed that several major components of
the Hornet were not with the airframe, including the wing fuel
drop tank, located four thousand meters north; the centerline
fuel drop tank, pinpointed 2,500 meters north; the canopy, found
670 meters northeast; and the cockpit, which, as noted, was
gone. A post-crash fire plus erosion by the elements had contributed to the breakdown and disintegration of the structural
components manufactured from composite material, such as the
wings.

Investigators started at the nose of the F/A-18 and roped off
an area to excavate. It looked to them like the wreckage had been
searched by people who knew what they were doing. A pile of
backfill, a mound of sand dug from somewhere else, had been
heaped near where the cockpit should have been. Popped rivets
lay on the ground nearby. The backfill, the experts thought, was

less than a month old. Components from the Hornet's computer had also been removed. To begin their own excavation, the team's investigators initiated the process where the cockpit should have been, an area that exhibited signs of recent manual digging. The ground was excavated to a depth of fifty centimeters, to culturally sterile soil, according to a DPMO memorandum prepared by Lieutenant Commander Kevin J. Wilson, who worked in the office of the assistant secretary of defense for international security affairs/DPMO, and sent to Michel Cageneaux in the operations division of the ICRC in 1997. Excavation continued along the aircraft's midline until it became readily apparent to investigators that there was no significant cockpit debris, pilot-related materials or pilot to recover.

Analysis of the engines concluded that both engines were in relatively good shape. Post-crash analysis later concluded that the engines had shut down in flight. With the cockpit section and ejection seat missing, most of the key evidence of missile damage was absent. There was just enough, however, to tell that the missile that had detonated under Scott Speicher's Hornet was a high-explosive warhead. Damage from an air-to-air missile detonation had cut the Hornet's fuel lines and blown the starboard wing flaps off of the aircraft—killing the airplane but not the pilot. "The damage was consistent with an AIM-54C Phoenix missile," admitted one of the crash investigators on condition of anonymity, but he was not permitted to include that finding in his report. The Phoenix has a 135-pound warhead and throws out a continuous rod belt that is designed to bring down an airplane. With a range of over one hundred nautical miles, the Phoenix is the Tomcats' longest-range missile. The wing and centerline drop tanks found north of the crash site had their pylons still attached. The pylons were torn from the fuselage in-flight, indicative of excessive aerodynamic forces over a short period of time that were consistent with the aircraft being subject to a violent spin or falling leaf configuration.

As the work near the jet continued, other members of the team formed skirmish lines, spreading out and walking slowly to look for other evidence. Buran was paired with his peer in the Iraqi Air Force, who went by the pseudonym Mohammed, a MiG pilot who had been shot down twice in the air war between Iraq and Iran. He had a bad back after parachuting out of his stricken aircraft the second time, and no longer flew. Mohammed had received his mishap-investigation training in Great Britain. Out in the middle of the western Iraqi desert, he and Buran talked frequently. On one such occasion, the Iraqi pilot stopped Buran as they strode over the site looking for clues and inquired about the need for aircraft investigators in other countries. "Are there jobs for people like us?" he asked. "Oh, yes," said Buran. "Lots of them." The Iraqi pilot grinned. Later, he gave Buran a set of his Iraqi pilot's wings—one pilot to another. Buran still has them.

During their recovery effort, the team surveyed a circle of roughly ten kilometers in diameter centered on the aircraft crash site. Approximately thirty meters north, east and south of the site, the team noticed several low, rectangular piles of rock. Dr. Tom Holland shovel-tested the rock piles near the wreckage in search of a possible gravesite, but none appeared to have been subjected to subsurface disturbance within ten years prior. No human remains were recovered from Holland's rock pile examinations. More important, no personal pilot-related items were recovered at the crash site. In fact, the only cockpit items gathered from the wreckage site—aside from the DSU—were two switches and one warning light indicator. Nothing else.

Two thousand feet to the north, they spotted something man-made—a tall arch sitting upright on a sandy knoll. As they got closer, they saw that it was the frame of the canopy, or at least, what was left of the transparent shield that covers the cockpit. It looked as if Bedouins had stood it on end as a landmark. A Bedouin boy had scrawled graffiti in Arabic across the bottom of the canopy frame, lamenting how much he hated it there. Both canopy-jettison rocket motors had been fired, which produced even and complete burn marks on the wreckage. While it was clear as they picked through the evidence on the ground that the pilot had ejected, mishap investigators later determined that he initiated the jettison—an important determination in favor of Scott's survival. To the south, they found the missing HARM missile Speicher was to drop on the first night of the Gulf War. This did not, as Albano had commented earlier, suggest that Speicher had jettisoned one of his three HARMs to regain control of his jet, as the missile was clearly torn from the plane.

A couple of days later, Navy flight mishap investigator Bruce Trenholm got an incredible call on his radio. Iraqi officials present at the site notified the team that a young Bedouin boy claimed he had encountered a flight suit while herding his sheep. The flight suit was about 3.5 kilometers northeast of the wreckage. Trenholm drove there and found members of the ICRC team standing in a circle. Standing close by was the boy's "uncle," a robe-clad, impeccably dressed gentleman wearing polished wing-tip shoes, hardly the attire of a shepherd. The boy had complained that the flight suit "smelled bad" and he didn't touch it, but Trenholm and the others were not permitted to interview him further. But most important, the flight suit was not on the ground when discovered. "It had been handed to us," remarked Buran. "That's a big difference."

Trenholm could see that what the team had been given was a U.S. Nomex flight suit, standard aviator coveralls resistant to fires up to several hundred degrees. He also could see that it had faded somewhat from its usual olive color to a more greenish yellow. "I was told that it was Michael's flight suit," recalled Trenholm. "But all I said at the time was 'Well, all I can tell you is it's a flight suit. I don't know whose it is.'" He'd have to run tests to make sure it was Speicher's. As they stood in the desert, more questions were raised than answered. "I mean, you know, the deal was we were looking for Michael Speicher. That was our task. You know there's a flight suit, but it's just like an Easter egg hunt basically, and here's his flight suit. 'This is his.'" Trenholm was suspicious of the sudden appearance of such important forensic evidence. "I can't verify whose it is," he said. "I don't see anybody wearing it. That's just the way I work. If I don't see you wearing it, then I'm not really sure it's yours." And the circumstances surrounding the flight suit's discovery were fishy. Nothing fit. During previous visits to the crash site, neither the Qataris nor other American CIA agents who'd "gone native" and explored the wreckage and surrounding area between 1991 and 1993 found a U.S. Nomex flight suit lying about the desert floor. So the "discovery" of the flight suit begged questions. Where had it been all this time? Where was the pilot who wore it? And was he Scott Speicher?

Near where the flight suit was recovered, a cluster of pilot survival items or aviation life support system (ALSS) equipment was also found: an ejection seat upper-leg garter fragment, three survival raft fragments, pieces of straps from a parachute, an inflatable raft, a twenty-millimeter shell from the Hornet's nose cannon, and six pieces of an anti-G suit that a pilot wears to lessen aerodynamic forces. They also found a signaling flare. Someone had tried to light both ends, one used for daytime and the other one for night. The pyrotechnics were still inside the night end, which meant maybe the flare hadn't worked. But the bottom line was clear: The flight suit and all the aviation life support equipment recovered by the team had been cut with a sharp object. Much of it also had bloodstains, but none suggesting massive external bleeding.

"The flight suit was cut up the back not including the collar," recalled Trenholm. The cuts up the back included the legs and the crotch, where the suit was notched or cut around the straps and fasteners of Speicher's torso harness, leaving a diamond-shaped cut by the groin area of each leg. The flight suit, if it was indeed Speicher's, had obviously been places other than the desert, due to the presence of foreign trace evidence of carpet fibers, dog hair, and the like—but where exactly? How long had Scott worn or kept his flight suit, if it was, indeed, his, before he was discovered?

The Iraqis made it more difficult to answer these questions by denying the investigators access to nearby Bedouins. "The Bedouins in that area out there, they're nomadic tribes and they go from Point A to Point B to Point C, and they do this all year round," Bruce Trenholm recounted. "They are like gypsies— they just travel. There was a small Bedouin tribe not too far away, but we never had any dealings with them at all. The Iraqis were there. I think the whole Iraqi army was there." Aside from General Khaldoun Khattab (head of the Iraqi Air Force) and Iraqi regulars present at the crash site, Saddam had dispatched his intelligence operatives to the site as well. "Every time the Bedouins tried to tell us something, or even looked like they wanted to tell us anything," said Mike Buran, "one of these intelligence guys intervened."

The Iraqis had also determined that the team could search only the area negotiated before the investigators' arrival. The mishap area was circular in shape and extended outward eighteen to twenty meters at its widest portion. Anything outside the coordinates provided by the ICRC was off limits. "Bruce [Trenholm] had taken some wind drift calculations that he thought we should've looked at," recalled Buran. "But the Iraqis didn't want us going outside the predetermined search perimeter. We thought that perhaps given the winds that night, he [Speicher] might have ended up slightly beyond where we initially thought." Buran and Trenholm were also not permitted by either side—the U.S. or Iraq—to search the area in which Speicher's ground-to-air signal had been detected on satellite imagery. They could see the area but were not allowed to walk into it. "Our hands were tied," said Buran. "The Iraqis said no."

Later, DPMO would issue an analysis of Speicher's ground-to-air marker. In that statement, DPMO remarked that the ICRC team "searched the entire vicinity and noted nothing they considered to be any type of survival symbol," when, in fact, the team had not been permitted to look at all. The DPMO's statement (undated and forwarded by the Office of Naval Intelligence in March 2002) further fabricated that team analysts "noted that Iraqi military units routinely draw designs in the desert sand during training exercises. The site of the unidentified marking is in the general vicinity of an Iraqi military training area." The facts of the matter are altogether different.

"There's nothing out there—nothing but sand, dirt and rocks," said Trenholm. "Nobody goes through there but the native people." His colleague, Mike Buran, iterated that the only population in that part of the desert were Bedouin sheepherders—and "lots of sheep. We're talking a lot of them. The entire crash area was covered with sheep droppings—everywhere you looked."

The DPMO debunked itself further in regards to the tracks radiating out from the crash site, by stating that "the marking could not be associated with any known Iraqi military unit." The ICRC team did not make any claims to having seen evidence of motorized vehicles in the area, even though DPMO stated in the report that "analysts believe the ground marking may have been caused by tire tracks left by some unidentifiable vehicle. Motorized vehicles have been noted in this area." This was simply not the case. "The site was in the middle of nowhere—and I mean nowhere," Trenholm later emphasized. One other thought picked at Trenholm's brain. It was freezing cold. This was December. Speicher was shot down in January. If it was cold for the ICRC team now, in a tent with plenty of layers of blankets and thick sleeping bags, Trenholm knew it would have been bone-chilling for Speicher.

After the team's fourth full day in the desert, as the site investigation wound down, Trenholm, Buran and the others headed back to their tents from the field. The Iraqis had piled next to the team's tents material from the aircraft and crash site that was not found in the mapped debris field. When asked where they'd gotten it, the Iraqis pleaded ignorance. Among the items was the one thing from the aircraft that investigators had most hoped to find—its data storage unit. The DSU had been blown out of its case and shut down immediately—Buran and the others would later learn that this had happened while the jet was still airborne. Wrenched from its case, the DSU fell away from the Hornet before the plane impacted the desert floor. The bottom plate of the memory unit had a fissure along the midline roughly half its length. The edges of the tear were jagged and displaced outward from the center of the unit. The front faceplate, with the handle and the motherboard, were missing. If the information could be recovered from it, the DSU, though damaged, would unveil a minute-by-minute mechanical account of Speicher's last flight. There was only one problem—getting it out of the country. Buran downplayed the DSU's importance in front of the Iraqis, but offered the Bedouins money for it. They accepted. He smuggled the DSU out in some of his personal gear.

Getting the DSU out of Iraq was important. But Mike Buran had one more thing he wanted to do before leaving the western Iraqi desert. He cut the tailhook off Speicher's airplane and brought it back for Michael Scott Speicher, Jr., who was eighteen months old the last time he had seen his father. He turned it over to Scott's former commanding officer, Michael T. "Spock" Anderson, to clean up and present properly to Speicher's boy. To carrier aviators, the hook is a cherished symbol of their flying career. At least young Michael would have something of his father's airplane to remember him by.

The team pulled out of Iraq on December 16, 1995, carrying its physical evidence and preliminary findings.

The Pentagon would now have to tell Joanne Speicher what had been found in and around her husband's aircraft. Details of the International Committee of the Red Cross mission were bound to become public, and the Pentagon didn't want her to read about it in the papers. In actuality, the cat was already out of the bag. The ICRC had been intermittently asking the Iraqi government to account for Speicher and Lieutenant Commander Barry Cooke since the war, but Joanne wasn't told by the Navy or the U.S. government about those inquiries. Whether Buddy Harris, working in the Pentagon on the case, mentioned the information to her as it became known is speculative. But Harris's proximity to the Speicher family was closer than anyone had imagined at the time. When the U.S. government enjoined the ICRC to ask Iraq about coming in-country to survey and excavate Scott's Hornet, the Navy then decided it was time to contact Joanne. And as plans were made, and next-of-kin considerations were discussed, Buddy Harris knew he had to come forward with one more piece of information for his bosses in the Pentagon.

Over two years before, on July 4, 1992, Harris had married Joanne Speicher. He never mentioned the marriage to his colleagues in the Pentagon as he investigated the case, certainly not to his superiors. While some investigators working with Harris purportedly knew that he had married Joanne Speicher, most did not. It was a clear case of conflict of interest, no matter how well intentioned or how much Buddy felt his presence on the team boosted the case before his superiors. Across the Pentagon in a very different quarter of the building, Harris's marriage to Joanne had not been missed. In the course of his work on the Speicher casualty file for the Navy POW/MIA Office, Lieutenant Commander Jeff Manor discovered the problem of next-of-kin rights.

"Technically, Joanne was no longer the next-of-kin since she was remarried. [Speicher's] father was." But he also recalled that his office had had a tough time tracking down Wallace Speicher back when they were performing DNA testing on the Iraqi remains. "Nobody knew if he was dead or alive." Wallace was very much alive in late 1994, but suffering the end-stages of Alzheimer's, much as his wife had. Manor tracked him down to a nursing home, but did not pursue it further. Back during the war, Manor recalled that Wallace had sought attention for what happened to his boy. "I think," said Manor, "[one reason concerned] money because of Scott's loss. Add to that, he was not Scott's natural father," which further complicated the next-of-kin issue.

Speicher's children are not eligible to become next-of-kin until they reach the age of eighteen. The difference between the semantics of "primary next of kin" and "member of the immediate family" became an important distinction as the case progressed. "We didn't know what we were going to do if they declared Scott missing again—all that retroactive pay had to go to someone," Manor said. The term "primary next of kin," in the

case of a missing person, refers to an individual authorized to direct disposition of the remains of the person. But the term
"member of the family" in the case of a missing person means the
spouse of the person (if they have not remarried or divorced the
service member); a natural, adopted or recognized illegitimate
child of the person if they have reached the age of eighteen (if
the child or children are not eighteen, a surviving parent can
speak for them); a biological parent, unless the law has revoked
custody by court decree and it was never restored; or a brother or
sister of the person, if eighteen years or older. Under these
guidelines, once remarried, Joanne Speicher was no longer Scott
Speicher's primary next of kin, nor was she a member of the family. In fact, it was—and is—Sheryl Long, Scott's adopted sister,
who is the primary next of kin, and as such, it is Sheryl Long who
should have received any of Scott's retroactive pay after July 4,
1992. However, the Navy continued to make these payments,
once in 1996 and again in 2001, to Joanne.

Later, Manor remembered how forthcoming a captain from
the Chief of Naval Operations' Special Operations group had
been with him during their meeting. "He told me right away
about the mess with Buddy Harris. I think it was then that I informed him that things were even worse because Joanne was not
the primary next of kin. It was a wrinkle that I don't think they
initially considered. I'm not sure what I would have done in
Buddy Harris's place. I know that Admiral Arthur secured a
promise from him that he would not release anything to Joanne
until the Navy decided to do so. I'm not sure why all this stuff
was not code word since it involved possible special ops."

Admiral Stan Arthur pulled Harris into his office after the
revelation of his marriage to Joanne was brought to his attention.
They talked for about an hour. Arthur told Harris he wouldn't
have been on the investigating team if Arthur had known the sit-

uation, but it was just as well. "Basically he said he's sorry," said Harris. Arthur took full responsibility for what had happened to Speicher. During the war, Arthur had been in charge of naval operations in Desert Storm. He thought his staff had made serious mistakes. Now, Arthur said, he was going to do everything he could to make it right, to get the answers to all the questions that have been asked since Scott's jet went down. It was a heartfelt promise, if not one that Arthur was actually able to do.

Commander Chip Beck, who had been pulled from the CIA in 1991 by the Navy to go back on active duty for nearly a year, had been tasked by the Navy as its official combat artist for Desert Storm. In that capacity he worked directly for Admiral Arthur. "I was on the USS *Ranger* the night that the air war commenced on January 17, 1991," he said, "the night that Scott Speicher was shot down. I believe from the comments I heard at the time that the Navy, and certainly Admiral Arthur, believed the initial reports that Speicher was killed in the shootdown of his aircraft. Exactly why a SAR [search and rescue] bird was not sent into the area, I don't know." But Beck got to know Admiral Arthur over the forty-seven-day period he was assigned to the theater. "He was a caring and competent leader and a human being who would not knowingly leave one of his men in the lurch. Like most people at his level, he accepted the professional assessments of his subordinates, and had too much else going on to probably focus on the details that might have caused him to question the analysis. After all," Beck noted, "that is what his subordinate staffs, and DPMO, were supposed to do at their stages of the action or post-action investigations."

Buddy Harris would now have to watch from the sidelines after his closed-door conversation with Arthur. "Instead of being part of the group and listening to what everybody else had to say, my tasks became more menial." Rather than unearth, evaluate and present information to others, Harris was relegated to gathering information and passing it to a captain to present in group sessions. "The group tended to always have meetings when I was not there, or they wouldn't have any time to notify me. I was slowly put on the outside," he recalled later. "I understand. I'm not sure I would do anything different. So at that point, I had to go tell Joanne."

When asked how he approached that conversation, he didn't want to go into it. The conversation could not have come easy. In the meantime, everyone hoped the crash site would divulge hard evidence, and clear up the mystery once and for all. They did not yet know that what the Hornet wreckage revealed would only make them feel worse.

Secretary of Defense William F. Perry wanted to know how long it would take to resolve the issues in the case. "I told him it'd be thirty to forty days," Bruce Trenholm said later. In the meantime, J. Alan Liotta, deputy to the deputy assistant secretary of defense (POW/MIA Affairs or DPMO), briefed Senator Robert C. Smith, a ranking member of the Armed Services Committee, to tell him what the group had found. Smith, a New Hampshire Republican, had tracked the Speicher case since the Qataris found the wreckage in 1993. Smith's own father was a naval aviator who was killed near the end of World War II during a training flight over the Chesapeake Bay, two days before Smith's fourth birthday. On January 17, 1996, during his briefing with Liotta, Smith heard grave news: The Red Cross team had found nothing to suggest that Speicher could have survived.

CHAPTER 8

Dead or Alive?

A few weeks after the ICRC wrapped up its inquiry, the aircraft investigators, life support experts, aviation engineers and anthropologists filed their reports. Their findings colored in a fairly thorough picture of what had happened to Speicher during his final mission. That picture differed sharply from what Senator Robert Smith had been told by Liotta. On January 12, 1996, just days before Smith's briefing, a McDonnell Douglas investigative team extracted the information from Scott Speicher's DSU. The team consisted of Jeff Edwards, an aircraft investigator; Scott Reynolds, an F/A-18 product-safety analyst; Kevin Schmitz and Jeff Staudacher, DSU data retrieval; and Glen Patterson from Hamilton Standard (the manufacturer of the DSU), all of whom performed retrieval and analysis of data contained on the DSU. They reported a detailed time line of Speicher's last flight. The McDonnell Douglas Aerospace team successfully retrieved about 93 percent of the DSU's data, despite significant damage to the memory unit. Data is recorded on the memory unit in pairs of a low and a high chip. The power loss to

Speicher's DSU was proven to be abrupt, and occurred between data being written from the low chip to the high chip.

Scott Speicher's data began recording to the DSU at 1:35:39.25 Baghdad time. The plane's throttles were set to 98 percent, or military power. Weight off wheels occurred at 1:36:18.44 as Spike lifted the Hornet off the deck of the *Saratoga*. Everything in his flight was normal during the climbout and Speicher cruised between 21,000 and 23,000 feet. But within eight minutes of takeoff, his jet started recording a lengthy series of maintenance status panel (MSP) code and built-in test (BIT) code failures, several having significant impact on the outcome of Speicher's flight and his mission.

At 1:43:30.65 A.M. he got a warning indicating a HARM command launch computer (CLC) failure (MSP Code 375). One, two or all three of his missiles might have been inoperative. Seconds later, he had a HARM/RWR (radar warning receiver) interface fail (MSP Code 377). The HARM CLC failure would either degrade or eliminate the HARM to RWR interface that enabled the HARM missile to characterize threats. At 3:46:25.95, two hours and ten minutes into the mission, as Scott was nearing his first target, the jet's computer recorded another code: an ALR-67 radar warning receiver analyzer fail (MSP Code 111). The device would have detected threats from air or land. The MSP code for the analyzer's failure corresponded to a detected BIT failure of the ALR-67 radar warning receiver: the countermeasures weapon system (BIT Code 94). The read-only memory (ROM) on the second of two processors was declared failed, which caused the analyzer to declare a failure. Though the severity of this failure can range from minor degradation to complete loss of displayed threat information, in investigator Mike Buran's opinion, "he was totally blind" to air-to-air threats.

The severity of this degradation is displayed to the pilot on the azimuth indicator on the right side of the cockpit instrument panel, so Speicher could have looked at another gauge to calculate how well the device was working. Significant corresponding avionics BIT code failures were also recorded. Ten minutes after weight off wheels, several of Speicher's HARM BIT codes indicated failures of the following HARM functions: general function fail, target of opportunity mode (TOO) fail, self-protect (SP) mode fail, HARM mode degraded, HARM command launch computer No Go, CLC fail and ALR-67/HARM interface fail. Reynolds and his team at McDonnell Douglas were unable to determine exactly which HARM station or stations were declared failed from the information available on the memory unit, or which had been damaged.

At 2:31:15.05, approximately fifty-five minutes into the flight, BIT Code 114—the signal data computer (SDC)—recorded its first failure. The SDC controls the four main electronic displays: the HUD, the right and left digital display indicators (DDIs) and the lower-middle navigation (NAV) display. A second failure was reported twenty-two minutes later, at 2:53:30.65, roughly one hour and nineteen minutes into the flight. The failures are believed to have been induced during one of three in-flight refueling events that took place before Speicher's inbound run to the target. The Hornets had followed the tanker during their ingress over Saudi airspace, topping off as necessary.

The BIT code failures seemed more than normal to Bob Stumpf. "He does appear to be having a bad day with the jet." But, he continued, "we train to function with multiple degrades and it appears Spike decided he could accomplish his mission with what he had, just as I decided I could make it with the lesser amount of fuel I had." He pointed to the fact that on that night, they all had considerable motivation to get their HARMs on the mark. Strikers [F-117s] were coming in below and were depending on the

Hornets' shutting down the Iraqis' missile batteries. "Those are the tough decisions that pilots have to make in the combat environment," Stumpf said.

Speicher received several advisories during the flight to keep him abreast of autopilot engagement. The last autopilot advisory indicates that autopilot was selected at 3:38:56.55, about two hours and three minutes into the flight. He disengaged autopilot roughly eight minutes later, at 3:49:42.75. He'd been at 28,160 feet, traveling at 364 knots.

"It does not surprise me," said Stumpf, "that Spike was on autopilot. We were on a very benign profile and the autopilot does a great job of keeping on this sort of profile." The autopilot permits the pilot to concentrate on other flying aspects besides navigating. "I'm sure we were all on autopilot for much of the flight," Stumpf added.

Seventeen seconds later, something slammed into Speicher's Hornet so hard that it experienced abrupt power loss. The information taken five seconds prior to the last recorded frame on the DSU indicates that Spike had dropped to 27,872 feet and increased his airspeed by four knots—he was dropping into his target run. This slight nose-down input by the pilot ten seconds before the loss of power is the only anomaly on the tape. The input was correlated by the loss of altitude and increase of indicated airspeed from 340 to nearly 370.

Mike Buran's Naval Safety Center analysis was submitted on February 15 to Alan Liotta at DPMO and Army Major W. L. Ray at CILHI. Engineers concluded that both of the Hornet's engines crashed with very little to no rotation. Because both engines were found in relatively good condition, and given the post-crash witness marks on the engine components, the qualified assumption by Buran and the engineers at Naval Aviation Depot Jacksonville was that both engines were no longer getting fuel and had shut down in flight. There were no entrance or exit wounds on either engine to indicate battle damage. The evidence pointed to a proximity detonation under the cockpit area of the aircraft. Whatever had damaged Scott Speicher's jet cut the fuel flow to the engines.

The wing and centerline drop tanks that had been located north of the crash site with the pylons still attached were also analyzed and documented. The pylons were torn from the fuselage, indicative of excessive aerodynamic forces over a short period of time—perhaps two or three seconds—due to the Hornet's altitude and approximated airspeed of 540 knots, or .92 Mach. Charles Sapp, unit manager of flight load limits at McDonnell Douglas, estimated that the maximum G-load and sideslip that caused the tanks to leave the airframe with their pylons still attached were six Gs and sixty degrees of sideslip. However, by the time the aircraft had plummeted into a falling-leaf configuration, Scott Speicher had already ejected.

Buran's engineering investigation reported that the rocket motors that blast the canopy from the aircraft had burned even marks on its frame. "The pilot had to have initiated the jettison," wrote Buran in his report. There are only two ways for the canopy to be jettisoned in an F/A-18 Hornet: the pilot pulling either of the two jettison release handles, one on the left side of the canopy, the other located between his legs. By the canopy alone investigators couldn't determine which one Scott Speicher had pulled. But in the end, what they did know was that he had ejected successfully.

Buran hypothesizes that the Hornet's engines were likely shut down from an impact that took place on the port side of the aircraft. This is the same side as the DSU, the mission computer and the recovered cockpit indicators. The throttle configuration on the F/A-18 is designed in such a way that if the throttle's cable is pulled forward, the aircraft loses power. If an explosion and/or airframe damage resulted in the throttle system being displaced forward enough, then the engine shutdown could also have been caused by that.

Buran's portion of the investigation also clearly stated that the pilot was not incapacitated by the missile's initial impact. One of the engineers wrote: "This pilot was over enemy territory, in extremis situation and sitting in the middle of a hot cockpit fire. Logic dictates that the only way this pilot is getting rid of his canopy is by ejecting." When he consulted flight surgeons and aircraft life support systems experts about the survivability factors facing the pilot, they assured Buran that Scott Speicher had an 85 to 90 percent chance of surviving the flash heat and fire and aerodynamic forces of the initial impact. Collene Swavely, a physical scientist in the protective-clothing division at the Naval Air Warfare Center in Warminster, Pennsylvania, told Buran that three- to four-second exposure to temperatures of 650 degrees Fahrenheit will result in second-degree burns on exposed areas of skin. If Speicher were burned in the ejection, it might have been on the back of the neck and any other areas that were not protected by clothing, such as his face if his visor was up. Swavely's studies had proven that a ten- to twelve-second exposure to temperatures in excess of 700 degrees Fahrenheit are needed to cause burns on a pilot because of the survival vests, anti-G suits, Nomex flight suits and cotton underwear that the heat has to pass through to get to the skin. The interior canopy bubble of Scott's jet was determined to have been exposed to only a few seconds of 400- to 500-degree heat. But this differs from the findings of Dr. Thomas D. Holland, team anthropologist, who suggested in his report that the cockpit was exposed to a fire "possibly reaching 650–700°F."

Trenholm's report picked up with the ejection. He determined that the canopy's distance from the wreckage meant that when Speicher pulled the ejection handle, it separated as it should have. As he worked on issues pertaining to the parachute and flight suit, Trenholm placed a call to "Spock" Anderson, who was now out of the Navy and working for McDonnell Douglas. He wanted to ask Anderson some questions about the flight suit, particularly if he'd authorized his pilots to wear their name tags on the mission. Anderson said he'd think about it and get back to him. "But when someone says this and doesn't get your phone number to call back, you aren't likely to get an answer," said Trenholm.

The *Sunliners* wore red name tags, usually stitched with their call signs—in Speicher's case, it read: "Spike." Trenholm was trying to figure out if the Iraqis cut off the left-breast Velcro for the "Spike" name tag or if the Bedouins had simply started to cut all the usable Velcro and metal fasteners off the suit for practical use. Much depended on whether Anderson let his pilots wear the name tags. He didn't, but Trenholm did not get that answer from Anderson then. He concluded that Anderson's negative interest was an admission, and that admission meant permission had been given. But the real answer came much later—well after his investigation was over. And it came from Speicher's former roommate and close friend on the *Saratoga*.

"We sanitized our flight suits," said Tony Albano recently. "We did not wear our name tags. Perhaps Trenholm was thinking of the tag on the inside back collar that we used to write our names and 'last four' for the ship's laundry. But we didn't have any name tags or patches on our flight suits that night or any other during the war." The "last four" Albano referred to were the last four digits of a pilot's social security number. If the Iraqis had Speicher's flight suit for any length of time, they knew exactly who they had—Scott Speicher. "The laundry label would've had Scott's last name on it," Albano concluded.

Trenholm began taking the flight suit around to various organizations for analysis. He was not the only one suspicious of the flight suit's origins. In his comprehensive report, Tom Holland addresses the flight suit "found" by the Bedouin boy—with the word "found" clearly in quotes.

One of the commands looking at the recovered flight suit was the Body Mounted Systems Branch at Naval Air Warfare Center, Warminster, Pennsylvania. Upon completion of the branch's evaluation, it was determined that the size of the suit was 38 Long and its type was CWU-27/P. But the leg inseam was based on a rough measurement due to the fact that fabric was missing from the flight suit examined. Investigators estimated a 30.5-inch inseam. Speicher's anthropomorphic data was estimated as 71 inches tall and weight approximately 168 pounds, but his Navy personal information sheet—on file with the DIA POW/MIA automated database—listed his exact height as 71.7 inches (5 feet 11 inches) and his weight at 154 pounds. Investigators suggested he wore a 38 Long flight suit. Maybe, but maybe not. Aviators typically wear flight suits slightly larger than their actual size to provide greater mobility. But after going to various reference materials and making some photographic comparisons, the idea that the flight suit was in fact Speicher's began to add up for Trenholm. In Trenholm's words, the suit "started quacking like a duck. I basically, for the most part, said that it was 'probable' it was his flight suit. [Now] I'm ninety-nine percent sure, just not a hundred percent sure. Personally, you know, you have a professional opinion and a personal opinion, right? My professional opinion is that most probably it's his. My personal opinion? Yeah, it's his. That's just the way I have to look at things."

The flight suit proved to be a pivotal piece of forensic evidence with a chain of custody arguably as convoluted as its discovery in the desert. On January 9, 1996, Deputy Assistant Secretary of Defense (POW/MIA Affairs) James W. Wold had sent a letter to the director of the FBI asking for assistance from the agency in analyzing a flight suit "recently recovered near a desert crash site." According to the letter, "The flight suit is presently being evaluated to determine if it belonged to the aviator involved in the loss incident. In particular we are interested in any evidence," the request continued, "of body fluids or foreign material remaining on the flight suit that may be used for DNA analysis and identification at a later date." The request further stated that "DNA testing is not desired at this time. The flight suit has already been examined by military crash investigation experts for heat damage and other crash-related evidence."

Special Agent Joe Errera was informed that the loss incident in question "is receiving high-level DoD, State and NSC attention." Wold wanted results back by February 6. Due to the suit's strict custody requirements, the flight suit was submitted to the FBI by Bruce Trenholm and he was the only person outside of Commander Mark D. Jensen, a Navy helicopter pilot working for Wold, authorized to receive the flight suit once the FBI concluded its testing. Trenholm delivered the flight suit in a bag to the FBI laboratory in Washington, D.C., ten days later, on January 19.

The FBI laboratory issued its preliminary findings on January 31. Technicians found brown Caucasian body hairs, which they determined were not sufficient for significant comparison purposes. A dark, reddish-brown dog hair was also found in the debris removed from the suit. Blue and brown carpet-type fibers were removed from it and preserved on glass microscope slides for future comparisons. "A preliminary chemical test for the possible presence of blood was positive on stains found on the flight suit," but strangely, the FBI laboratory refused to confirm whether the stain was actually blood. The samples tested were three dark splotches on the suit, each about an eighth of an inch in diameter. There were also a moderate number of dark brown-ish stains from the left arm cuff to the Velcro closure. Both Vel-cro closures on the sleeves were intact. Samples of stains on the crotch and armpit were also taken for possible DNA analysis. Holland, in a report not issued until March 19, 1996, states: "FBI chemical tests of the flight suit were positive for possible blood residues." But the FBI report still never definitely identifies the stains as blood—it simply hints at it. It also found a small amount of sand and whitish plant debris. The samples were placed in en-velopes to be retained along with the flight suit until it was picked up by the two individuals Wold authorized to take cus-tody. A separate fingerprint examination of the suit was con-ducted but its results had not been entered into the FBI file as of February 6, when Wold wanted the information. While it wasn't explicated in any detail, the FBI did run a serology workup and limited DNA testing, but the examiners agreed not to talk about their findings. It is known, however, that they did agree on what-ever the results showed.

All the FBI would say in the report about the suit aside from the tests was that it belonged to either "an unknown suspect, un-named victim—or a missing person." The report described the flight suit as "olive green, very worn, heavily soiled with multiple pockets with zipper closures, a few snaps, and no inside labels." Laboratory technicians observed that it was hard to tell the top of the suit from the bottom—entire portions of it were, in fact, missing. "Completely torn and shredded" were the terms the FBI analysts used to emphasize the condition of the flight suit. But there were still several Velcro areas sewn to the suit for squadron patches, as well as Velcro intact on the cuffs. From the

FBI analysis, it was learned that the laundry tag had been partly cut and only small portions were actually readable. What was left had faded badly, but investigators determined that the legible portions told them it was a U.S. Air Force summer-issue flight suit. The FBI also photographed the suit.

The FBI examination of the suit was ordered discontinued completely on February 7, and a facsimile of final results sent to Trenholm at China Lake.

On February 8, 1996, Commander Jensen—Wold's assistant—signed out the flight suit, specimens and test results from the FBI, and took the specimens to the DNA Identification Laboratory, Armed Forces Institute of Pathology (AFIP) at Rockville, Maryland, for DNA analysis. His was the last name on the log that provides the only documentation, at least with any certainty, of the flight suit's exact whereabouts. The items examined included a small Ziploc bag containing stained green material; two portions of the left arm cuff, which had moderate-size stains that looked like dried blood; a crotch cutting and an armpit cutting. The specimens were analyzed using short tandem repeat (STR) analysis, but nothing conclusive was recorded. The report was signed off by two DNA analysts, Richard E. Wilson and Jeanne M. Willard, as well as Dr. Mitchell M. Holland, branch chief of the Armed Forces DNA Identification Laboratory, and Dr. Victor Weedn, the same DNA expert who had five years earlier run tests on the one-and-a-half pounds of flesh the Iraqis claimed belonged to a pilot named "Mickel."

During the time the flight suit made the rounds of East Coast laboratories, Bruce Trenholm sent five small fragments of Scott Speicher's canopy bubble to Marlowe V. Moncur at Pilkington Aerospace on February 2. Moncur returned them five days later with a report that indicated the stretch acrylic that once made up Scott's canopy bubble had undergone "shrinkback," a process in which the thickness increases and in-plane dimensions decrease. "Surface shrinkback forces caused the fissuring and thickness increase evident in all the samples." Based on the degree of damage, Moncur estimated that the canopy surfaces reached temperatures of 400 to 500°F or higher while the core temperature remained below the minimum shrinkback temperature—230°F. In other words, the canopy was exposed to intense heat that lasted only seconds, an assessment that gave Trenholm a better idea of the flash fire's intensity and duration. The picture of Speicher's last moments in the air was starting to come together, but key elements were still missing.

Trenholm's report reviewed F/A-18 ejection history, which subsequent investigators would come to memorize. The first ejection in a U.S. Navy F/A-18 squadron aircraft occurred on July 17, 1985. Up to the time of the Speicher investigation in 1995-96, there had been fifty-eight aircrew ejections from fifty-two aircraft. Of the fifty-eight aircrew who had ejected, forty-one had done so over land and seventeen over water. Of the fifty-eight pilots, six received fatal injuries. The six fatalities were due to the fact that three pilots were outside the safe envelope for ejection; one pilot's parachute melted during descent as a result of direct contact with the aircraft fireball; one pilot was not connected to his parachute; and one aircraft experienced a strike—the pilot ejected and was subsequently wrapped in the ejection seat because of a freak asymmetrical drogue deployment. In no instance was it determined that a parachute had been packed incorrectly. Of the forty-one successful ejections over land, roughly 70 percent of the aviators received injuries (both minor and major) that were the result of the shock loads created during parachute opening and/or the descent and landing.

Based on the condition of the materials recovered and reviewed from past F/A-18 mishaps, Trenholm accepted or rejected parachute scenarios, or ruled them probable. "The parachute was a variable, not a factor, in the investigation," stated Buran. "We recognized that the parachute packed in Speicher's ejection seat was responsible for more injuries in the fleet than any other, so we gave it proper attention in the report." He is referring to the GQ 1000 Aeroconical parachute.

Trenholm rejected the possibility that the aircraft canopy had failed to separate from the aircraft. Based upon wreckage analysis, the pilot—Scott Speicher—had clearly initiated the ejection sequence. Trenholm also rejected the notion that the ejection system had failed to function. The condition of the aircraft canopy and of all the life support items recovered was not consistent with aircraft impact. When the ejection system fails to depart from the aircraft prior to impact, life support equipment packed with the seat experiences almost complete destruction either as a result of extreme heat and/or the impact with the ground or water. The scenarios of the drogue parachute system failure or main parachute failure were also rejected on the basis of the near-spotless record of the fifty-eight previous F/A-18 ejections. From what was found in the debris field in December 1995, investigators determined that Speicher's GQ 1000 Aeroconical opened during parachute descent. Although they could not say with 100 percent certainty if Scott opened his parachute or the GQ 1000 deployed on its own, "it can be safely assumed it was opened based on the pieces of life raft found." The life raft, located in the seat pan of the ejection seat, normally disintegrates during a successful ejection. Interestingly, the GQ 1000 was not recommended for over-land ejections per NATOPS Flight Manual A1-F18AC-NFM-000.

Based on Speicher's quick exit from a hot cockpit, Trenholm noted probable injuries or incapacitation from shock and the result of a hard landing. Warren Ingram of the Emergency Egress and Crashworthy Systems Division at Naval Air Warfare Center

Weapons Division at China Lake conducted a descent rate analysis based on a suspended weight of 218 pounds, which consisted of the pilot's body weight and his life support equipment, as well as the meteorological conditions of the crash site as of Scott Speicher's loss date, January 17, 1991. On the day Scott Speicher went down, a frontal system brought very low temperatures and cloud cover with bases raised to eight thousand feet, and ceilings from twenty to twenty-five thousand feet. Winds whipped from the south-southwest at six to twenty knots, increasing at higher elevations to over one hundred knots aloft. There was a patchy ground fog in west central Iraq, and blowing sand and suspended dust reduced visibility to thirty-two hundred meters during the afternoon along the Saudi Arabia–Iraq border. Ingram's analysis demonstrated a minimum total velocity rate of descent of twenty-six feet per second and a maximum of thirty-three feet per second. In other words, the parachute might have dropped Speicher to the desert floor below too fast—a possibility that no one could know for certain. The calculated rate of descent for Scott in the parachute may have been sufficient to inflict injury upon landing. Injuries could have been anything from a bloody nose to compound fractures, but there was no indication looking at the flight suit that any of this was the case for Scott Speicher.

Shortly before Bruce Trenholm issued his final report on the flight suit, Tony Albano got a message during a training flight that Trenholm was trying to track him down. By that time, Albano was executive officer of VT-19 in Meridian, Mississippi. Albano and Commander Mark Fox, another squadron mate from VFA-81, who was actually commanding officer of the *Sunliners* when Bruce's call came, agreed to meet Trenholm at Florida's Cecil Field. Prior to the interview it was requested that squadron patches and any photos taken of Scott Speicher in the flight suit be submitted as evidence for the investigation. Four photographs were provided.

In Jacksonville, Trenholm explained that he had been on the International Red Cross mission to the Iraqi desert. While there, Bruce told Albano and Fox, the team found a flight suit, and he wanted Albano to look at it and see if he thought it was Speicher's. He told them about the Bedouin boy who the Iraqis said had found the suit, and that most of the Red Cross team members figured the Iraqis had planted it. He told them that the legs were slit in the back, in a manner that an emergency worker or doctor might cut a suit off someone who was facedown. He told them he'd estimated Speicher's height at 71 inches, his weight at 168 pounds and his flight suit size at 38 Long. Then Trenholm reached into a brown paper grocery bag and pulled the suit out.

The last time Albano figured he had seen that suit, Speicher was wearing it, and they were slapping hands, wishing each other luck on their first wartime mission. Now here it was. "He just pulled it out of the bag like it was nothing," remembered Albano later. "We'd been talking and then there was the flight suit." Albano saw that the suit was torn and tattered. Pockets were missing and the patches were gone. He knew that pilots remove those patches to "sanitize" their flight suits before flying into enemy territory. Albano also noticed something else: scorch marks. "The material of the flight suit won't scorch [flight suits have a chemical retardant that prevents them from burning; the material flakes away]. But there were scorch marks on the shoulders—they were too symmetrical for normal burn marks." He looked at Trenholm. "I'm positive that's his flight suit," Albano said. Then Fox hopped into his car, went to his house and grabbed his old flight suit. A circular patch of Velcro fastener on Speicher's right sleeve matched Fox's "*Sunliners*-Anytime-Anyplace" patch. An oval of

Velcro on the left sleeve lined up perfectly with a patch their squadron gave out to those that earned it that read, "F/A-18 Hornet 1000 Hours." Trenholm then told Speicher's squadronmates about the condition of the jet, and the canopy and the parachute straps and the life support gear. Five years after that awful night, there seemed to be even fewer answers. And the same old question. "Oh God," Albano thought. "Well, what happened to him?"

While Albano explained that all the identification patches on their flight suits were removed prior to combat operations, including the name tag over the left breast pocket, Trenholm maintained that the latter was on the suit and that Spock Anderson had given his pilots permission to wear them. "That is not true," maintains Albano, now a captain and commodore of Training Wing Two. "Nobody wore any squadron identification, including the name tag. That's fabrication. There were standing orders to every aviator in the fleet to take all that off their flight suits on a mission."

In the end, the flight suit was determined to be the one "most likely worn by VFA-81 naval pilot LCDR M. S. Speicher." But there was no way to tell whether Scott wore the name tag that night. Odds are that he didn't.

Bob Stumpf remembers getting a telephone call shortly after the ICRC team returned from the Iraqi desert and analysis of their findings was well under way. The caller said, "Hey, I saw his flight suit. They found a canopy." Stumpf thought, "Holy shit." Then he learned that there had been an option to go in and examine the wreckage covertly and apparently it hadn't happened. "That just blew me away. We have a contract with our soldiers—it's black and white—'You go down, we're going to come get you. It doesn't matter if it takes a while. We're not going to forget you.'" But that's not what Stumpf saw happen with Scott Speicher. The evidence mounted in just the opposite direction. "Basically, what we said was, 'Screw you, Speicher. We're not going to honor our commitment to you. You gave your life for your country and we don't care.'" The canopy was not with the wreckage, which indicated an ejection. The flight suit was in pretty fair shape—not soaked in blood—so all the clues pointed to Scott Speicher walking away from the ejection. What happened to Speicher, in Stumpf's opinion, "should be unheard of. You can't do this job without some high level of patriotism and trust. It has to go both ways. The Pentagon . . . just lost its teeth. Where is the spirit, the military spirit and tradition we've had for two hundred years? Where is it?"

Trenholm coordinated with other crash investigators about the evidence, too. Physical evidence gathered at the crash site, analyzed and laid up against other bits and pieces of pilot gear, started to sculpt the picture of what happened to Scott Speicher. They had located several pieces of Speicher's anti-G suit. The anti-G suit is made of a fire-resistant aramid cloth outer shell that houses a polyurethane bladder. The outer shell has waist and leg slide fasteners, adjustment lacing areas with lacing covers, and leg pockets with slide fasteners. The bladder system is constructed of polyurethane-coated nylon cloth and covers the pilot's abdomen, thighs and calves. The life support material recovered in the vicinity of Speicher's Hornet wreckage in the Iraqi desert was consistent with portions of a CSU-15/P anti-G suit issued to Navy aircrew. The six fragments found by investigators included the hose, a waist slide fastener, adjacent material to the slide fastener and two pieces of spacer/reinforcement material roughly thirteen inches and three inches in length. Although the upper sleeves of Scott's flight suit showed signs of heat exposure, there was no evidence that the anti-G suit material had been exposed to the flash fire that preceded Speicher's ejection from his stricken aircraft.

Perhaps one of the most encouraging finds among the debris

collected by the ICRC team was an SJU-5A ejection seat upper leg garter. The upper leg garter, connected to the pilot when seated in the aircraft and worn approximately three inches above the knee, is unique to the F/A-18 aircraft. Its purpose is to ensure that the pilot's legs will be pulled back upon ejection, thus enhancing the ejection seat's stability and preventing the pilot's legs from flailing during ejection. The garter was found in two pieces with about three inches missing. Like the anti-G fragments, the garter had not been exposed to heat.

By February 26, Bruce Trenholm was ready to issue his final report on Speicher's aviation life support system equipment recovered from the crash site. Trenholm's opening statement was a double-edged sword. His area of expertise, by his own admission, is parachutes. Bruce Trenholm is a parachute-mishap investigator and mishap-investigation support team leader with some twenty years of experience. He'd investigated some 350 aircraft mishaps, but none that had been as protracted as Speicher's. From the pieces of the life support equipment found in the search, Trenholm concluded, "Speicher ejected from the aircraft." Even though the F/A-18 Hornet has an 85 to 90 percent survival rate on ejection, and no significant amount of blood or body tissue was on any of the equipment recovered, Trenholm still insisted that "the pilot may have been injured/incapacitated (perhaps fatally) due to trauma associated with ejection, parachute deployment, or ground impact." Though the conclusion didn't seem to marry up to the facts, there were still unknowns about Speicher's condition after he had ejected.

Before the ICRC mission findings and accompanying forensic documentation were submitted up the Pentagon chain of command, Secretary of Defense William Perry was informed by J. Alan Liotta's office that material recovered from the crash site was insufficient to determine Scott Speicher's fate. The date was

February 16, 1996—almost two weeks before most of the investigators finished their analyses.

"When it came to Speicher, Liotta was simply not up to the task of conducting a challenging and competent investigation against the Iraqis about the topic of a potentially live and covertly held American," said Commander Chip Beck, the former CIA station chief and naval intelligence officer. Beck was working with DPMO at the time Liotta went to the field to oversee the crash-site investigation in December 1995. "I had known Liotta for some years previously when he was a low-level and unexceptional analyst at CIA." Liotta did not actually go into Iraq, as some news agencies reported by omission of details, but remained on the Jordanian side of the border while the ICRC-led team went across with Iraq's permission. According to Beck, Liotta sat on the Jordanian-Iraqi border long enough for the battery on his Land Rover to die. When Liotta came back to DPMO's offices in Crystal City, he gathered the DPMO staff in a small conference room to go over the team's "findings." "After telling us of the ejection seat and lack of forensic evidence, Liotta amazingly, to me, concluded to the staff that: 'We found no evidence that Lieutenant Commander Speicher survived the crash.'" The silence from those gathered was both deafening and telling to Beck. After a few seconds, Beck was the only one in the room to speak up and challenge Liotta, saying out loud: "Excuse me, Alan, but you didn't find any evidence that he died, either. You basically didn't find any evidence to support a conclusion of any type, so the investigation has to continue." Beck's comments were met with surprise and a glare from Liotta, but no rebuttal or answer.

It soon became readily apparent that the Iraqis had some agenda of their own to spin in the press. After all, they had sent two of their own crash investigators to work beside the predominantly American ICRC team. More significant than that, Saddam had dispatched the head of the Iraqi Air Force to the site. General Khaldoun Khattab had his men set up a large, heated tent across the steppe from the makeshift ICRC camp. Behind the general's tent were two Russian-made Mi-8 Hip helicopters, which the Iraqis used for observation and for the general's transportation during the ICRC visit. Bruce Trenholm remembers being invited to Khattab's tent for coffee: "[We were] eating dates or something, he leans over, grabs my arm and says, 'The woolufs eat him.' " Not understanding, Trenholm asked Khattab to repeat what he said. "He was trying to say, 'The wolves ate him.' This was all too contrived and I almost didn't understand what he said at all." Later, as media began to pay closer attention to emerging details of Speicher's story, Khattab repeated his pronouncement to them about the wolves. But even then, Chip Beck knew the Iraqis were lying.

"I was probably the only DPMO officer who had spent three or more years in North African and Middle East deserts and had seen what desert wolves do to bodies," noted Beck. "First of all, they are more like big, mangy coyotes than the timber wolves we know, and they don't consume the bodies and bones in a way that would totally obliterate a pilot's remains." Beck had seen the bodies of fishermen washed up on the coastline of the Sahara being "played with" by these desert wolves. "They can be pretty effective at spreading the remains around an area, but they are sloppy eaters and leave enough behind for a recovery team to find a fairly substantial amount of remains—certainly enough for DNA and forensics identification. The wolves would not likely eat the skull or the teeth, for instance, even if they broke [the skull] open for the soft tissue." In fact, Beck found whole skulls in the desert in areas where he personally witnessed wolves eating bodies. "I approached these 'wolves' unarmed to see what they were up to with the fishermen's bodies, and they ran off. I never felt threatened at all."

The Iraqis lied blatantly, assuming Americans wouldn't have a clue about the wolves' habits. Perhaps the Iraqi general was trying to mix fact and fable. The Koran, the primary religious text of the Islamic faith, recounts the story of Joseph, whose brothers sought to kill him to gain their father's favor. Similar in many aspects to the story of Joseph in the Bible, in the Koran version, Joseph's brothers put him down a well, but tell their father a wolf ate him. To quote from the Koran, "They showed him the shirt with blood on it. [Their father] said: 'It is not so, you have made up the story.'" Joseph was found by a caravan, which happened to pass and use the well. "'What luck,' said the man [in the caravan]; 'here is a boy;' and they hid him as an item of merchandise; but what they did was known to God. And they sold him as worthless for a few paltry dirham." The Iraqis were lying, but the deception begged the question: Why were they lying? It was almost as if the story of Joseph mirrored what had happened to Speicher—where Joseph's father rejected the news of his son's death, so did the American military reject the remains the Iraqis had given them as belonging to their own lost son. Like Joseph, Speicher was also picked up by a caravan (in this case, of nomadic Bedouins), who were looking to sell him back into freedom before Saddam's soldiers intervened.

"I think we can conclude," Beck remarked, "that they were hiding their knowledge of what really happened to Speicher." But they spun it neatly in the form of a proverbial lie, partly for an incredulous American public, and perhaps also as a frightening tale of wolves devouring dead bodies that would send a message to their own people to avoid the area around the crash site.

The Iraqi-spun story might have also been a prescient metaphor for the deception and the lone-wolf agendas that seemed to surround the ICRC-sponsored crash investigation. Buran noted that he was there to find his evidence as everyone else on the mission fanned out across the desert in search of his own. Everyone had an agenda. The biggest one by far was Liotta's: to find the body under the plane. "What a way to go—what a way to send off a mission that could have gathered so much more," remarked a chagrined Dussault.

DPMO and the Joint Chiefs of Staff had all the information they required to keep Scott's case open. But their views and objectives—conflicted, in some instances—got in the way, leading to the absolute crime of leaving Scott Speicher behind not just once, but also when several additional opportunities presented themselves as the years ticked by. Chip Beck noted that he and Norman Kass, chairman of the Joint Commission Support Directorate (JCSD), spent eight hours of closed-door testimony before Congressman Bob Dornan's subcommittee on prisoners of war in October 1996. DPMO has traditionally demonstrated lackluster results investigating the fate of unrepatriated POWs from all wars. "We believed that in the case of Vietnam, in particular, and to a certain extent the Cold War, Korea, World War II and World War I as well, this failure was intentionally contrived by longtime analysts, many of whom had been in DPMO (and its previous iterations) for twenty-five to thirty years, to cover up the inaccuracy of their initial statements on live Americans," Beck observed.

Not only was Liotta not up to the task on the Speicher case, but nothing in his background prepared or qualified him to conduct or oversee such an investigation. He had never served in the military, nor had he worked in the clandestine service of the CIA. Liotta was an overt analyst. He was not an investigator and his research instincts were not honed by original research or firsthand collection experience. Beck, who had been a case officer, chief of station, a Navy Criminal Investigations Division and Naval Criminal Investigative Service agent during his career, had worked with Kass as a special POW investigator from November 1995 through October 1996. But Liotta was so opposed to Kass's special initiative aimed at fleshing out the truth concerning unrepatriated POWs held for decades by Soviet and Soviet Bloc intelligence services "that he actually became part of an internal DPMO effort to sabotage and end our investigations along this path," Beck said. DPMO's actions, Liotta's in particular, cast a pall over the Speicher case before it could gain momentum. "[Speicher] may just be the last—or most recent—in a long line of ghosts who did not die when we wanted them to be dead," said Beck.

The mire surrounding the Speicher debacle deepened with the purported "loss" of the flight suit, one of the most important pieces of key forensic evidence in the case. When Bob Dussault requested the suit in the spring of 1996 for independent testing, Liotta's office told him it was lost. Liotta blamed the FBI for "misplacing the suit," but all Dussault knew at that time was that it could not be located. Liotta had fudged the truth. Commander Mark Jensen, working for James W. Wold—Liotta's boss—had signed the flight suit out of FBI custody on February 8, 1996. After taking the suit and samples up to the Armed Forces Institute of Pathology in Maryland, Jensen brought it back to Wold's offices. "At some point," recalls Bruce Trenholm, "the flight suit gets sent back to me. I had it for over a year. But around Christmas 1997, I decided to send it by mail to the CILHI. They say they never got it." Shortly after the holiday, Trenholm got a telephone call from somebody in the Pentagon who wanted the flight suit again, "but I had to tell him: 'Sorry, buddy, no can do.'" Trenholm explained that he'd tucked the flight suit, specimens and test results into a mailing envelope and dropped them in the mailbox during the Christmas rush. Nobody had told him, he said, that there was anything particularly important to the flight suit now that Speicher had been reaffirmed KIA/BNR.

Admittedly, the status change that retroactively placed Speicher in an MIA status up to September 30, 1996, only to switch back the next day to KIA/BNR, confused those who'd investigated Speicher's case. "He's dead, so what's the big deal about the flight suit?" Trenholm thought. But the whole chain of custody nightmare surrounding the flight suit also smacked of people who couldn't get their story straight. "Somebody has it and they consider it terribly sensitive to mention who—either because it reveals too much that they do not want others to know, or because they mishandled it and did not do the proper testing of all the evidence available. That would make them look dumb if that came out," observed Dussault.

Either way, the flight suit that held important clues in the Speicher case was lost at the end of 1997. With it went the specimens, DNA analysis, fingerprinting results and forensic reports that could have played a crucial role in the investigation had they not gone missing. Nearly two years later, in July 1999, DPMO told the Senate Select Committee on Intelligence that the flight suit and some other equipment appeared to have been literally cut away from whoever was wearing them, and that their condition suggested the wearer was severely injured or dead at the time. Another report stated the flight suit was in tatters, with portions of the legs missing altogether. Other reports about the flight suit and ALSS equipment suggest just the opposite. Without the flight suit as physical evidence—and with Pentagon agencies now denying access to flight suit photographs, claiming that they couldn't find them—which was it?

CHAPTER 9

The Driver

Despite Secretary of Defense Perry's declaration that nothing found at the crash site had helped the Pentagon determine the fate of Scott Speicher, on October 2, 1996, Navy Secretary John H. Dalton modified Scott's presumptive finding of death from May 23, 1991, to September 30, 1996. Dalton's pronouncement made Scott Speicher MIA retroactive to the day after his original placement in a KIA/BNR status. Speicher was also promoted to full commander on the basis of time in grade during the period in which he was now declared MIA.

But Dalton did not leave Speicher in an MIA status. The Navy later reached an agreement with Joanne Speicher Harris to reaffirm Scott's KIA/BNR status as of October 1, 1996. She was given his unpaid pay and allowances, totaling $330,858, on top of the $150,000 in Servicemembers' Group Life Insurance and the $50,000 special death gratuity she'd received in 1991 when Scott was first declared KIA/BNR. But Joanne Harris was technically no longer Scott's primary next of kin. Primary next of kin reverted to Wallace L. Speicher, Scott's father, after Joanne's marriage to Buddy Harris on July 4, 1992. Scott's mother passed away on October 14, 1991, never comprehending her son's death. Alzheimer's had also severely debilitated Wallace Speicher as well, and he died June 15, 1995. If he had still been living, Scott's unpaid pay and allowances would've gone to Wallace. Scott's children are ineligible as primary next of kin until the age of eighteen, so the next family member in line would be Sheryl Speicher Long, Scott's younger sister and only sibling. She was also adopted as an infant by Wallace and Barbara Speicher. But Sheryl had not been kept in the loop. Ask her about Scott's loss and the pain is still on the surface. She remembers their childhood. He liked to play practical jokes, "especially on me," she said. "When we walked to school, he'd make me—little sister— tag along a dozen paces behind." Later, he'd fly over her house on Jacksonville Beach. "Didn't you see me fly over your house today?" he'd ask her. "C'mon. Didn't you see it?!" He'd waggled his wings. She'd always say no. There were so many airplanes, she'd tell him, flying overhead all day. After Scott was gone, Joanne gradually cut ties with the Speicher family. There's no contact today, according to Scott's sister.

The story might have ended there, with the reaffirmation of Scott's KIA/BNR status, but just when it seemed there was nothing more to investigate, when there was no more hope that Speicher might have survived, new information began trickling out of Iraq.

Buddy Harris, the ex–Navy pilot who had married Speicher's wife, was assigned a Navy officer to keep him up to date. It seemed like every week or two, Harris would get a call about a rumored Speicher sighting. Some guy in Canada had been in an Iraqi camp and had been given a Colt .45 pistol that was taken from an American pilot. No, Harris told investigators, Speicher didn't have such a gun, but they checked it out anyway. Intelligence agents traced the gun and found out that Harris was right.

They tracked another pistol, a .45-caliber Beretta automatic that supposedly belonged to Speicher, all the way back to the British experience in Iraq after World War I.

In another story, an Iraqi doctor was said to have performed a physical on Speicher. Another man said he had seen Speicher's name on a file when he was moving records to hide them from UN weapons inspectors. Many of these leads were dead ends. Some couldn't be verified, others could—only time would tell. All of them tormented Buddy and Joanne. One day Scott was dead, the next day he had been seen alive. Meghan and Michael, Scott and Joanne's children, were now nine and seven. Buddy and Joanne had since had two children of their own. Whenever they didn't know what to do, they asked themselves a question: "If Scott walked in today, could we lay it on the line, say 'This is what we did' and feel comfortable telling him we had done everything possible to keep our family normal and get him out?"

In the meantime, Senator Robert Smith began to wonder about what he had been told after the Red Cross team returned. He had been assured by the Defense Department's POW/MIA office that there was no evidence to support the idea that Speicher had survived his F/A-18 crash. But Smith had sources in the Pentagon telling him otherwise: There's more to it than you're being told, they said. Smith wanted to believe the officials at DPMO, but the more he thought about it the less certain he became: At first, Speicher's Hornet was blown to bits in the sky, then they found it nearly intact in the desert. At first, they said they sent a search team in for Speicher, then it turned out they didn't. The inconsistencies seemed too numerous.

Admiral Mike Boorda, now chief of naval operations, was given an overview of the Speicher case on May 14, 1996 after his staff determined that Scott had survived the ejection and was on the ground. "We felt very confident," said Buddy Harris, "that he was alive on the ground. We went to Boorda and told him." Harris has never forgotten Boorda's reaction when people in Harris's office told the admiral what they knew about the case from the developments that arose out of the ICRC mission. Harris wasn't permitted in the briefing, but senior staff told him that Boorda was completely taken aback. "They said his jaw just hit the desk. He couldn't believe it." Boorda just listened to the evidence, thanked the staffers and asked a couple of minor questions: You sure? You positive? They explained everything Boorda asked about. "His staff knew he was going through tough times, so they didn't want to push it," Harris said. The next day, Boorda wrote two suicide notes. On May 16, 1996, he committed suicide in the sideyard of his navy yard residence. "I think [the briefing] was one of the nails in his coffin," said Harris. "Boorda had so much on his plate at that time." Admiral Boorda was embroiled in issues ranging from females going into combat and flying combat aircraft, to making hard political decisions that were, in Harris's opinion, not good for the Navy. "I think when they went in and told him about Scott, it was the final blow."

Then, on a day in early December 1997, Senator Rod Grams's staff read a *New York Times* story that floored them. The *Times*'s Tim Weiner used Pentagon documents and military sources to construct a time line of the handling of the investigation. Among other things, the story reported that after the Qataris found the aircraft, the Pentagon tasked a spy satellite over the crash site. The satellite images "detected a man-made symbol in the area of the ejection seat," a ground-to-air signal, the kind a pilot is trained to put down to attract collection platforms' attention. DPMO claimed that the symbol did not match Speicher's assigned symbol, but that turned out to be a gross misrepresentation of the facts. Grams's staff called him in Africa, and then they contacted Senator Smith. Armed with misleading correspondence catching DPMO in an outrageous lie, Grams issued a press release stating that Congress had been purposefully misled.

Days later, Senator Smith fired off two letters. The first, dated December 10, he addressed to the assistant secretary of defense for international security affairs, Franklin Kramer, whose office had shepherded the ICRC crash-site mission. Smith said he was extremely concerned about the article, especially considering what he had been told about Speicher's chances of survival. He asked for a meeting with Pentagon and POW/MIA officials, as he stated in his letter: "Especially in view of a briefing I received on this case by Alan Liotta from DPMO on January 17, 1996, where I was told that there were no indications that Commander Speicher might have survived his loss incident." Smith further instructed Kramer, Fred Smith and Alan Liotta to meet with him on Monday, December 15, to discuss both the intelligence and the policy DoD had pursued regarding the case. "I would also request," he wrote Kramer, "that you bring the documentation referenced in the *New York Times* article, including the document referencing the detection of 'a man-made symbol in the area of the ejection seat.' " The second letter went to Senator Richard C. Shelby, a Republican from Alabama and chairman of the Senate Select Committee on Intelligence. It was cosigned by his colleague Rod Grams. Senators Smith and Grams asked that the committee open an inquiry into all intelligence information that had been gathered on the Speicher case. "The enclosed article published in *The New York Times* this past Sunday raises serious questions as to whether both of us may have been misled by the Administration," they wrote.

Shelby took it from there. He contacted CIA Director George J. Tenet and asked for computer files, documents, memos, raw reports, operational messages—anything and everything Tenet had on Speicher. He also asked that Tenet explain which intelligence agency considered itself responsible for the investigation.

Smith then called Grams to join the meeting with Kramer, Fred Smith and Liotta on December 15. A few days earlier, Senator Grams had issued a statement on the Speicher case that reverberated throughout the Pentagon and the Clinton administration. "An American pilot is missing. I have directly questioned the administration about his fate, and frankly, their answers don't square with the facts. In light of this apparent misinformation, it is the Senate's obligation to step in and discover the truth."

Senator Smith entered the meeting angry. He wanted answers; what he got was appeasement. Fred Smith sent an e-mail to Franklin Kramer and copied it to Alan Liotta at 5:57 P.M. on December 15, the afternoon of the same day he'd met with Senators Smith and Grams. He wrote, "It started out rather testy, but after responding to several of [Senator] Smith's questions, he became more relaxed and we had a civil discussion. Grams was concerned about a letter to him from Jim Wold (then deputy assistant secretary of defense for POW/MIA Affairs) earlier this year. Grams claims the letter was misleading."

Fred Smith said he looked at the letter Grams received from Wold and agreed. The letter, dated March 3, 1997, and copied to the Navy Casualty Office and the secretary of the Navy, documents information that the senators found misleading. Wold writes: "Mr. Daly [Richard Daly, one of Grams's Minnesota constituents] first asks if there is any evidence that Commander Speicher survived his crash. At present, we do not have any evidence that he survived his loss incident. Our specialists have investigated the probable crash site and Commander Speicher's F/A-18. Evidence from this site is undergoing analysis and will be released when the investigation is complete and Commander Speicher's family has been fully informed."

But this "investigation"—at least the part concerned with the ICRC mission in 1995—had already been concluded. Secretary of Defense William Perry had been informed on February 16, 1996, that material recovered from the crash site was "insufficient to determine the fate of the pilot." By that time, of course, the flight suit had been relegated to a paper sack in Bruce Trenholm's office and no further tests had been run on it—there was no need. After all, Scott Speicher had been reaffirmed KIA/BNR.

Yet when Richard Daly expressed interest in evidence of Speicher's man-made symbol on the ground, he was told through Senator Grams that the investigation was not complete. "Mr. Daly's final question is whether any pilot distress symbols were found near the crash site," wrote Wold to Grams. "Again, we do not possess any evidence that evasion codes assigned to Commander Speicher were located near his crash site." In a follow-up letter on April 21, Wold wrote: "Our investigation of this incident has found no symbols that correlate to civilian or military distress symbols or evasion codes." The conflicting statements piled on each other, deepening the confusion.

Much of the hour-and-a-half December 15 meeting centered on the report of a man-made symbol in the vicinity of Speicher's crash site and the fact that the Navy had declared Speicher KIA/BNR. "On the latter," wrote Fred Smith, "I assured [Senator] Smith that the Navy's designation of the case has no bearing on how we prosecute it. It is an active case." Senator Smith seemed reasonably satisfied. But the senator wasn't the trouble as far as Fred Smith was concerned. Senator Smith was "handled" in the meeting. "The problem," Frederick Smith wrote to Kramer, "is his staffers. These guys will probably be spurred on by what they heard today and continue to press the issue in some form, possibly a hearing at a later date." Though Senator Smith hardly realized it, he'd been outmaneuvered by a glib-tongued master. Frederick Smith had quelled the senator's anger with answers, whether they were the right answers or not, and then, when he knew the tenor of the meeting was on solid footing, he offered to meet Senator Smith for another breakfast. "[Senator] Smith was pleased to hear that," he wrote. Then, he added this: "Footnote: The first and last thing [Senator] Smith wanted to talk to me about was baseball. He still remembers the fact that you [referring to Kramer] and I are Dodger fans."

In reply, Alan Liotta e-mailed Fred Smith the following morning, at 11:01 A.M. to tell him that the previous night CILHI had sent him a map of where the ICRC team searched, and the site of the symbol, Liotta told Smith, "was well within this area." "In fact," Liotta continues, "NIMA [the National Imagery and Mapping Agency] says the symbol is about nine hundred meters (less than a kilometer, or a click) away, but the team searched five clicks out. I still think you should call Smith and Grams, but insist on talking to the members, not staffers." Recall that the ICRC team was not permitted by the Iraqis into the area where the symbol was sculpted in sand. And NIMA had not evaluated the film and certified it—JSSA had done that.

Liotta also continued to debate the letter that Wold sent Grams and that Grams found misleading: "By the by, I still disagree with you that our letter was misleading. If you look at the original constituent letter, how that was sent to us by Grams, and the facts surrounding the case (including the classification of the imagery and the analysis), our response was factual and accurate. Could it have been more robust? Possibly, although we then would have been treading dangerously close to disclosing classified information. Should we have called to brief Grams? In hindsight, yes. But given the way the request was received from his office, we had no indication of any particular interest in this case. We'll be more sensitive next time."

Liotta seems to have been hiding behind classification to prevent two U.S. senators from finding out that his office had skewed the findings of the original ICRC investigation. JSSA had reviewed Speicher's ground-to-air signal and certified it as his, yet Liotta swept that information, like so many other key pieces of evidence, under the rug. The significance of this emerged much later, when Tim Connolly was informed of the JSSA evaluation of the ground-to-air signal, and of its exclusion from the discussions about the decision to go with either the covert or diplomatic route in 1994. "Well, that's a one-eighty out from what was said then. Knowing about the man-made symbol would've made a huge difference—the diplomatic option would've been taken totally off the table." The man-made symbol specifically indicated a pilot in distress on the ground or in the general vicinity.

Almost four years after it was brought to DPMO's attention, Alan Liotta requested an analysis of the Kuwaiti colonel's An Nasiriyah sighting of Speicher first reported by Tim Connolly. In an e-mail from David M. Rosenau to Gregory K. S. Man, and copied to Gary C. Sydow, Lieutenant Commander Kevin J. Wilson, James R. Caswell, Robert T. Pasquerella, Melvin E. Richmond, Jr., and Jo Anne Travis (all staffers within different offices in the Department of Defense), dated February 18, 1998, Liotta's staff issued a one-page evaluation of the event. First, the evaluation noted that the information provided by the Kuwaiti colonel did not marry up to any known American loss incident. The only possible correlation they found linked the sighting to a British GR-1 Tornado crew shot down on January 19, 1991. Flight Lieutenants Robert Stewart and David Waddington were injured during ejection from their aircraft. Both were treated for their injuries then transported to Baghdad. But even though the DPMO analysts tried hard to link the British aircrew to the Kuwaiti's sighting, it didn't dovetail perfectly. Colonel al-Jairan had stressed he'd seen an American pilot roughly fifteen days before he reported the sighting on March 4, 1991. Because Liotta's office concluded the Kuwaiti couldn't have possibly seen an American, DPMO stated, "It is possible the Kuwaiti is reporting hearsay information as firsthand."

Because An Nasiriyah is some 230 miles southeast of Lieutenant Commander Speicher's crash site, and based on known Iraqi POW handling procedures, DPMO concluded Speicher would not have been taken to An Nasiriyah. "All Allied pilots shot down and captured west of Baghdad," the evaluation reported, "were transported along the East-West Highway directly to Baghdad where they remained until release." The assumption was made that Speicher was caught the day he was shot down, which was decidedly not the case. But the assumption was also made that Speicher was the only U.S. pilot who might have been hospitalized as the result of ejection injuries. Might it have been Lieutenant Commander Barry Cooke or Lieutenant Robert J. Dwyer, both off the USS *Theodore Roosevelt*? Could it have been another American pilot who survived for a period of time and later died in Iraqi custody, his remains returned? No one ever put photographs in front of Colonel al-Jairan for identification as Connolly and Pritchard requested. Had they done so, the outcome might have shed light on any number of POW cases. If DoD POW/MIA Affairs and its successor agency, DPMO, had dogged Connolly's report four years before, could they have connected with the Kuwaiti colonel and asked for his assistance in identifying the pilot he saw? Perhaps. But the point is that DPMO, rather than investigate a possible lead on a case that was under its mandate, instead attempted to debunk a credible report, to cover its missteps. The report's conclusion was a baseless one: "The Kuwaiti intelligence officer did not see LCDR Speicher." Yet how would they know it? No one has attempted to find the colonel since he was repatriated in 1991 to Kuwait City. He was not given the chance to view any pilots' photographs and he was asked no names. How could it be concluded so easily that he had not seen an American pilot given his genuine attempt to help his U.S. liberators? Facts seemed to be lost in the supposition and innuendo of Liotta's report.

In March 1998, Senator Shelby wrote to CIA Director George Tenet again. He wanted a report that consolidated everything they knew about Speicher from the Defense Intelligence Agency, the National Imagery and Mapping Agency, the Office of Naval Intelligence, the National Security Agency and the Joint Chiefs of Staff.

On March 10, Kevin Wilson wrote an e-mail to Bob Pasquerella (a Pentagon staffer) that had originally been classified "SECRET." In reviewing the material to be handed over for Shelby's report, Wilson said, "Bob, Mr. Liotta liked the overall package. Couple of things. He wants to be more specific on areas of interest. Please look at the three items and try to be more definitive on the area." The first item stated, "LCDR Speicher is suspected of being shot down by an air-to-air missile fired from an Iraqi aircraft or by a surface-to-air missile fired from an unidentified antiaircraft battery. Provide any records that relate to the shootdown of Coalition aircraft on 17 January 1991." The second item was redacted.

The third was a statement of Iraqi forces on scene after Scott Speicher was on the ground. "Air Defense and/or Republican Guard units were most likely active in the area of LCDR Speicher's loss location. Identify and make available for interview any individuals from Air Defense or Republican Guard units in the area at the time of the loss that may have information pertaining to this incident or LCDR Speicher's fate." What is maddening is that it had long been established that Scott Speicher was not shot down by a surface-to-air missile. Buddy Harris's call to the CIA years before had cleared that up. Then-Captain Michael "Carlos" Johnson, SPEAR director, had corroborated an air-to-air missile scenario and eliminated the SAM possibility after SPEAR scrubbed surveilling aircraft tapes and aircrew debriefs. No one, including the A-6E Intruder crews wearing night vision goggles, saw a SAM fired in the vicinity of Speicher's Hornet. The ICRC crew that examined the actual wreckage concluded that the damage was caused by an air-to-air strike.

Even so, two months later, Pasquerella sent an e-mail back to Kevin Wilson, copied to Greg Man and Gary Sydow. Originally classified "SECRET," and dated May 11, 1998, Pasquerella's e-mail read, "Sir, the below information will assist in the effort to identify the cause of LCDR Speicher's shootdown. I recommend reviewing the imagery within a 25NM [nautical mile] radius of the crash site located in 1994 at 330114N/0421528E (UTM 38S KB 43810 56910)." Again, Pasquerella made the statement that "the most likely scenario is that LCDR Speicher was shot down by an AAM launched from a MiG-25 Foxbat; however, it is also possible he was shot down by an SA-6 SAM fired from an unidentified location."

Despite all that had been vetted in previous investigations years before, Pasquerella and the rest of the Pentagon staff to whom the various e-mails were copied still would not make clear what empirical evidence had shown time and again. While it had long been a known fact that a SAM did not shoot down Commander Speicher, DPMO analysts and their DIA counterparts could not get off the notion that a SAM had something to do with Scott's incident. The time wasted rehashing old information was reaching the point of being ludicrous.

Luckily, after what he'd read in *The New York Times*, Senator Robert Smith wasn't about to let the issue drop. There hadn't been anything in the *Times* piece he hadn't seen before, but the mainstream media had begun to pick up on the story. The family had been misled from day one, and Smith had been given the runaround by elements of the Pentagon and federal agencies. "Members of the intelligence community had been misled and it's all pretty outrageous," declared Smith recently. "The fact of the matter is there's a great amount of evidence and testimony that Mr. Speicher could have survived the impact, may well have survived it and been taken to prison." From all the information he had seen, Smith now knew for sure that Scott Speicher had not been killed when his Hornet impacted the desert floor. But there was even more information to come.

In early 1999 a man defected from Iraq with a story that was hard to believe. The defector, who has come to be known as "the Driver," was asked by Iraqi officials to go from Baghdad to another town in Iraq and pick up an American prisoner. The Driver told U.S. investigators that he had indeed picked up a pilot, who was still wearing a flight suit. The pilot had no significant injuries, other than a small amount of dried blood on his flight suit. The Driver's report of Speicher in his flight suit cast doubt on the origins of the tattered flight suit recovered by the ICRC in December 1995. The Driver took the pilot to Baghdad and turned him over to military authorities. U.S. intelligence agents asked the Driver to look at a lineup of mug shots. He quickly pointed out Speicher as the pilot he shuttled to Baghdad. Investigators then asked about the chronology of this story   was Speicher picked up four to six weeks after his shootdown from some townspeople who'd roughed him up? The Driver told them no—he'd picked up Scott Speicher much later—years later, in fact.

The DPMO was in on everything related to the Driver's interrogations thanks to a native linguist working for DIA. Despite the importance of the Driver's statements, including the fact that he pointed investigators to the exact location Scott was taken to—and why—DPMO continued to issue statements to the effect that Scott was dead.

For weeks, investigators kept grilling the Driver. He passed one lie detector test, then another, then yet another. They interrogated him throughout 1999 and into 2000, trying to be certain he was telling the truth. Maybe he's looking for money, a reward? They gave him a greed test: There's another missing American, they told him, whose family is offering a big reward—$10,000 in American dollars—if the pilot he saw was short in stature with blond hair. Are you sure he wasn't real short with blond hair? Maybe you saw a man who looked a little different? But the defector stuck to his story. Intelligence agents determined that the man was probably telling the truth.

"A lot of things like that went on early because anything that was found of a positive nature was kind of shoved aside, disbelieved, because 'he's dead,'" said Buddy Harris. He described the mentality of investigators: "We just want information on the fact that he's dead." Finally, around 1997 or 1998, that attitude began to change somewhat because of the volumes of information coming in that there was a reasonable chance Scott Speicher had survived. "All of it started stacking up," Harris continued, "started moving in a different direction. We'd get information from various sources. I had some friends that I had met from the Pentagon and who were still working on the case." Harris said that they'd call him and say, "You need to look up this, you need to look up that—something's going on here." Harris would call the Pentagon and press for the information, and usually ended up going to Washington for a meeting. The first question out of the mouths of those sitting across the desk from him would inevitably be "Well, how do you know this?" He'd reply, "It's what I heard, so what's going on?"

Harris met Navy Secretary Richard B. Danzig as often as he could. "He took it seriously and he wanted to get it solved." Danzig, according to Harris, had politicians to deal with in the Clinton administration who didn't want to touch the case. "They didn't want the State Department involved," Harris said. "They mainly used the argument that if they changed his status it would kill him, that as soon as the Iraqis saw that he was an MIA now, they'd know the U.S. was coming after them. They'd be scared and kill him."

Navy data showed that nine of ten pilots who eject from F/A-18s survive. And the Iraqis had swiftly tried to find and capture every pilot who was shot down during the war, often succeeding. But if Speicher was taken to Baghdad, as the Driver had claimed, what had happened then? Could he still be alive? Would Saddam Hussein, knowing that the U.S. government had quickly pronounced Speicher dead in 1991, keep a pilot incommunicado indefinitely? Why wouldn't he use the prisoner as leverage against sanctions, ongoing U.S. air patrols or UN weapons inspections?

Investigators didn't have those answers, but they did have some historical insight. In April 1998, Iraq released an Iranian pilot from prison. Hossein Lashgari's plane had been shot down in southern Iraq during the beginning of the Iran-Iraq War. He was captured on September 18, 1980, and held as a POW for more than seventeen years. "Baghdad and other Arab nations," Harris remarked recently, "but Saddam Hussein in particular, have a real tendency to hang on to people. They like souvenirs.

Saddam Hussein *really* loves souvenirs." He pointed to the Iranians in Saddam's jails since the 1980 to 1988 Iran-Iraq War and the 605 Kuwaitis Saddam abducted from their country when he occupied it in late 1990 and early 1991. Lashgari was one of hundreds. "An American pilot would just be a huge boon to him," Harris said.

With the Driver's story in hand, Senator Smith spent much of 1999 and 2000 pushing Navy officials to back down from Speicher's killed-in-action status. More appropriate, Smith said, would be missing in action. Smith and Grams wrote a letter to Richard Danzig on March 19, 1999, requesting that the secretary exercise his authority under Title 37 USCS, Section 555 (a) and 556 (d) to reconsider and change or modify the "finding of death" determination made by Vice Admiral Boorda on May 22, 1991, with respect to Lieutenant Commander Speicher. According to their correspondence, Scott was not covered by the Missing Persons Act, Title 10, USCS, Sections 1501–1510, as amended, because he was still listed as KIA/BNR, thereby making action under Title 37 the most appropriate form of action.

The letter to Danzig reviewed Congress's entire exposure to the Speicher case from 1996 on: "The results of the crash site investigation," Smith and Grams wrote, "were briefed to Congress in the winter and spring of 1996. In December 1997, we were further briefed on this matter by the Principal Deputy Assistant Secretary of Defense for International Security Affairs, Frederick Smith, in response to concerns generated by the attached *New York Times* story." While Congress was still being briefed, the Department of Defense had written Speicher off—perhaps unknown to Senators Smith and Grams at the time—not once, but many times over. Secretary of Defense Perry determined on February 16, 1996, that evidence gathered at the crash site was "insufficient" to determine what happened to Scott on the basis of what he was hearing from Fred Smith's office. Yet Congress was still making inquiries. In February 1998, Congress received a classified follow-up briefing on the case provided to the Senate Select Committee on Intelligence (SSCI) by DPMO. That September, pursuant to Smith and Grams's earlier inquiries on the issue of Scott Speicher, the intelligence community and the Department of Defense provided SSCI a classified chronology outlining intelligence community activities bearing on the issues raised as a result of Speicher's loss. On the basis of what they read in the briefing materials and the chronology, Senators Smith and Grams strongly believed that the information contained therein supported their request to change Scott Speicher's status from KIA/BNR to MIA.

In a separate letter addressed the same day to President Clinton, Senators Smith and Grams pointedly stated, "We are writing to express our grave concerns that you and your Administration have not done more to gain an accounting from the Government of Iraq for U.S. Navy Lieutenant Commander Michael Scott Speicher." In their second paragraph, the senators remind the president that "Speicher is the only serviceman still unaccounted for from that conflict," which was, of course, not the case. They were seemingly unaware at that time of the two other Navy pilots, Cooke and Dwyer, whose cases are KIA/BNR from the Persian Gulf War—unlike Speicher, both have open files with DPMO.

"We understand," they wrote, "that requests by Department of Defense officials to have this matter further pursued with the Iraqi Government through the International Committee of the Red Cross have been placed on hold by your Administration for three years now 'because of the state of U.S.-Iraqi bilateral relations.' We further understand that your National Security Council may not have focused on this matter during the last several years." They implored him to act as commander in chief of the armed forces. It took the president of the United States and the United States Navy nearly ten months to do so.

In a recent interview, Senator Smith shed light on the issues that prompted him to write these letters. "There was all kinds of things left out," he said. "We were just getting it in bits and parts. When I started the process, I just assumed the man was dead. And frankly, my source that I had, I didn't believe my source. I thought, 'Well, hey, the guy's killed in action. Where's all this stuff coming from?'" He couldn't believe that he'd been so blatantly misled. "We were told by DPMO office personnel that there was no other information." Then he found out what DPMO was trying to obscure. "We found out there was a canopy, there was a piece of the plane, there was a uniform, there was a live sighting report and on and on and on."

In July 1999, Senator Pat Roberts asked SSCI to conduct an inquiry into the intelligence community's input to the U.S. government's decision to list Commander Speicher as KIA. The Senate Select Committee on Intelligence's interest centered on the role and impact of intelligence in the government's accounting for Scott Speicher, and what the committee increasingly came to view as the discrepancy between the available intelligence information and the Navy's determination that Speicher was killed in the wee hours of January 17, 1991. The committee held a closed briefing on September 15, 1999, and a closed hearing on October 28, 1999, to examine the case in secret. They received testimony from Vice Admiral Thomas R. Wilson, DIA director; Brigadier General Roderick Isler, the associate director of Central Intelligence (DCI) for military support; and Admiral Michael Ratliff, director of naval intelligence.

The purpose of the hearing was to review the intelligence community's analytical input concerning Speicher's status as either a prisoner of war, missing, or killed in action; determine how the intelligence community is organized to carry out the DCI's statutory responsibility for analytical support of POW/MIA issues; and consider recommendations for handling analysis of POW matters in the future. The committee concluded that information existed suggesting Scott Speicher may have survived his aircraft being shot down. And as such, he may at one time have been—and conceivably could still be—a prisoner of war. The committee's interest prompted the establishment of a secretary of defense "tiger team," which included members of the DIA and the Office of the Secretary of Defense (OSD), to reassess the Speicher case.

Smith and Grams expressed their dismay that between 1996 and 1999—three full years—the DoD refused to authorize any further approaches to the Iraqi government through the State Department because of the tenor of U.S.-Iraqi relations. "Nonetheless," they wrote on March 19, "our offices were informed during a briefing we received on March 12, that the official publicly stated position of the Department of Defense POW/Missing Personnel Office (DPMO) with respect to whether the available evidence indicates Lt. Cmdr. Speicher perished in his aircraft incident, is 'we don't know.'" DPMO, as the senators correctly point out, is charged to develop, implement and oversee policy on unaccounted-for U.S. personnel for the Department of Defense. But in this and other Gulf War cases, DPMO had failed miserably.

Worst of all, Smith and Grams realized the depth of the lies they'd been told. "I was told that the man was killed in action. He was classified as KIA. I was told this by sources in the intelligence community." But Smith had his own sources in the intelligence community who were telling him that this was not, in fact, accurate, and that there was a lot of information indicating that Speicher may have survived his incident. "Because of that," said

Smith, "I began doing my own digging with my own sources, and through a series of briefings over the years, we began to get information that in fact he should never have been classified as KIA." Scott Speicher should have been classified MIA all along, Smith learned. Finally, the Senate Select Committee on Intelligence enlisted the assistance of Vice Admiral Tom Wilson, DIA director, someone who happened to agree with Senator Smith that Scott Speicher should have always been categorized as missing in action. Wilson's challenge would be to convince the staff of his own agency of the same.

For Buddy Harris and Joanne Speicher Harris, the year 2000 was a mix of progress and setbacks. DIA Director Vice Admiral Wilson and some of the people on his newly formed Speicher tiger team were, in Buddy Harris's words, "more skeptical than we wanted his office to be, and we didn't think they were pushing as hard as they should. A lot of agencies that should have been involved were not," to Harris's knowledge. Whether Scott was KIA/BNR or MIA, once a war is declared over, the responsibility for servicemember repatriation or remains recovery resides with the State Department, NSA, CIA and any number of federal agencies necessary to initiate a black box or black ops (covert) program to get answers. These agencies inevitably reach out to the Pentagon and its associated agencies, such as JSSA, for assistance in accomplishing the mission. Harris made a statement to the effect that, "when you have a KIA/BNR, it's their choice whether they want to be involved, but if it's an MIA case, they have to be involved. They have no choice." This is not a valid observation, especially in this case, where so much information continued to be gathered from the period just after cessation of hostilities at the end of Operation Desert Storm to the present.

Although scheduled to produce a joint report on March 13, 2000, DIA and OSD were unable to agree on findings, so no report was published. SSCI held an additional closed hearing on April 4, 2000, and testimony was heard from Admiral Wilson; Jerry M. Hultin, the undersecretary of the Navy; and Paul Lowell, director of naval intelligence. During the hearing, Senator Pat Roberts and others reviewed the intelligence community's all-source analytical input to the secretary of the navy and the tiger team concerning Speicher's status, reviewed the intelligence community's responsiveness to the secretary of the navy's intelligence needs regarding the Speicher case, and sought to determine better means for the intelligence community to support POW/MIA issues, which had not been addressed properly to that point. At the hearing, members of the committee learned, much to their dismay, that no comprehensive analytic review of all-source intelligence had been produced on the fate of Commander Speicher since his plane was shot down back in 1991. As a result of what they learned, the committee directed a comprehensive analytical assessment of the intelligence pertaining to Scott Speicher.

Continuing their active oversight function on the Speicher case, the Senate Select Committee on Intelligence passed the Intelligence Authorization Act (Section 304 of Senate 2507, 106th Congress; Senate Report 106–279, May 4, 2000), requiring the director of central intelligence to establish in the intelligence community "an analytic capability with responsibility for intelligence in support of the activities of the United States relating to prisoners of war and missing persons." The final version of the bill stated that the reason for doing this was the inadequacy of the intelligence information provided in support of a Department of Defense decision to make a presumptive finding of death for Scott Speicher.

Another closed hearing was conducted by SSCI on July 25, 2000, to update members on efforts to obtain the fullest possible accounting for Commander Speicher. By that time, the committee was deeply troubled that the Navy's conclusion that Speicher was killed in action during the Gulf War did not reflect the information being provided by the intelligence community. Federal regulations state that a finding of presumptive death is made when a survey of all available sources of information indicates, beyond doubt, that the presumption of continuance of life has been overcome. Information available to Congress simply did not support that conclusion.

The closed-session testimony varied broadly between those who wanted to see Scott Speicher's status changed to MIA, and others with instructions to do all they could to subvert the Senate's investigation. Commander Graig M. Hoeffer, an S-3 Viking pilot on staff in Riyadh, was dispatched from CENTCOM by Army General Tommy R. Franks with instructions to do everything he could to squelch the Senate's investigation of the Speicher case. Franks and his predecessor, Marine Corps General Anthony C. Zinni, did little to aid Senate investigators looking into the Riyadh paperwork concerning Scott Speicher's situation. No information was forthcoming as to special or black operations with Speicher's name on them. But why work so hard to end the Senate's inquiry? Hoeffer was merely a "talking head" sent on a mission to muddy the waters. In the end, the committee didn't buy Hoeffer's or others' testimony that blatantly attempted to throw them off from looking at CENTCOM for the answers as to why Scott Speicher was left behind on several occasions—all under CENTCOM's nose.

The Senate was looking for documentation on Scott Speicher's whereabouts since the war—the years between 1991 and 1995—when he was being held in the company of Bedouins keeping him for his blood chit until a suitable arrangement could be made to turn him over. The committee specifically asked the CIA to report to the committee on the matter by September 15, 2000.

Prodding Richard Danzig forward, the senators closed their letter by urging the secretary of the Navy to exercise his statutory authority to change the status of Lieutenant Commander Speicher back to MIA—"a status that more accurately reflects the available evidence and provides a presumptive 'benefit of the doubt' to Lt. Cmdr. Speicher. We owe nothing less to Lt. Cmdr. Speicher and his family." Although the Navy had earlier stated that it was not reviewing the Speicher case, it also said it remained an open issue. The Navy later appeared to have been somewhat swayed by the evidence available on Scott's status, but it wasn't completely sold on a change of status to MIA.

Danzig, under increasing pressure from Senators Smith and Grams's offices, asked Harris to give him a good argument for Scott Speicher's status change to MIA. Danzig, and many others, had one major concern with the status change. Maybe the Iraqis would think the United States was going to come after Speicher. If Speicher were alive, it might get him killed. "Give me a good argument," Danzig said. Harris had thought about this before, and he had an analogy. "I look at him like a guy with either cancer or a brain tumor," he told Danzig. "We can keep you living in a hospital, and you'd be drugged up most of the time and have to stay in this hospital. Or we can do surgery, and it could kill you or it may set you free to live your own life. And after ten years, personally, I'll take the surgery." Danzig thought that was a good argument for the change. He took the case to Clinton. It was still risky, and embarrassing. The government basically would be admitting that Speicher had been classified wrongly for a decade.

Buddy and Joanne Harris were thrust into strange territory with Smith and Grams's effort to have Scott declared an MIA. If there were the slightest chance that Scott could still be alive, shouldn't they get behind the senators' plan and ask for him to be declared MIA? They asked themselves that question again: If

Scott walked in today, would they be able to say that they'd done everything they could? The answer had changed. Even though the media crush could ruin the normalcy they'd tried to carve out for themselves and the children, they thought it might also put pressure on the government. The greater concern, however, seemed to be what the Speicher children might think of them for not doing something to help their father. "I don't want these kids coming up to me, at any time, and saying, 'Why didn't you do this?'" said Harris, of Meghan and Michael Scott Speicher-Harris.

Danzig ultimately relented, and began to make preparations so that Commander Scott Speicher could be declared an MIA. The status would be retroactive to cover the period between October 1, 1996, and April 30, 2001. Again, Joanne Harris would receive his unpaid pay and allowances totaling $292,747. Beginning May 1, 2001, she would also begin receiving Scott's monthly pay totaling $6,313 per month, which was based on a commander's pay scale. That figure did not include the commander's allowances and career incentive payments, which edged the payments closer to $8,000 a month.

CHAPTER 10

Missing in Action

Any day now, the call would come. Scott Speicher's former wife, Joanne, and her husband, Albert "Buddy" Harris, would be told on which day Speicher's status would be officially changed to missing in action. President Clinton had signed off. It was early January 2001, ten years since Speicher's F/A-18 had been shot down over Iraq, nearly as long since the Navy had declared him killed in action. What was about to happen would make history. No American service member, from any war, had ever been taken off the KIA list and switched back to missing in action. Joanne and Buddy knew the story would stir the media. They would have to talk to Scott Speicher's children, Meghan and Michael. They had been three years and eighteen months old when their father was shot down. The couple worried that this would upset their lives again. "The worst thing that's going to happen," Buddy remembers telling them, "is that somebody is going to come back into your lives who loves you more than anything else. Having more than one person love you can't be bad."

Representatives from the U.S. Department of State met Akram Jasim al-Duri, head of the Iraqi Interest Section, in the

Algerian embassy in Washington, on January 10. "The demarche and diplomatic note demands that the Iraqi government provide an accounting for Commander Michael Scott Speicher," said State Department spokesman Philip T. Reeker, in his morning press conference the next day, "which they are obligated to do under international law," or the Geneva Convention. Al-Duri received the communication, but he was in no position to reply, so it was forwarded to officials in Iraq. "We don't have a response from Baghdad. And a similar message is being delivered to Iraq through their representatives in New York and also in Geneva," Reeker reported. The official in New York was Iraq's permanent representative to the United Nations, Said Hasan al-Musawi. Saddam's permanent representative to the U.N. in Geneva was Muhammad al-Duri. None of them acted surprised to receive the diplomatic communication on Speicher.

"The simple point is," said Reeker, "that we believe that the Iraqis hold additional information that could help resolve the case of Commander Speicher, and they are obligated to provide that information to the United States." The delivery of a demarche, or diplomatic note, was not done often between the U.S. and the Iraqi government, Reeker explained. The continuing antagonism, including the ongoing low-intensity conflict and air warfare that had included spurts of daily air engagement between the U.S. and Iraq, had made diplomacy difficult. U.S. government personnel had been pulled out of the Iraqi capital due to obvious security concerns. "We don't have particularly close relations with Iraq, as you are well aware," Reeker said. "Our decision to demarche them on this issue was entirely driven by the humanitarian need that we see to resolve the case of Commander Speicher." The same day, the Pentagon and the White House gave similar briefings.

During a scheduled private security briefing with the Joint

Chiefs of Staff, President-elect George W. Bush, joined by Dick Cheney and Colin Powell, heard pointed presentations on Iraq, including information regarding the soon-to-be-announced status change for Scott Speicher later that day. Before George W. Bush could take the oath of office, his administration had the Speicher hot potato tossed in its lap. Why did the Clinton administration wait so long to change the status when Senators Smith and Grams had begun petitioning for Scott Speicher's MIA designation in 1999?

After the State Department leaked word of Scott's status change to MIA, reporters surrounded the Harris house in Orange Park, Florida, but Joanne and Buddy had packed up the family and left town for a week. The Navy announced Speicher's status change on January 11, 2001, in a four-paragraph statement, and that same day President Clinton created a frenzy. "We have some information that leads us to believe he might be alive," Clinton told reporters. "And we hope and pray that he is. But we have already begun working to try to determine whether, in fact, he's alive, if he is, where he is and how we can get him out."

Alive? What did the government know? Or had Clinton, ten days before leaving office, gone too far? Hours later, he tried to temper the statement. "Well, I don't want to say more than we have," the president said. "All I want to say is we have evidence which convinced me that we can't ensure that he perished. I don't want to hold out false hope, but I thought it was wrong to continue to classify him as killed in action when he might not have been."

The next day the story was splashed on the front page of newspapers across the country. Speicher's squadronmate Barry Hull and Senator Bob Smith appeared on CBS's *The Early Show.* The show's anchor, Jane Clayson, asked Smith why the U.S. government had waited seven years from the time Speicher's jet was found to try to locate the pilot. Smith said he couldn't understand it either. Up until 1998 he had been misled, and he promised to deal later with those who had steered Congress awry. There's not one shred of evidence, Smith said, that shows where, how or even if Speicher died. "This pilot, if he's alive, has been there for ten years with nobody looking for him. And that's just plain outrageous."

Hull began by saying hello to his combat buddies. "And, Spike, if you're out there, we're thinking about you, buddy," he added. The anchor asked him if he really thought Speicher could be alive after ten years. He didn't think so, Hull said, but he couldn't be sure. "I believe I read somewhere where the North Vietnamese held French prisoners for twenty years. So it has happened before. And there's no assurance that he's dead." He went on to say that the question had haunted him, his squadron-mates, Spike's friends and the government for a decade. It confounded them more, not less, as each year passed. "This is a situation where the pieces of the puzzle don't fit and no one knows exactly what happened to him. And for all we know," said Hull, "he is still alive. And that makes this tragedy so much worse."

At a Pentagon news briefing on January 16, Kenneth H. Bacon, assistant secretary of defense for public affairs, reminded the deluge of reporters that Scott Speicher's status change did not mean the Department of Defense was admitting that they knew he was alive. As Bacon answered pointed questions pertaining to the shift to missing in action, he claimed the Iraqis said they didn't have records of such matters as missing pilots. "But some of their statements have been somewhat disingenuous because they only go back to 1995, when we, as you know, sent representatives in with the International Committee of the Red Cross to look at the crash site. So we have asked the Iraqis to provide whatever information they have about what happened between 1991, when the plane was shot down, and 1995, certainly, and thereafter, if they have information." The interesting issue, Bacon pointed out, was what happened right after the crash. But the Iraqis didn't have custody of Scott Speicher in that time frame, so the Pentagon through the State Department was asking the Iraqis for the impossible.

For Scott Speicher, the status change also meant he was now covered under United States Code Title 10, Chapter 76, commonly referred to as the "Missing Persons Act." He had rights, particularly the right to have a lawyer. Section 1503(f)(1) states this clearly, "The Secretary appointing a board to conduct an inquiry under this section shall appoint counsel to represent each person covered by the inquiry or, in a case covered by subsection (b), one counsel to represent all persons covered by the inquiry." The secretary of the Navy was obligated by the law to appoint legal counsel—a judge advocate general (JAG) attorney—for Scott Speicher.

Cindy Laquidara, the attorney hired by Joanne and Albert Harris to represent them, does not meet the requirements of the law under Title 10, Section 1503(f)(1). Counsel under this paragraph may be referred to as a "missing person's counsel" and represents the interests of the person covered by the inquiry—not any member of that person's family or other interested parties. The secretary of the Navy has not provided Scott Speicher with his own legal representation as required under the Missing Persons Act, which is a breach of public law. Section 1503(f)(3)(A) states that the missing person's legal counsel "shall have access to all facts and evidence" considered by a board of inquiry into the case for which the counsel is appointed. A missing person's counsel may assist the board in ensuring that all appropriate information concerning the case is collected, logged, filed and safeguarded. The importance of Scott having legal counsel of his own becomes more relevant when looking at classified information that might determine action on his behalf.

Much of what appears in Scott Speicher's files has some level of classification attached. In fact, a good portion of it reaches the threshold of special compartmentalized information, special access or code word. Because he has no counsel of his own, much of the information that might be used to make determinations in his favor has not been brought to light.

The Speicher flight suit photographs are a good example of the abuse of classifying information that does not impact national security. Jumping ahead a few years, Scott Speicher's flight suit photographs were obtained by CBS's *60 Minutes II* for national broadcast in April 2000. The reply to two requests made later, on December 19, 2001, and January 8, 2002, stated, "J. Alan Liotta, Deputy Director of Defense Prisoner of War Personnel Affairs Office (DPMO), an initial denial authority, has denied in their entirety the photographs responsive to the 'flight suit' portion of your request, the release of which would circumvent the DPMO Congressionally mandated mission to account for U.S. personnel missing as a result of this Nation's conflicts. Accordingly, the denied photographs are withheld pursuant to 5 USC, 552(b)(2)(High) governing Freedom of Information Act [FOIA]." This second category of information covered by Exemption 2—internal matters of a more substantial nature, the disclosure of which would risk the circumvention of a statute or agency regulation—has generated considerable controversy over the years. Liotta was trying to use what is commonly referred to as a "High 2" to stop disclosure of the photographs.

In *Crooker* v. *ATF,* adjudicated in the Court of Appeals for the District of Columbia Circuit, the circuit court fashioned a two-part test for determining which sensitive materials are exempt from mandatory disclosure under Exemption 2. This test requires both (1) that a requested document be "predominantly internal," and (2) that its disclosure "significantly risks circumvention of agency regulations or statutes." The flight suit photographs do not meet the law's rigorous litmus test. First, they have already been released for public view on national television. Second, when the head of the Department of the Navy's FOIA Policy Branch, Doris M. Lama, requested the photographs for release, suddenly DPMO couldn't locate them. Were they now "lost" like Scott Speicher's flight suit?

The law is clear on another count, too. Whenever any U.S. intelligence agency or other element of the government finds or receives information that may be related to a missing person, the information is required to be promptly sent to the office of the service secretary. In this case, the secretary of the Navy is to receive copies of all intelligence information gathered by the different government intelligence agencies so that proper determinations may be made with regard to the missing person's status. The Speicher investigation within the Department of Defense and the alphabet soup of intelligence agencies—namely the Defense Intelligence Agency (DIA), the Central Intelligence Agency (CIA) and the National Security Agency (NSA)—has been hobbled by each agency's refusing to share important information.

Even after Speicher's status was changed to MIA on January 10, 2001, Senator Bob Smith wrote to National Security Advisor Condoleezza Rice saying that he had "serious concerns that elements of the U.S. government have misled the Congress on this tragic case." A month later, he wrote to Senator Bob Graham (D-FL), chairman of the Senate Select Committee on Intelligence, and Richard Shelby, his vice chairman, to ask them to formally investigate the intelligence community's performance on the case and the inspector generals' glowing review of the intelligence agencies' performance. He also questioned the ability of the inspector generals to conduct an independent investigation on the case. In May, the Senate Select Committee on Intelligence agreed to formally investigate the intelligence community's work on Scott Speicher. A few months later, after September 11, several of those agencies would be questioned over lapses similar to the Speicher investigation: Did they share information? How good were they at analyzing data? Could they oversee and critique their own work?

In addition, nowhere in the United States Code does it state that primary next of kin can request a hold on release of classified information or block the declassification of information for the public file to protect their own privacy. The excuse that the Speicher family wants the information to remain classified to protect their privacy and the sanctity of an ongoing investigation is stretching the purpose of classification, period. Joanne Speicher-Harris ceased to be Scott Speicher's primary next of kin, by law, when she married Albert Harris in July 1992, and with it went her ability to dictate the terms of classification of Scott's file to the United States Navy and the Department of Defense. The Navy realized this fact around the time that Buddy Harris revealed to Admiral Arthur that he had married Scott Speicher's wife. Still, this is what Senator John McCain's office was told in response to a letter he addressed to Secretary of Defense William S. Cohen on January 9, 1998. McCain wrote Secretary Cohen to express his concern about the manner in which Speicher's case had been handled, to request a briefing on the status of the case, and to urge that all information pertaining to the case be made public as soon as possible. The Department of Defense responded by letter on February 13, 1998, expressing to Senator McCain that it was the Speicher family's wish that information not be released to the public to protect their privacy. He was then accorded a classified, closed-door briefing.

Shortly after Scott's change of designation to MIA, on February 7, 2001, Senator Pat Roberts of Kansas participated in a hearing of the Senate Select Committee on Intelligence on worldwide threats to U.S. national security. A portion of this hearing was devoted to Scott Speicher. Roberts summoned George Tenet, director of the Central Intelligence Agency; Vice Admiral Thomas Wilson, DIA director; and Thomas Singer, acting assistant secretary of state, to answer pressing questions concerning progress on the Speicher case. In his opening statement, he said, "Lieutenant Commander Michael Speicher, KIA in 1991, MIA in 2001. President Clinton said the following, as of last month, when he indicated that the commander might still be alive: 'We've already begun working to try to determine whether, in fact, he's alive; if he is, where he is and how we can get him out,' the president said, 'because since he was a uniformed service person he's clearly entitled to be released, and we're going to do everything we can to get him out.'" Senator Shelby, Senator Smith, who came on the issue in 1996, and Roberts, who got involved in 1998, expressed to the panel that they felt they'd lost one of their own. He was left behind, they said. "We think the system failed, and we're trying to fix it," said Roberts. This could be done partly by setting up intelligence analysts who would cover POWs and missing persons. "We passed that in the authorization bill," pressed Roberts. "We hope that there's been a big change, and I need to know the progress you've made in establishing this capability in regard to status, budget and the breadth of its activities."

Roberts asked pointed questions. To what extent has the new capability drawn on the resources of the DIA? "I want to thank Admiral Wilson for his excellent work in this respect. I want to make sure that Admiral Wilson's right arm knows what your left arm is doing or vice versa." He also wanted to know if the intelligence agencies were cooperating. One Senate staffer said that

while they had done a fairly good job, he took exception to the
circuitous route it took them to get there. "If somebody smacks
you in the face and says get going, and you do a good job after
that, you are commended for doing a good job. But you don't get
a check in the box that says, 'Initiative.' "

Two months before the hearing, the inspector generals of the
CIA and DoD had given a "noteworthy" assessment of the intelligence community support of the Speicher case, and of the general quality of intelligence support for POW/MIA matters. "I
don't agree" with the assessment, said Senator Roberts. "I think
it's noteworthy, all right, but it's not the same connotation that
was in that report. Were the factors that contributed to this allegedly high-level work in place in the early and mid-1990s,
when most of the effort now regarded as incomplete—and that's
the nicest way I can put it—in regard to the Speicher case, were
they considered in that inspector general's report?"

"I don't know, sir," replied Tenet. "I'll have to check for you. I
don't know. Do you know?" he asked, as he leaned over to
Thomas Singer.

"Did the inspector general look back as far as we had records
dealing with the issue?" asked Singer. "But I . . . it was an independent investigation . . ." His voice trailed off.

"From '91 up to '96, were those factors considered, Tom?"
Roberts queried Singer.

"As far as I know they were, sir," said Singer.

"How on earth could anybody reach the conclusion that they
were noteworthy and excellent? That's beyond me," an agitated
Roberts shot back.

Later, during a separate interview in May, several months
after the SSCI hearing, Wilson himself would say that though
he'd established a working group—a tiger team—to aggressively

investigate the Speicher case within the DIA, interagency cooperation "doesn't seem to have been effective yet."

Meanwhile, Iraq responded angrily to the demarche they had been served. In a Reuters report dated February 11, 2001, several days after the senators' deliberations behind closed doors, the Iraqis renewed their accusations that United Nations weapons inspectors were looking for a U.S. Navy pilot shot down during the Persian Gulf War rather than trying to uncover evidence of Iraq's weapons of mass destruction. The report, originally carried in the Iraqi weekly newspaper *Nasirriya*, referred to a period of time well after the war when UNSCOM teams were repeatedly in Iraq, until they were expelled at the end of 1998. "I was informed by former UN weapons inspector Scott Ritter," said Hussam Mohammed Amin, head of the Iraqi National Monitoring Directorate, "that a team of UN weapons inspectors was looking for the body of the American pilot." Amin accused the team of looking for the downed pilot in an area where there were no military sites or inhabitants, reported Reuters. In this respect, Amin was telling the truth. There was nothing in the vicinity of where Scott Speicher had gone down.

The UN weapons inspectors had been monitoring Iraq's weapons of mass destruction since April 1991 as part of the Gulf War cease-fire agreement. In its response to a recent inquiry, the Iraqi Foreign Ministry stated that one of the commission's missile inspection teams—UNSCOM 24—had surveyed and inspected Iraq's western area between December 17 and 19, 1991. "The team's chief, Scott Ritter," the Foreign Ministry reported, "admitted later that he had been asked by the U.S. administration to search for the body of an American pilot." Ritter has publicly denied this, but it was because of this search that the Iraqis

became particularly jumpy during his attempts in 1998 to access
Abu Ghraib, Iraq's largest and most notorious prison, near Baghdad, with more than fifteen thousand inmates, just before inspectors were forced out of the country completely in December.

The showdown at Abu Ghraib pitted Lieutenant Colonel Dr.
Gabriele Kraatz-Wadsack, of the German Army Medical Service, and her UNSCOM Inspection Team #215 against savvy
Iraqi record keepers who didn't want them to find hard intelligence that the Iraqis had used prisoners for live human experi-
ments with biological agents in 1994 and 1995. Now, three years
later, the team appeared at the gate to the prison, wanting answers. Biologist Dr. Kraatz-Wadsack, unbeknownst to the Iraqis,
had learned enough Arabic to know what she was looking for in
their files. "She did not anticipate finding any forensic evidence,"
wrote Tom Mangold and Jeff Goldberg in their 1999 work
Plague Wars, "but the Iraqis are paper-crazy when it comes to bu-
reaucracy, so she marched straight to the prison's administrative
offices to demand prison records for 1994–5." They weren't
there. She saw records from 1992 and 1993, but nothing else.

Iraq's sensitivity to the Speicher case, heightened by the State
Department's demarche, also showed the pressure they felt on another front. Iraq continued to insist that Speicher was dead, but
its officials weren't offering any substantive proof. Nor were they
cooperating with a mandate passed by the U.N. Security Council.

United Nations Resolution 1248, enacted on December 17,
1999, stated, "The repatriation and return of all Kuwaiti and
third country nationals or their remains, present in Iraq on or
after August 2, 1990 . . . have not yet been fully carried out by
Iraq." To accomplish this, the resolution established a subsidiary
body of the UN Security Council called the United Nations
Monitoring, Verification and Inspection Commission (UN-
MOVIC). Under the new mandate, UNMOVIC inspectors

would be accorded unrestricted and unimpeded access to any and all areas, facilities, equipment, records and means of transport to fulfill their mission, as well as the right to interview all officials and persons under the authority of the Iraqi government. The U.N. Security Council directed the Iraqi government to extend all the necessary cooperation to the ICRC, and called upon them to resume cooperation with the Tripartite Commission to discuss missing person's cases. The Tripartite Commission is an eight-country commission, chaired by the ICRC and responsible for locating and securing the release of remaining prisoners of war, which started almost immediately after Operation Desert Storm. Iraq has rebuffed participation in the commission as late as March 8, 2002, when the ICRC forwarded another message to them about Scott Speicher.

After the Persian Gulf War, there were initially 628 Kuwaiti cases, which were eventually pared down to 605 left unresolved, and the Saudi government claimed another seventeen cases. But Iraq admitted to only 126 Kuwaiti detainees and even then didn't provide enough information to determine what had happened to them. Only three Kuwaitis had been accounted for since 1995, when Iraq and Kuwait in January opted to increase the frequency to every other month of their own meetings on the Iraq-Kuwait border, with American, British, French and Saudi representatives present. But Iraq stopped attending the meetings after Operation Desert Fox in December 1998. Shortly after Resolution 1248 was passed, a retired Russian diplomat named Yuli Vorontsov was put in charge of sorting out the issues of missing Kuwaiti persons and illegally seized property. Vorontsov, however, has never been permitted into Iraq.

The ICRC has been doing its part all along. In 1998 it held three meetings in Geneva with the set objective to account for remaining missing persons. Nine meetings were held in the demilitarized zone on the Iraq-Kuwait border, and in both Iraq and Kuwait the ICRC continued to monitor the treatment and conditions of detained persons from the Gulf War. In Kuwait, the ICRC visited detainees with no diplomatic protection, mainly stateless persons and Jordanians, Sudanese, Yemenites and Palestinians without travel documents. In Iraq, they visited seventy-eight foreign nationals (in 1994 this figure had been 353 foreign nationals) held at the Abu Ghraib detention center. The ICRC was also responsible for a repatriation that took place at the Safwan border crossing point in February and March 1998 involving two Kuwaitis and two Saudis who had been held in Iraq illegally. If there is any doubt as to the existence of Kuwaitis in Iraqi prisons and vice versa, it should be resolved by the fact that the ICRC forwarded 10,744 Red Cross messages in one direction and 9,189 in the other between families in Kuwait and relatives from whom they were separated as a result of the Gulf War. They also exchanged 22,000 messages between families in Iraq and their relatives abroad. The number of incarcerated foreign nationals falls only as they die off. By 2000, the number of foreign nationals visited by the ICRC in Abu Ghraib prison had been reduced to sixty-four. The number of messages collected was down to 6,855, and those distributed in return, with the help of the Iraqi Red Crescent Society, had dropped to 8,565 messages. But repatriations and reprieves are few, especially from Abu Ghraib.

On July 19, 2000, the U.S. Congress passed concurrent resolutions in the House and Senate. The language of the Senate resolution was particularly strong. Punctuated with words like "immediately" and phrases such as "fullest possible accounting," the Senate was trying to float a message not only throughout government in Washington, but abroad to Iraq. The Senate document mentioned eyewitness reports from released prisoners of war, which indicated that many of the missing Kuwaitis, for example, had been seen and contacted in Iraqi prisons. Most important, the Congress "demands that the government of Iraq immediately provide the fullest possible accounting for U.S. Navy Commander Michael Scott Speicher in compliance with UN Security Council Resolution 686 and other applicable international law."

The House of Representatives passed its resolution four days later in an attempt to exert further pressure on the Clinton administration to demand that the UN Security Council focus the spotlight on the fate of Scott Speicher as well as persons missing from Kuwait and other Middle East countries. "There are 605 Kuwaiti MIAs, many of whom are civilians, and they have been held for over ten years now," said California Congressman Dana Rohrabacher. "To put this in proportion for the people of the United States, this would be the equivalent of an enemy of the United States holding two hundred thousand Americans for a period of ten years. Think of what the suffering among our people and the emotional upheaval in our country would be if two hundred thousand Americans were being held by an enemy of the United States."

The resolution states that Iraq, under the rule of Saddam Hussein, has failed to locate and secure the return of all prisoners of war being held in Iraq, including prisoners from Kuwait and nine other nations. The original draft of Resolution 275 did not include Scott Speicher's name, even though it had been proposed by Congressman Robert Wexler, a Democrat from Florida, Scott's home state when he disappeared. The week before it was presented for vote, Rohrabacher amended the document. "Michael Speicher, a patriotic young American who volunteered to serve his country, has not been well served by his country," he said. "During visits to Kuwait in 1998 and again in 1999, I asked intelligence officials at the American embassy about Lieutenant Commander Speicher. They told me that there is a legitimate reason for concern about whether he survived his crash and was taken prisoner." These same officials told Rohrabacher that they welcomed congressional support to determine Speicher's fate. Rohrabacher also had an addition made to the preamble to the resolution that stated, in part, that Scott Speicher had been declared dead by the United States Navy "without the conduct of an adequate search and rescue operation, however subsequent information obtained after the Persian Gulf Conflict by United States officials has raised the possibility that Lieutenant Commander Speicher survived and was captured by Iraqi forces."

On September 15, 2001, the DIA POW/MIA Office was created as a direct result of ongoing congressional inquiry into the Gulf War case of Scott Speicher. Congress had not forgotten its recent history with DIA vis-à-vis missing soldiers. Historically, DIA has had a central, two-pronged role in U.S. efforts to account for POW/MIAs. First, it is responsible for investigating and analyzing reports of live sightings and evidence that American prisoners may still be held in foreign lands. Second, the Department of Defense relies heavily on DIA for analysis to draw conclusions about the fate of missing servicemen. In 1993, the Senate Select Committee on POW/MIA Affairs drew several negative conclusions about DIA's performance in this capacity. The agency has been plagued historically by lack of resources, guilty of overclassification, defensive toward criticism, handicapped by poor coordination with other elements of the intelligence community and slow to follow up on live sightings and foreign-generated intelligence reports. Several of those who reviewed the workings of DIA during this period in the early 1990s also faulted DIA's analytical process and referred to it as a "mindset to debunk" live-sighting reports. Committee members expressed particular concern and disappointment that, on occasion, individuals within DIA had been evasive, unresponsive and disturbingly incorrect and cavalier, diminishing the work of others who'd performed professionally under extraordinarily difficult circumstances. This second attempt at a DIA POW/MIA office held greater promise, but Congress was careful to focus this latest effort on current operational POW/MIA issues, should they reach crisis proportion. Those in the new office carry with them some firsthand field experience from the Gulf War and the legacy of Scott Speicher.

A further development occurred on February 14, 2002. In a letter to Secretary of Defense Donald H. Rumsfeld, Senator Pat Roberts stated that a recent U.S. intelligence community assessment of the Speicher case indicates "Commander Speicher probably survived the loss of his aircraft, and if he survived, he almost certainly was captured by the Iraqis." Senator Roberts doesn't indicate when he believes the capture to have occurred. "This strongly suggests the more appropriate designator or status of POW," he writes. "I believe the status of POW sends a symbolic message not only to the Iraqis, but to other adversaries, current and future—and most importantly to the men and women of the U.S. armed forces and the American people."

Senator Roberts's proposal to change Scott Speicher's status to POW raises interesting issues. Commander Chip Beck makes the argument that "a POW is a POW, not an MIA. This is true even if the enemy knows that the person is a POW, but our side does not. As long as one party, in this case the 'holding party,' knows that the person is alive and captive, then he is a POW." This may apply to Scott Speicher, and Beck emphasizes that even when and if a POW expires in captivity, he does not become an MIA. There are those in the Pentagon who will argue, Beck has said, that all POWs and MIAs are MIAs, which is not the case. "This lack of distinction serves the enemy's interest," he writes, "not ours. It requires us to only track down those men and women who were killed in the conduct of battle, not kidnapped by the forces they confronted." Roberts pushed for POW status because its standard of accountability is considerably higher.

Thanks to the efforts of several dedicated senators, and other courageous voices within the military establishment, the U.S. government has taken long strides toward ensuring that what happened to Scott Speicher will not happen again. Yet the fate of Scott himself remains in doubt. He is still trapped inside a country run by a ruthless dictator. The release of this brave pilot must be granted by Saddam Hussein.

CHAPTER 11

Daniel in the Lion's Den

Charles A. Forrest was just about to conclude his meeting in Tehran with members of the Supreme Council for Islamic Revolution in Iraq (SCIRI) when one of its key participants asked him to look at the report of a captured American pilot. Forrest's group, INDICT, was established in late 1998 to campaign for the creation of an ad hoc international criminal tribunal to try leading members of the Iraqi regime on charges of war crimes and crimes against humanity, including genocide and torture. The group's chair, Ann Clwyd, a member of the British Parliament, is also chair of the UK All-Party Human Rights Group. INDICT collects the evidence that can be used in prosecution of Saddam Hussein and his top leadership. The meeting in Tehran in the fall of 2001 was one of several that Forrest has had with SCIRI, a group dedicated to the overthrow of Saddam and the ruling Ba'ath Party. Forrest found the report unsettling. "There's a certain voodoo to keeping an American in the basement," he said recently. "And why—it looks like it's been incredibly successful to [Hussein]. You can't believe that his doing this hasn't had some impact on U.S. policy with Iraq." The report had been made by an Iraqi who left the country via Tehran, contacted the SCIRI members there, and then left for Beirut, Lebanon, where several thousand Iraqis now live. These expatriates have emigrated for different political, economic and security-related reasons, and many have stories that defy the imagination. A number of them have appeared in the *Al-Hayat* newspaper. "We receive a lot of Iraqis," said *Al-Hayat* reporter Hazem al-Amin, "because they believe the newspaper reaches many in the Arab world."

The former prisoner who contacted SCIRI was Hussam Al Mousawi, a twenty-six-year-old arrested ten years earlier by the Iraqis, in 1991, in the city of Hillah in the governate of Karbala, along with his entire family. His father had been executed earlier, in 1986. During his first period of incarceration, the young man told al-Amin in a May 4, 2001, *Al-Hayat* article, that two of his brothers were executed. "I had only one brother who had remained alive, and I later discovered that he was in prison like I was," Al Mousawi said. "He had been put in the same prison where I was." During his ten years of imprisonment, Al Mousawi was incarcerated in three different prisons, the first two for one month each and the rest of his time in the third, which he established at some point to be in or near Baghdad, and which is believed to be Abu Ghraib. "In the third prison, I was put in a cell on the fourth level underneath the ground level of the building. This was a big prison consisting of three buildings."

Saddam has a number of large prisons with underground holding areas, including the one in which Al Mousawi was detained. A defector, a sergeant in an all-volunteer unit called the Fedayeen Saddam, who worked in one of these secret sites outside Baghdad, said recently of such prisoners: "They were kept in an underground cell. They were rarely let out, usually once for a very brief time every three or four months, and only when the camp was empty."[20] He revealed that the site was at Salman Pak, just outside Baghdad. The prison was covered with date palm trees, with only an air vent visible above ground. The Iraqi government maintains other secret sites like the prison the former Fedayeen Saddam guard describes. In all of them, the conditions are overcrowded and common prisoners are crammed into cells.

The cell in which Al Mousawi was placed was no more than four meters long and three meters wide. When he entered it, there were eighteen prisoners there. "But this figure sometimes went up to as high as forty prisoners," said Al Mousawi. "For every prisoner or person arrested, the initial period of imprisonment, with its interrogations, was one of the hardest phases of prison life. But in Iraqi prisons, torture is used all during a person's period of imprisonment." He described some of the brutal methods employed. "Today I am a young man, but I have no sexual sensations. During my interrogations, they destroyed that area of my body with electrical instruments of torture. And, as you can see, my jaw was broken, and was put back together the wrong way. This is because the interrogator kicked my jaw with his foot until it fell apart. These disfigurements on my hand are because I was burned with cigarette butts and because pincers with electricity were used on me during interrogations."

Enduring the conditions of the prison—little food, abominable sanitary and living conditions, and almost constant torture of some kind—Al Mousawi followed the rules of the Iraqi security service and avoided angering the interrogators. One day in 1997, however, a security service man came to the cell door and requested him by name. Al Mousawi's prison uniform was filthy and he smelled. "A disgusting smell emanated from my body because of the putridness and humidity," he said, "and I had had scabies and whole areas of my skin had been worn away." The prison security service cleaned him up, gave him new clothes and told Hussam that he'd be permitted to pass out food to other prisoners—always accompanied by prison security. It was as a "feeder" that Hussam Al Mousawi encountered the "foreigners' floor," which was set aside for non-Iraqi prisoners. The inmates on the foreigners' floor were a mixture of Kuwaitis, Palestinians and four Western foreigners, one of whom was an American pilot. "There was also another one whose nationality I did not know," said Al Mousawi, "and who had gone insane."

Al Mousawi was permitted to pass out bigger portions of food on the foreigners' floor, particularly since most of the rooms were solitary confinement cells. One day, while he was passing out food, the security guard accompanying Al Mousawi announced that an intelligence inspection committee had suddenly made a surprise appearance on the floor. He shoved Al Mousawi into the nearest cell and secured the door. "I was passing the cell of the American prisoner. The security man had me go in there, and he closed the door from outside. [The American] was the only one there, and it appears that he had learned to speak a little Arabic. He said to me: 'You are a temporary prisoner. They often set free those whom they choose for the job of distributing food.'" The American pilot told him that he was taken prisoner after his airplane was shot down during the Gulf War. According to al-Amin's article, he asked Hussam if he could send a message to his command after they freed him. "I refused even to talk to him," Al Mousawi said, "and I remained silent until the cell door was opened again. The officer took me out of the cell and inspected me carefully. He asked me if this American had talked to me about anything, and I said that he hadn't. I did this not out of concern for him, but rather out of fear that they would have suspicions about me." His first encounter with the pilot was very brief, but he was still afraid any contact with the American would mean the end of his chances to get out of the prison.

The following year, in 1998, Al Mousawi noticed that the prison routine changed radically on the foreigners' floor. Some officers and soldiers working in the prison had tried to smuggle documents, photographs and information concerning Kuwaiti prisoners back to their country, and Saddam's security forces caught them at the border and executed all of them. From that time on, an electric gate was erected at the entrance to the foreigners' floor, and the prisoners were forced to don masks before feeders entered their cells. One Kuwaiti prisoner who refused to put on his mask was hauled out of his cell by a security officer and taken to an open gallery area. There, the officer beat him over the head until he died.

As a food distributor, Al Mousawi said that one of his collateral duties was to clean rooms—including the interrogation rooms, where he often found inmates' bodies, blood and remains. "One could look at the body," said Hussam, "and tell how the person was killed. Some of them had been given injections, after which their bodies shriveled up. Others had been tortured so much by the interrogators that they had been accidentally killed by them. Still others had died out of fear and had had heart failure.

"I had a second chance to be with the American prisoner in the same room," he continued. "He was afflicted with extreme exhaustion and was very sick, and this led to a doctor visiting him and giving him a vaccine. The doctor, an officer, ordered me to stay with him about two hours." During that time the American again asked Al Mousawi if he would pass a message to his command if they set Hussam free. "He repeated to me words, which, if I recited them and they were heard, would prove his identity."

The later conversation between Al Mousawi and the CIA in regards to these words is classified.

In 1999, Qusay Saddam Hussein, the dictator's son, took personal charge of the prison in which Hussam Al Mousawi was incarcerated. New jailers were brought in—and the executions started in earnest. One prisoner familiar to Hussam had read a paper that stated they were in a general security prison in the General Security Directorate of Baghdad. For his trouble, the young man was crudely hanged. The chief interrogator opened a door and made sure Hussam saw what happened to those who read and talked about such papers. "His neck seemed very long," Hussam told al-Amin. "The skin and flesh had been torn away, and only the bones were connected to the body. And before he was hanged, they had cut out his tongue. The interrogating officer made sure that we knew this additional fact. He went and stood up on the chair and opened the mouth of the hanged person so that we could see that his tongue had been cut out." Shortly thereafter, Hussam was called into the office of the interrogator, who informed him that he had been pardoned by Saddam Hussein and would be leaving the prison immediately.

The American embassy in Beirut contacted Hazem al-Amin, the *Al-Hayat* newspaper reporter, in September, several months after his article about Hussam Al Mousawi appeared, and asked him if Hussam would like to talk to someone from the embassy. "We asked him," said al-Amin, "and he agreed on the condition that we be present at the meeting. We went with him to the meeting, which took place at the Phoenicia Hotel." Accompanying the military attaché were three agents from the CIA. "They asked to talk to him alone—without us," al-Amin reported. "They went up with him to a room in the hotel. When he agreed to this, we excused ourselves to leave and since then we lost contact with him." Hussam Al Mousawi hasn't been seen about Beirut since then. No one there knows what's happened to him.

Was the pilot in question Scott Speicher? If Al Mousawi is correct and the pilot stated that he'd been in the prison since he was shot down during the Gulf War, then the answer is no. Scott was not captured at the time his jet went down. He was not in Iraqi custody for several years, but in the care of a Bedouin tribe. Could he have been one of the other missing aviators—Cooke, Dwyer or another pilot whose remains the Iraqis claimed to have returned? That is possible.

The tantalizing question of where Scott is now cannot be answered definitively, but talks with inside sources offer several possibilities. The first step is to understand more about Saddam Hussein himself. Scott Speicher is not held where more than a small number of people are going to see him. Whether or not the prisoner who spoke with Hussam Al Mousawi was Scott Speicher, the fact that he is a prisoner is not in doubt. A defector who escaped Iraq in 1998 kept prisoner records for the government. He'd shuffle the records from one location to the next ahead of UN weapons inspectors, trying to keep U.S. officials, in particular, from getting a look at them. Yet in one location weapons inspectors did see a file with Scott Speicher's name on it. It was a medical record, showing that an Iraqi physician had given Scott checkups in 1997 and 1999. When investigators later interrogated the doctor, who'd defected earlier, he couldn't remember the place where he'd treated him. So the question remains, where is Scott being held?

Saddam never shared Scott's whereabouts with his sons-in-law Lieutenant General Hussein Kamel Al-Majid and Saddam Kamel Al-Majid, who defected in 1996 to Jordan and who were later executed on return to Iraq. When interviewed by U.S. intelligence, they knew nothing of Scott Speicher, but Hussein Kamel Al-Majid told his interrogators that it didn't astonish him at all. "It wouldn't surprise him if he had Scott," related Buddy Harris of Al-Majid's conversation with officials. "It wouldn't surprise him if he didn't know about it because Saddam is like a stolen art dealer." The stolen treasures can't be shared with the world—only a limited inner circle. "He can't tell anybody," says Buddy Harris of Hussein, "because they'd gain so much power just by going down and looking at it. And that's how he [Al-Majid] described Saddam Hussein, that's just the kind of guy he is."

Charles Forrest of INDICT believes that the situation has gone on for ten years precisely because the U.S. believes that a diplomatic approach will ultimately work where Scott is concerned. But Saddam's patience is endless, and diplomacy means nothing to a man whose reign has been defined by extreme violence. The corpses stacked like cordwood throughout his country should be proof enough of that. In addition, Saddam Hussein hates the United States with a vengeance that has few parallels in the world. "It is hatred intensified by a tribal culture of the blood feud—one that he has embraced since Mr. Bush's father defeated him on the field of battle," wrote Richard Perle, former assistant secretary of defense, in a December 28, 2001, *New York Times* op-ed piece. Every day Saddam gets joy knowing he has Scott, a prize possession of his enemy the Great Satan—the U.S.—even more so since the demand for his return. From the captor's point of view, why kill someone who provides daily pleasure—sadistic as that is—and who has some bartering value? Saddam knows that it would serve no purpose to kill Scott now. It would be better for Saddam to return Scott alive as a humanitarian gesture than to continue to keep him. But it might be better still if Saddam could show the Arab world that he will release Scott only if concessions are made.

"Know thy enemy" is no longer a hollow phrase where Saddam Hussein is concerned. Despite his penchant for wiping out perceived enemies en masse, Hussein is a devout Muslim who takes many of his cues from the Koran—even some from the Christian Bible. At least 20 percent of Iraq's population is Christian, including its deputy foreign minister, Tariq Aziz. Chris Toensing, executive director and editor of *Middle East Report* for the Middle East Research and Information Project, concurs that Americans don't want to have to understand Saddam or Arab culture in general. "Americans can be obtuse and disparaging of the culture. They don't want to know it. They don't want to understand it. It's easier to dismiss it as beneath our own, as violent and devoid of morality."

One place to look for Scott Speicher may be tied to Hussein's desire to resurrect the glory days of Nebuchadnezzar and the Babylonian Empire. General Wafic al Samarrai, former head of Iraqi Military Intelligence, commented, in somewhat fractured English, "He's much fond of going into history. Perhaps, when you go to Babel, where there are these ruins . . . of Nebuchadnezzar . . . there's this building with a little inscription saying, 'This was rebuilt, reconstructed during the days of Saddam.' He's very much fond of going into history as a great leader."[21] Of course, Nebuchadnezzar is famous for capturing Palestinian Jews and transporting them by the hundreds to Babylon (Iraq) and holding them prisoner for years.

"The memorials to Saddam are legion," said Dr. Phebe A. Marr, retired Institute for National Strategic Studies senior fellow at the National Defense University. "As far as Babylon is concerned, he has completely renovated the hanging gardens and the ancient remains in Babylon, 'restoring' them to what they were, with his name stamped on all the bricks." Saddam's construction efforts at Babylon have been under way for more than ten years. He wants to be remembered as being comparable to both Nebuchadnezzar and Hammurabi, who had their names and seals put on each brick. He is also recording on clay or bricks his history of events and placing them under archival corners. Selected corners of ancient buildings had a space below the foundation stone—a place where the king ensured that his histories and archives would be placed like a time capsule to preserve the history of his achievements. Saddam has many such records from kings of the past in his museums.

Saddam rebuilt the six hundred–room palace of Nebuchadnezzar in the center of Babylon, the ancient capital of modern-day Iraq, and shortly before Operation Desert Storm, Saddam ordered a huge statue of himself constructed over the restored gate of Babylon. This parallels King Nebuchadnezzar's actions in Daniel 3:1–7. During the restoration, archaeologists uncovered a plaque on the right-hand side of the ancient city gate, placed there by Nebuchadnezzar and proclaiming the ancient ruler's greatness. Saddam ordered stonemasons to place another plaque on the left-hand side of the gate, glorifying the greatness of Saddam Hussein. In addition to emblazoning bricks with his own name, Saddam has had some cast with the phrase "Babylon is rising again" on them. But there is no tokenism in this massive project to rebuild Babylon. Every effort is being made to reproduce exactly what existed in the days of Nebuchadnezzar, including his opulent throne room.

Less certain is what all the Russian and Chinese technicians moving in and about the ancient city of Babylon are doing. Has Saddam had Nebuchadnezzar's great palace strung with the sophisticated and far-advanced fiber-optic network already suspected in the West, a system provided by the Chinese to give Saddam a deadlier integrated air defense (IAD) system? Is this Saddam's means of hiding his technology, placing it inconspicuously within some of Iraq's great religious sites, most of which are archaeological and historical treasures important to the rest of the world? A National Security Directive issued by President Bush on January 15, 1991, stated that the United States intended to "reduce collateral damage incident to military attacks, taking special precautions to minimize civilian casualties and damage to nonmilitary economic infrastructure, energy-related facilities, and religious sites." It was not the president's intention to bring harm to the culturally significant sites in Iraq, and Saddam knew it—and he believes the U.S. and its allies would not bomb these facilities today, because of the backlash it might cause in the Arab world.

By the same token, could he not use one of the rooms in the gigantic palace to hide Scott Speicher?

In any case, a British MI6 (military intelligence agency) source provided startling information to the CIA and DIA in the fall of 2001 regarding Scott Speicher. The British intelligence source had recently been in Baghdad and learned about Speicher. Just as was suspected all along, only a handful of Saddam's closest associates were allowed to see him, including Uday Saddam Hussein, Saddam's eldest son, and the chief of the Mukhabarat, the Iraqi intelligence service. The Mukhabarat, which attempted to assassinate former President George Bush during his visit to Kuwait in April 1993, maintains its principal command and control complex in Baghdad. The primary prison under its control is Abu Ghraib. The MI6 source told U.S. intelligence officials where the pilot is being held and the latest reports indicate that British intelligence now possesses several photographs of Speicher in Iraqi custody, gleaned from sources inside Saddam's regime. There are indications that Speicher has facial scars and walks with a limp.

The U.S. agencies sat on the information for six months before it was leaked by Capitol Hill to the Washington media. There is no doubt in the mind of several sources who worked the case that influential people with the ability to help or thwart Scott's chances had a mindset that would prevent "ninety-nine percent of all chances of a successful recovery from being planned or executed" (in the words of one case insider) because their image or credibility or political position would be negatively affected if a successful mission brought Scott Speicher home. "They are political beings," said the insider, "who are not focused on the operator [Speicher], but totally unable or unwilling to give the operator the benefit of the doubt."

Nonetheless, the day after the announcement in the first week of March 2002 that Scott Speicher was possibly being held in Baghdad, the media picked up the story, and it reverberated around the country. The Scott Speicher story was once again headline material.

Then came word that previously, in January of 2002, Dutch intelligence had made contact with an Iraqi defector about an American pilot. The defector said that Speicher had been moved to a military facility after the events of September 11—when airliners destroyed the World Trade Center and careened into the Pentagon—a temporary move made to protect Scott Speicher, Saddam's trophy, from being damaged. As a result of the media blitz, Richard Boucher, State Department spokesman, said in his Monday morning, March 11, 2002, briefing that the United States delegation led by U.S. Ambassador to Kuwait Richard Jones underscored that Iraq had continued, "to shirk its responsibility to answer the many unresolved questions about Commander Speicher's fate."

On March 26, retired Ambassador Frances D. Cook attended a seminar on Iraq hosted by the Washington Institute for Near East Policy featuring Amatzia Baram, an Israeli historian and arguably the world's best expert on Iraq. "He reads all Iraqi newspapers every day, has tons of informants, and has spent a lifetime's scholarship on the subject," said Cook. "He also has clear evidence that Saddam reads everything that he writes." The subject of Baram's lecture was "Iraq: Post-Saddam." After the talk was over, Ambassador Cook went up to Baram and raised the question of Scott Speicher. "As a lot of folks were crowding around, I only got to ask if he thinks Speicher could still be alive." In answer, he said, "It would be very like Saddam to keep an American all these years, and not tell us about it. Very, very like Saddam." Baram remarked that the U.S. absolutely needs to send someone to Baghdad to officially confer on the matter—but not to expect anything but propaganda in return. The Iraqis believe that the U.S. has abandoned Scott and that they have a right to possess him, because of that abandonment.

The Iraqi's November 6 response to questions regarding Speicher's status, sent by the author and Lon Wagner through the *Virginian-Pilot*, reflects this belief. "After almost another five years' silence," wrote Dr. Fahmi El-Qaisy (the Iraqi minister of legal affairs), "U.S. President Clinton raised on January 12, 2001, once again and on a large scale, the issue of the pilot, Speicher. Accordingly, the status of the pilot, Speicher, has been changed from killed in the operations into a missing person. The United States headed for the first time to the Tripartite Committee and asked to present a fact-finding file for the pilot ten years after his death." The U.S. either attended or had ICRC representation at two Tripartite Commissions in 1991 and 1993. On both occasions, information on Scott Speicher was requested from the Iraqis. The Iraqis even replied to the latter entreaty in 1993 for the missing pilot. Of course, what they said was that they had no knowledge of an American pilot still in Iraq.

The question of how to conclusively get Scott back, whether by patient and conciliatory diplomatic means, or by brute force—overtly or covertly—remains an issue that is hard to resolve.

Knowing Saddam's megalomaniac psychology helps to gain insight as to why he might have held Scott for so long, and possibly the best way to approach the dictator in order to get him home again. But in the end, one thing is certain: Unless the United States is committed to a consistent, proactive and relentless strategy to get the Iraqis to admit that Speicher is within their borders, and to work to bring him back to American soil, it would seem as if Scott will have to continue to endure the lion's den, as he has so bravely for the past ten years.

Afterword

Theodore Roosevelt once said that "all the resources we need are in the mind," and that to attempt life's greater triumphs, "far better it is to dare mighty things, to win glorious triumphs, even though checkered by failure, than to take rank with those poor spirits who neither enjoy nor suffer too much, because they live in the gray twilight that knows not victory or defeat." Roosevelt would most likely concur that the worst thing anyone can do is exactly what was done so often in the Speicher case: nothing.

It is time to do something. Despite further skepticism and obfuscation on the details of the case, it becomes overwhelmingly hard to deny that Scott Speicher is still waiting for someone to bring him home.

When discussing the probability of Speicher's survival for the last ten years, Vice Admiral Charles W. "Willy" Moore, Jr., deputy chief of naval operations for readiness and logistics, wrote the following: "I too believe he is still alive. I know him very well. I was his weapons training flight instructor when he first started out in the A-7 Corsair II back in 1981/2. He is one of the finest young men I have ever served with, and I have never had the feeling that he is gone. I often," he continued, "fantasize about how joyous it would be if he were to find his way out of there." Moore's e-mail, dated November 18, 2001, while he was still in Manama, Bahrain, as commander of U.S. Naval Forces Central Command and Fifth Fleet, notes that he'd worked closely on Scott's issue when he was J33 (Current Operations), Operations Directorate, on the Joint Staff in Washington, D.C., "so I have a keen interest in his whereabouts and welfare." Moore was privy to all the highly classified intelligence coming in on Scott during his back-to-back tours with the Joint Staff. He was in the loop from 1993 through 1999, a key period in the Speicher investigation.

"There are several others—general officers, staff officers, survival instructors and mission planners—who were also involved and knew some of the amazing and shocking events related to this case," wrote Bob Dussault on January 11, 2002. "I think the evidence the government has to deal with can be responded to in two ways. Look at it, giving [Speicher] the benefit of the doubt, i.e., assume he is alive until this is proved otherwise, or give the info no credibility and believe Speicher is dead and did not survive until he walks in the room." Dussault stresses the need for action. "At this stage of the game for me, I must do the right thing for the person and the right thing for the nation. It is the principle of liberty in its simplest form. We must do it for Scott and all our military personnel, or we do not do right for any." To do any less for Scott Speicher goes against our obligation to him and to all of our military. "Leaving a single operator forgotten or totally on their own, when they have been taught to expect allegiance, love and recovery efforts by their own country, is wrong."

Barry Hull, Scott's squadronmate, says it is an obligation that's part of the deal from day one. "When I hang my ass out and I go across the border, if I get shot down or something happens to me,

I absolutely know, there is no question in my mind, that those snakeaters are coming to get me. Those guys are going to do whatever they have to do to get me." If he were in Scott's situation, he said he would have thought, "If they in their minds know I'm dead, well, they're probably not going to come get me now. [But] if it's three or four years later and they find out something different, they better get their ass over there. And we had an opportunity to do it, and we made a conscious decision not to."

Like many others, Hull will live with what happened that night over the Iraqi desert for the rest of his life. He thinks often of what he might have done differently that could have prevented Spike's loss. There's a twinge of guilt that he's never shaken. "There is not another Navy pilot," he recalled recently, "that if you get five guys together somebody's not going to say something bad about him. Somebody's going to criticize everybody, that's the nature of the job and the mentality—except with Speicher. He was just a great guy, all around, and it sounds so phony to say that, but it's actually true in this situation. He was probably the best pilot in the squadron because he was just a naturally good pilot."

"I almost went down to Arlington today," said another one of Scott's former squadronmates, Craig Bertolett. He'd done it enough times in the past. "My wife and I invariably reflect on where we were and what we were doing and remember Spike on the evening of January 17." For others, it cuts to the heart of the code they live by and the code they have ingrained in their hearts.

There is an unspoken obligation in the U.S. military chain of command that they will leave no one behind over enemy lines without making every reasonable effort to recover that member. Among America's Special Forces branches, this guarantee is written code—rote memorized and lived to the letter—but its message is simple, easy enough to understand in peace *and* the heat of battle. "The warriors believed they had a responsibility," said

Admiral Stan Arthur. "You lose one of your own, you go back and find him."

It is thus ironic that in his farewell speech delivered at Fort Myer, Virginia, on January 17, 2001, ten years to the day after Scott Speicher's disappearance, Secretary of Defense William S. Cohen should choose to quote a statement from General William Tecumseh Sherman to Ulysses S. Grant. Sherman said to his old friend, "I always knew that if I was in trouble you'd come for me if alive." Chairman of the Joint Chiefs of Staff Henry H. Shelton had given Cohen a fountain pen with the phrase engraved on it. "Mr. Chairman," Cohen said to Shelton, "I always knew that if I were ever in trouble, that you would always be there for me as you've been there for all of the men and women who wear our uniform. You are a warrior and you carry the warrior's code not only on your sleeve, but in your soul."

Will the warriors go get Scott Speicher, knowing now that he is alive?

At least some warriors are still trying.

On March 20, 2002, a special session of the Senate Select Committee on Intelligence was held, chaired by Senator Pat Roberts. Perhaps frustrated at the Pentagon's beginning to circle the wagons and deny the leaking intelligence about the Speicher case being reported in the press throughout the beginning of the year, Roberts called in CIA Director George Tenet and DIA Director Vice Admiral Tom Wilson to testify yet again on the Speicher case. Roberts was making no bones about the situation. He wanted an answer for the record, and would brook no ambiguity in the matter.

Directing his oratory at Tenet and Wilson, he pointedly asked the question that was on everyone's lips: "Given all the information in your possession, is Scott Speicher alive today? Tell us all now," he demanded.

There was silence. Tenet and Wilson paused. Roberts waited. "Yes, he is," they replied.

One can only hope that this long overdue admission will be the turning point in the Spiecher case, and perhaps serve as a watershed moment where POW/MIA affairs are concerned.

"Certainty" is a relative term in all matters. There were plenty of people along the road to recovering Scott Speicher who wanted more of it, who spouted policies and politics of convenience that had little to do with conviction and character. But there are certainties that lie in all of us—the ones that don't let us forget Scott Speicher and the men like him who have been left behind.

Admiral James Stockdale, a Vietnam-era POW, wrote: "In the end the prisoner learns he can't be hurt and he can't be had as long as he tells the truth and clings to that forgiving hand of the brothers who are becoming his country, his family . . . What does it all come down to? It does not come down to coping or supplication or hatred or strength beyond the grasp of any normal person. It comes down to comradeship, and it comes down to pride, dignity, an enduring sense of self-worth and to that enigmatic mixture of conscience and egoism called personal honor."[22]

Scott Speicher has met the test of personal honor. Have we? Certainty, I was told, is when he walks up to you and touches your face . . . and says, "I'm alive." Scott has done just that by doing everything he can to survive and come home. Before leaving on any mission, he told Joanne innumerable times he'd be home: "I guarantee it." His country owes him no less than to fulfill that promise Scott made to his family over a decade ago.

Retired Vice Admiral Carlos Johnson made an important observation: "America has some great Americans in it, it just doesn't realize it yet." Those great Americans must now choose the right course and make sure that Commander Michael Scott Speicher—a truly great American—is returned with honor.

Author's Note

This book is a compilation of more than five hundred inter-views; sixty-five hundred e-mail exchanges of information; government documents and correspondence; case files from U.S. intelligence, Pentagon agencies and the U.S. Navy; and fac-similied documents, personal letters, transcripts, maps and photographs obtained over an eight-year period beginning in 1994. But more than the sum of its parts, I am indebted to the aviators who have never stopped being Scott Speicher's friends—the ones who stood up for him and helped carry me through the writing of this book and across the finish line.

In particular, I feel especially indebted to the determination of the *Sunliners* who flew into harm's way over Baghdad on the first air strike with Scott—Barry W. "Skull" Hull, Philip "Chauncey" Gardner, Tony "Bano" Albano—and their effort to help recon-struct the events that led to Spike's disappearance. They also pro-vided background on Scott and the deployment from which he did not return. There were others, like Patrick R. "Roller" Rink, a former Marine Corps F/A-18 pilot, who stayed determinedly by my side throughout the research, often doing Herculean amounts of information gathering and communication among sources. I would like to thank Bob "Ripper" Stumpf and Dave "Frenchy" Renaud. Ripper was the executive officer of the VFA-83 *Rampagers*, the *Sunliners'* sister squadron aboard the *Saratoga*. Frenchy was one of his junior officers. Both were HARM shooters along with Spike on the first strike, and each contributed much to the book.

There is great thanks reserved for Craig "Bert" Bertolett, Scott's former squadronmate and a constant source of encouragement and information. Along with so many others who flew with Scott, Craig demonstrated the premise that friendship and courage and commitment—one aviator to another—can withstand the test of time and trying circumstances. There are no words adequate to express my deepest thanks to all of the people who took a leap of faith and trust and permitted me to include them in this book. They are all what Carlos Johnson called the great Americans that America doesn't realize it has yet. They possess the highest honor, they are indeed the best this country has to offer— and they tried to do the right thing for Michael Scott Speicher.

Peter Rubie, my literary agent and friend, made all this come together with Penguin Putnam and I thank him for making this book happen for Scott's sake. To Daniel B. Slater, my editor, I cannot thank him enough. He had a vision for *No One Left Behind* that makes the book's already powerful subject come to life off the page. Thanks, too, for the efforts of John Paine.

Finally, I would like to thank my family. I have a devoted husband in Ray, and three incredible children who are by far my greatest accomplishments. They stood by me throughout the research and writing of this book and were extraordinarily patient when I shouldn't have expected it.

Epilogue

Since the publication of the book in July 2002, the response to *No One Left Behind* has been overwhelmingly positive—and amazingly poignant. Some readers were numb after reading it, others sobbed uncontrollably. With each telephone call, e-mail, card, and letter received, I revisited many of the same emotions. I cried with you; I also steeled myself to stay focused. I inevitably ask myself the same question most of you do: Where do we go from here? Some days I feel completely useless to answer that question, and on others I'm focused and determined that we must endeavor to recover one of our own, Scott Speicher, from the bowels of Saddam Hussein's regime in Iraq. There have now been hundreds of newspaper and magazine articles, op-ed pieces, and television and radio programs pertaining to Scott, many of which I participated in, but all of which spotlight the tragedy of the Scott Speicher story. In a note to me dated July 8, 2002, Craig Bertolett, one of Scott's friends and former squadronmates, wrote this:

"The naval service and the nation must 'keep the promise' with those brave individuals who dedicate themselves to 'duty, honor, country.' Only by doing so will we be worthy of future selfless service. Thank you for researching, writing, and prodding this story along to awareness and action."

Significant changes in Scott Speicher's status have occurred since the book's publication in July 2002. Published and unpublished intelligence product gathered for the book has proved invaluable to Senate and Pentagon investigators tasked with resolving Speicher's fate, and analysis of that information against available—and current—intelligence continues to provide greater insight into his case. President George W. Bush, in his September 12, 2002, address to the United Nations, calling that international body to action against Iraq, noted that in 1991, the U.N. Security Council demanded through Resolutions 686 and 687 that Iraq return all prisoners from Kuwait and other lands. "Iraq's regime agreed," said the president. "It broke this promise. Last year the secretary general's high-level coordinator for this issue reported that Kuwaiti, Saudi, Indian, Syrian, Lebanese, Iranian, Egyptian, Bahraini and Omani nationals remain unaccounted for—more than 600 people. One American pilot is among them." President Bush has made Scott Speicher's return to American custody a condition Saddam Hussein must meet to avoid war with the United States and its coalition partners.

In his insistence that Iraq account for Scott Speicher, President Bush is exercising his right under U.S. Code Title 22, Chapter 23, Section 1732, Release of Citizens Imprisoned by Foreign Governments, which states unequivocally:

"Whenever it is made known to the President that any citizen of the United States has been unjustly deprived of his liberty by or under the authority of any foreign government, it shall be the duty of the President forthwith to demand of that government the reasons of such imprisonment; and if it appears to be wrongful and in violation of the rights of American citizenship, the President shall forthwith demand the release of such citizen, and if the release so demanded is unreasonably delayed or refused, the President shall use such means, not amounting to acts of war and not otherwise prohibited by law, as he may think necessary and proper to obtain or effectuate the release; and all the facts and proceedings relative thereto shall as soon as practicable be communicated by the President to Congress."

But the U.S. needs more than Section 1732 and a United Nations plea. The United States needs a permanent fix to written armistice documents to ensure each has a clause inserted authorizing military action into enemy areas postconflict to recover POWs and MIAs.

Since promoted to Navy captain, Scott Speicher was reclassified missing/captured on October 11, 2002, by Navy secretary Gordon England, a category that denotes that a service member has been seized as the result of the action of an unfriendly military or paramilitary force in a foreign country. Under terms of the Geneva Convention of 1949, the Navy's classification of Speicher to missing/captured is equivalent by the terms of the Convention to Speicher being a prisoner of war. A little over two weeks later, on October 30, President Bush signed into law the Persian Gulf War POW/MIA Accountability Act of 2001 [S. 1339] to provide an asylum program with regard to American Persian Gulf War POW/MIAs. This amendment to the Bring Them Home Alive Act of 2000, dubbed the Speicher Bill, grants asylum to any Middle Eastern national—and his or her family—who returns an American prisoner of war from the Persian Gulf War.

"It's not only for Scott; it's for every person who wears the uniform," said Senator Pat Roberts, the chairman of the Senate Select Committee on Intelligence, to reporters on January 6, 2003, referring to his renewed effort to meet with Iraq's permanent representative to the United Nations, Mohammed Al-Douri, to discuss Speicher. In clear-cut, insistent language, Roberts's letter to Saddam Hussein requesting a meeting with Al-Douri indicated that he sought Hussein's assistance in effecting a humanitarian release of Speicher. Roberts has waged a tenacious fight to increase U.S. efforts to recover Scott and has long maintained that Pentagon officials did not adequately investigate the incident and improperly listed him as killed in action. Even when intelligence data began to surface, little was done to set the record straight.

More recently, congressional staff visits to Southwest Asia indicate, according to Roberts, "there are signs that an American POW is in Iraq." A few days later, during a January 10 appearance on CNN's *Wolf Blitzer Live*, Senator Roberts cited this book as an aid in connecting the dots for Senate investigators. "I can't tell you what it's like if you look at one mistake after another," Roberts said. "We did actually leave somebody behind."

—Amy Waters Yarsinske
February 2003

Acronyms

A

ADS—air defense system
AFIP—Armed Forces Institute of Pathology
ALSS—aviation life support system equipment
AMRAAM—advanced medium-range air-to-air missile
AOCS—Aviation Officers' Candidate School
AOR—area of responsibility
APC—armored personnel carrier
ATO—air tasking order
AWACS—Boeing E-3 Sentry airborne warning and control
   system

B

BIT—built-in test
BuNo—bureau number
BUPERS—Bureau of Naval Personnel
BVR—beyond visual range

C

CACO—casualty assistance calls officer

CAG—carrier air group commander (also, carrier air wing commander)

CAP—combat air patrol

CDR—Navy commander

CENTAF—Central Command Air Force commander

CENTCOM—U.S. Central Command (also, USCENTCOM)

CIA—Central Intelligence Agency

CILHI—Army Central Identification Laboratory Hawaii

CLC—command launch computer

CNN—Cable News Network

CNO—Chief of Naval Operations

COMLATWING—commander light wing attack

CSAR—combat search and rescue

CTG—Combined Task Group

CTF—Combined Task Force

CVIC—carrier intelligence center

CVW—Carrier Air Wing

D

DCAG—deputy air group commander

DCI—director of Central Intelligence

DDIs—digital display indicators

DIA—Defense Intelligence Agency

DoD—Department of Defense

DoD POW/MIA Office—Department of Defense Prisoner of War/Missing in Action Office

DPMO—Department of Defense Prisoner of War/Missing Personnel Office

DSU—data storage unit

E

E & E nets—escape and evasion nets

EID—electronic identification

ELINT—electronic intelligence
ELT—electronic transponder

F

FBI—Federal Bureau of Investigation
FOD—foreign object debris
FOIA—Freedom of Information Act
FSU—Florida State University

H

HARM—high-speed anti-radiation missile
HET—heavy equipment transport
HUD—Head-Up Display
HUMINT—human intelligence

I

IADS—integrated air defense system
ICRC—International Committee of the Red Cross
IFF—Identify Friend or Foe
INC—Iraqi National Congress
INDICT—a London-based human rights organization
IQAF—Iraqi Air Force
IRNA—Islamic Republic News Agency

J

JCS—Joint Chiefs of Staff
JCSD—Joint Commission Support Directorate
JCS/JSOC—Joint Chiefs of Staff/Joint Special Operations
    Command
JFACC—Joint Force Air Component Commander
JMAO—Joint Mortuary Affairs Office
JPRA—Joint Personnel Recovery Agency
JRCC—Joint Recovery Command Center
J-STARS—Joint Surveillance and Target Attack Radar System

JSOC—Joint Special Operations Command
JSOTF—Joint Special Operations Task Force
JSSA—Joint Service Survival, Evasion, Resistance and Escape (SERE) Agency
JTF-SWA—Joint Task Force–Southwest Asia

K

KIA—killed in action
KIA/BNR—killed in action/body not recovered
KTO—Kuwaiti Theater of Operations

L

LCDR—Navy lieutenant commander
LCOL—lieutenant colonel
LT—lieutenant

M

MAJ—major
MIA—missing in action
MSP—maintenance status panel

N

NAV—navigation display
NAVCENT—United States Naval Forces Central Command
NAVSAFECEN—Naval Safety Center Norfolk
NAWCWD—Naval Air Warfare Center Weapons Division
NBC—nuclear, biological, chemical
NCA—National Command Authority
NIMA—National Imagery and Mapping Agency
NPIC—National Photographic Interpretation Center
NRCC—NAVCENT Rescue Coordination Center
NSA—National Security Agency
NSC—National Security Council
NSWC—Naval Strike Warfare Center Fallon (Nevada)
NVGs—night vision goggles

O

ONI—Office of Naval Intelligence
OSD—Office of the Secretary of Defense

P

PIREPS—pilot reports
PKIA—probable killed in action
POW—prisoner of war
POW/MIA—Department of Defense Special Office for Prisoners of
    War and Missing in Action
PSYOP—psychological operation

R

RHAW—radar homing and warning gear
ROE—rules of engagement
ROI—Republic of Iraq
RWR—radar warning receiver

S

SAM—Roland ADS surface-to-air missile
SAS—British Special Air Service
SCIRI—Supreme Council for Islamic Revolution in Iraq
SCUD—short-range ballistic missile
SDC—signal data computer
SEAD—suppression of enemy air defenses
SIGINT—signals intelligence
SNORT—Supersonic Naval Ordnance Research Track (China Lake,
    California)
SOCCENT—Special Operations Command Central Command
SPC—Army specialist
SPEAR—Strike Projection Evaluation and Anti–Air Warfare
    Research group
SPECWAR—Naval Special Warfare
SPINS—special instructions
SSCI—Senate Select Committee on Intelligence

T

TFW—Tactical Fighter Wing
TOO—target of opportunity
TOT—time on target

U

UNMOVIC—United Nations Monitoring, Verification and
Inspection Commission
UNSCOM—United Nations Special Commission for Iraq
USAR—United States Army Reserve
USCENTCOM—United States Central Command (also,
CENTCOM)

V

VA—attack squadron
VAW—carrier airborne early warning squadron
VFA—strike fighter squadron
VMFA—Marine strike fighter squadron
VT—training squadron
VX—a lethal nerve agent

Notes

[1]Miller, Mark Crispin, "Death of a Fighter Pilot," *The New York Times*, September 15, 1992.

[2]Casey, Kathryn, "The Wings of Love," *Ladies' Home Journal*, June 1991, p. 197. The *Ladies' Home Journal* interview was the first and only interview Joanne L. Speicher gave after Scott Speicher's loss. The Office of Naval Intelligence, which kept track of most media associated with the commander's loss and subsequent investigation, forwarded this article along with several others.

[3]Ibid., p. 197.

[4]Ibid.

[5]Ibid., p. 198.

[6]Ibid., p. 199.

[7]Ibid.

[8]Ibid.

[9]Ibid.

[10]Ibid.

[11]Ibid.

[12]This was presented April 21, 1994, as part of the investigation conducted after Speicher's wreckage was located.

[13]Miller, *NYT*, September 15, 1992.

[14]Ibid.

[15]Mann, Edward C., III. *Thunder and Lightning: Desert Storm and the Airpower Debates*. Maxwell Air Force Base, Alabama: Air University Press, 1995, from the second chapter.

[16]Carpenter, P. Mason, "Joint Operations in the Gulf War: An Allison Analysis, Thesis, School of Advanced Air Power Studies, Air University, Maxwell Air Force Base, June 1994.

[17]Ibid.

[18]Stumpf, Robert E., "Scott Speicher, Prisoner of War," *National Review Online*, Guest Comment, March 19, 2002.

[19]Ryan, Chris. *The One That Got Away*. London: Brassey's, 1998, p. 30.

[20]Hedges, Chris, "Iraqi Defectors Tell of Kuwaitis in Secret Jail in Baghdad," *The New York Times*, November 12, 2001, Late Edition.

[21]PBS *Frontline* interview first broadcast and published on January 20, 1996.

[22]Dedication, Report of the Senate Select Committee on POW/MIA Affairs, January 13, 1993.